THE AUTHORS

G. Theresa Wintour and Zachariah Evans are the bynames of two professional journalists who also have a wide experience of UK and international business affairs.

When they concluded with regret that city life was no longer for them they set off with high hopes of life and work in the countryside.

Now comfortably settled in their village they admit nevertheless to having made some mistakes along their country way. "The biggest blooper was **buying** a house. Its attraction was that it was old and picturesque but it cost a fortune to rebuild, with the plumbing being a particular nightmare. It finally dawned that it was crazy to have all that money tied up so we sold the house and **rented** another. The ideal is to rent with an option to purchase. That way you get the best of all possible financial worlds (country rents seldom have a true relationship to the capital value), plus the fact that, if you decide to take up the purchase option, you know the building and it's therefore easy to know to a few pounds how much any building works are going to cost if you want to upgrade and/or extend it.

"But whether you rent or buy we think the really sensible course is to use your house both to live in and to make money from. That way you can afford a big enough place to house both business and you in comfort."

Apart from seeing the need to use property assets more sensibly the couple also observed that many people did not appear to appreciate the changing possibilities of business in the countryside, mainly because of the lack of a raft of stimulating ideas.

They got to work and this guide is the result. "It's

only a pity such a guide wasn't around when we first went countryside. It would have saved us much money."

We hope that's exactly what it will do for you.

SATURDAY RICHMOND'S GUIDE TO VILLAGE RICHES:
COUNTRYSIDE BUSINESS VENTURES
THE PRIZES AND THE PITFALLS .

Copyright © SATURDAY RICHMOND PUBLISHERS 1990

Published by SATURDAY RICHMOND PUBLISHERS
Le Clos Fontaine. Little Sark. C.I.

First Edition 1990

Designed by CRAVEN DESIGNS
Set in Times Roman

Typeset, printed and bound in Great Britain
by THE GUERNSEY PRESS CO. LTD.,
Guernsey, Channel Islands

British Library Cataloging in Publication Data
Saturday Richmond's guide to village riches —
countryside business ventures: the prizes and pitfalls.
Bibliography
Index
1. Great Britain. Home-based small firms
1. Saturday Richmond Publishers
658.0220941

ISBN 1-872804-03-9

Saturday Richmond's

GUIDE TO VILLAGE RICHES

COUNTRYSIDE BUSINESS VENTURES

THE PRIZES AND THE PITFALLS

SATURDAY RICHMOND PUBLISHERS

INTRODUCTION

- For city-dwellers, learning to live in the country can be a culture shock but a pleasant one; for quite some time you tend to look for the catch.

- The empty roads strike you first, a part of you vaguely wondering when you're going to turn a corner and find the mother-and-father of all traffic jams.

- As you have no need to compete fiercely with other motorists you tend to get to and fro about your affairs with time to spare. This may tempt you to stop awhile and simply enjoy the view. You are reminded that this is still a very spacious and beautiful nation.

- Prepare for some pleasant surprises, e.g. that village neighbours actually are interested in you, yes, you, the human being, provided, naturally, that you make it clear that you're genuinely interested in them and the whole context of your new environment. Then there's the surge of vigour that will grow within you as the clean air does its work; the ebbing away of stress as you come to terms with your new rural life.

- However, what your instincts may not have told you is that by wanting to commit part or all of your life to the country you are sharing a feeling held by 72% of the UK population, according to a recent poll carried out by Gallup.

- With city conditions not getting any better it is unsurprising that over the last few years hundreds of thousands of people have migrated from the larger towns and cities, heading for a more rewarding future in smaller communities, with the majority favouring life in a village.

- So said the Henley Centre for Forecasting; another of their reports predicts that within the next few years some four million people will have re-thought their lives and will be working from home. Other reports put this figure higher and forecast that by early next century at least one-third of us will be working home-based.

- To us the only surprising thing was that using the house (and, of course, preferably one in the country) as both home and money-maker was not already more wide-spread.

- When we stopped to think about it, however, we realised that what was missing was a guide that people could refer to; that would stimulate readers to think 'money-making', then take them through the various steps essential to getting a country home-based business venture into play and on to fruition.

- Here is that guide.

CONTENTS

YES, BUT WHAT ABOUT . . . ?   1

THE VENTURES: 9

ADVENTURE GAMES   11
ANTIQUES APPRECIATION and
    RESTORATION   17
AQUA GROOMING and OTHER
    THERAPIES   21

BESPOKE   29

CALLIGRAPHY   35
COMPUTERS FOR THE PANIC-STRUCK   39
CULTS   45

DESIGN and DECORATION   49

ETIQUETTE   55

FAST READING, WRITING and RECALL   61
FINANCIAL SPECULATION   65

GAMBLING   69
GROWING THINGS   75

INVENTING THINGS   87

KITCHEN FACTORY   99

LANGUAGES   111
LAUGHTER   117

MAIL ORDER   125
MASTER DRIVING   133
MICROWAVE MAGIC   139

MOBILE PROFESSIONAL 145
MUSIC 149
MYSTERIES 153

NOSTALGIA 169

PAINTING, DRAWING and SCULPTURE 175
PERSONAL DEVELOPMENT 177
PHOTOGRAPHY 183

RECYCLING 191

SEMINARS 205
SNOW and ICE 219
SPECIAL EFFECTS 225

THE TEA CEREMONY 233
TELEPHONE DYSPHORIA 241

WEATHER MAN 247
WINE and MALT WHISKY 251
WRITING 259

HIT LIST 265

WHAT TO DO NOW: 281
  THE SR FORMULA 285
  YOUR PERSONAL STOCKTAKE 287
  YOUR VENTURE PHILOSOPHY 293
  THE CRITICAL SUCCESS FACTOR(S) 295
  MARKETING STRATEGY 297
  FUNDING YOUR VENTURE 301
  SELLING YOUR PRESENT HOME 311
  ACQUIRING YOUR COUNTRY
    PROPERTY 317
  MARKETING PLAN 323

FINALLY 327

BIBLIOGRAPHY, INDICATING POSITION
  OF SOURCE IN TEXT 329

LIST OF INDIVIDUALS &
ORGANISATIONS REFERRED TO
IN TEXT   340
INDEX   350
GIFT COUPON   368
NOTES   369

YES, BUT WHAT ABOUT . . . ?

- **Affording it.** Whether your country house is to be either your second or your only house you've obviously got to be able to see that you can achieve it without putting yourself in queer street.

- Here's how:

- Don't buy your property, **rent** it, maybe with an **option** to purchase. (See **ACQUIRING YOUR COUNTRY PROPERTY**). Then

- **Reinvent** it. Only the really well-off can afford to use a country home simply as a pleasant haven. For the rest of us the home must cease to be a money-gobbler; it must become a money-maker. As you read on you will see how the ventures outlined achieve this.

- However, material riches are not the only things in life:

- The riches of **self-fulfilment** will be high on every-body's list. Our suggested ventures reflect this.

- **Education** for your children:

- Clearly educational standards vary but there can be few if any exceptions to the general rule that your child will enjoy at least as good an education in the country as in the city. There will probably be smaller classes and these will be freer of **stress.**

- **Health.** You and yours will be much healthier living in the country. When you do need expert care however you'll find that the doctors, nurses and facilities are every bit as good as in the city.

- Worried about losing those old **friendships**? Two

things can be said: You will certainly make new friends in your new environment — and there's nothing to stop your old mates from visiting you. Your village home will be a great attraction!

- Difficulty selling your existing house? See our suggestions under **SELLING YOUR PRESENT HOME.**

- Worried about **training/retraining**? Don't be. Nationwide, there's an enterprise infrastructure that is well able to cope with such challenges. There has to be: more than **1 in 9** of all workers are now **self-employed** (and that's not counting the moonlighters!).

- However, the most important thing really is getting to an understanding of who **you** are; fitting that you into the **right** business is much more than half the battle won. (See **YOUR PERSONAL STOCKTAKE).**

- A final thought, if appropriate: have you considered having your cake and eating it by **remaining** in your job as an **employee** but doing your work from a country village home? The technology is there, if you're an expert at using it. Whilst you continue to earn your salary you could be setting up one of the ventures in this guide.

- As to **the ventures:**

- These are personal businesses and depend for their success on your fairly intimate commitment.

- Some of them are **green** — not to be trendy but because it simply makes sense and probably most profit to do it that way.

- Many of the ventures involve you in providing appropriate space in your home in which to

2

show **Paying Student Guests** (PSGs), of various ages, how to do things.

- For **SEMINARS** (which you may find instructive to read first) and some of the other ventures it will make sense to provide bed and board or, if this is quite impossible, track down local accommodation for your PSGs.

- Other ventures could involve daily visitors; others again leave you alone to get on with your project.

- Some of the ventures **could** involve staff **but** this is an area where caution is essential. See **INFORMATION CHECK LIST**.

- Some of the ventures require you to have a fair acreage of land but if this is not available with the desired house it is usually possible to rent the space needed from local farmers.

- Whichever venture you choose they can all be run profitably and enjoyably from a country home which may well be more spacious than your present dwelling.

- How comfortable you make your own quarters is governed by the rule that the **business** must have first call on finance available.

- The alphabetically-listed ventures are intended to stimulate. Modifications and mixing of ideas will be required to suit your personality.

- Some ventures call for skills. These you may already have but, if not, these **can** be learned and there has never been more training available than there is today.

- If you are not able to commit to the training others can be hired to do the job for you. But remember the bottom line.

• Some of the ventures need little explanation. Others are more complex. The descriptive material varies in length accordingly.

• Where it has been possible for us to quote figures we have done so. These are included for general guidance only so you will, of course, check closely into all numbers relevant to those ventures of interest to you.

• At the end of each venture section reference sources are quoted to enable you to begin fuller investigation. Altogether over **500 information sources** of various kinds are thus available to you.

• To enable you to assess ventures of interest and for how to eventually get your venture into play refer to **WHAT TO DO NOW.**

• Reference information correct at time of going to press but, of course, things can change, particularly (a) phone numbers, e.g. London is involved in the 071 and 081 code alterations, and (b) books can be in print one day and not the next!

• Finally, for our lady readers, in the text any reference to the male gender is purely stylistic and does of course include the female gender as appropriate.

••• INFORMATION CHECK LIST

• You may have a job that looks good career-wise. Before you allow that to deter you from countryside activity it might be worth your while taking the trouble to read AGE OF UN-REASON, by CHARLES HANDY, pub. HUTCHINSON, £10.95. Professor Handy forecasts: a **reduction** in full-time employment; that employment will not be consistent and that a 'major discontinuity will affect **every** family in **every** industrial country within the next generation'. He blames the emergence of the **shamrock organisation** for the underlying 'change-a-company' structure, which will increasingly be based around a core of essential executives and workers supported by outside contractors and part-time helpers.

- Contact STEPHANIE DONALDSON on 0707 - 58561. This lady runs CLASSES IN A COUNTRY HOUSE. The classes cover flower arrangement, conservatory gardens, special paint finishes, silk and china painting and other aspects of country house life. Consider visiting the house (it's in Hertfordshire) as much for the style of presentation as anything else. (Also get the lady to tell you about her time as a hippy before she became mistress of this rather fine house.)

- You're almost certainly not in the market for a stately home but for an insight into how the enterprising owners of these money-gobbling old piles go about generating money contact CHRISTIE'S (01 - 839 9060). Together with Savills, the estate agents, Christie's recently ran a series of seminars: FUNDING THE COUNTRY HOUSE AND AGRICULTURAL ESTATE IN THE 1990s. Get the reports and consider if possible going to some of the estates; e.g. LADY ASHCOMBE makes **exclusive furniture** at her Sudeley Castle at Winchcombe; Mr & Mrs DOCKER do a massive business in **dried flowers** at their Armscote Manor, Shipton on Stour; LADY GELBER specialises in **fabric** and **wallpaper** designs at Blenheim Palace, Woodstock; at Chenies Manor near Amersham, the family MATTHEWS profit from **potted herbs;** the DUCHESS of DEVONSHIRE specialises in **jams, chutneys** and **biscuits** at Chatsworth House, near Chesterfield and at Hagley Hall, Stourbridge, VISCOUNT COBHAM turns more than the odd penny by running **Murder Evenings, parlour music** and, most successfully, a **community of craftsmen** who restore clocks, furniture and pianos, make guns, handbags **and** invent and design things.

- Perhaps the biggest stately money-spinner is the most surprising. See details under **RECYCLING.**

- Some inspiration for you? If not, there's plenty more in this guide.

- You will find that we make frequent reference to the need for **research.** EUROMONITOR (01 - 251 8024) have two items that should interest you for general background: UK CONSUMER SPENDING TRENDS & FORECASTS, ISBN 0 86338 344 0 and LEISURE COMPANIES AND LEISURE MARKETS, ISBN 0 86338 332 7. However, as each report costs £375, try and track them down at your local large reference library or failing that, check with the SCIENCE REFERENCE LIBRARY division of the BRITISH LIBRARY (start with 01 - 323 7454).

- For those who fear some isolation when working away from what was perhaps a previously many-colleague'd environment there are some organisations who lend support:

- OWNBASE (0963 - 250764) is run by CHRIS OLIVER. £17.50 p.a. gets you opportunities to meet other people who work from their home in a variety of skills, six issues of the OwnBase Newsletter and a range of other facilities.

- Also consider HOME-START CONSULT-ANCY (0533 - 554988) run by MARGARET HARRISON who can put you in touch with local groups dedicated to helping you through that potentially difficult settling-in phase and finding new pals.

- As we have mentioned, experts predict that by the year 2020 **at least** one third of the population will be working from home.

- Pleasing though the prospect undoubtedly is, there is a knack: e.g. work time, space organis-ation, even leisure are all areas where some skills are required to ensure a successful outcome. Therefore also contact:

- The NATIONAL HOMEWORKING UNIT (01 - 643 6352) for their FACTPACK FOR HOME-WORKERS.

- We mentioned your children's education. There is a plethora of guides so to save you time it may be worth paying £10 to SCHOOLPLAN UK (0985 - 219732). From their extensive database they will provide you with a tailored short-list of schools according to your special geographical, financial and educational require-ments.

- We mentioned staff. It can cost anything up to £500 to recruit one 'permanent' member of staff, to which add training costs. Even then you may not have a winner. At least in the early stages, try and avoid employing others (far better use members of your family if possible); if unavoid-able then only employ on a 'cash casual' basis until you've checked them out. Also see **HIT LIST** comments.

- Finally, you will see very many reference source books quoted in this guide. If you cannot track them down in bookshops and libraries then go further afield. Whilst the BRITISH LIB-RARY (01 - 636 1544) is obviously the last resort, do also try local universities, business colleges, schools, even government departments.

- **Stop Press:** Although EUROMONITOR, market researchers, are quoted throughout the guide, we recommend you get KNOW YOUR MARKET, 220 WAYS and their information pack from KEY NOTE PUBLICATIONS LTD (01 - 783 0755), another muscular player in the major research field. Although it is extremely difficult to compare report prices, KEY NOTE certainly appear to be competitive.

THE VENTURES

• ADVENTURE GAMES

- Some say that man is the most dangerous, warlike creature on the planet.

- However, the fact is that modern man has to face the strong possibility that there are not going to **be** any more wars.

- Fine — if you overlook our current basic aggression.

- And as this is going to be within us for quite some time to come some of us need an outlet for all this raw energy.

- This is where adventure games come in.

- What are we talking about here?

- SAS-styled courses in karate (and possibly even less civilised unarmed combat), fencing, shooting (hand and rifle), orienteering (or survival), outdoor (and indoor) mountaineering and abseiling, horse riding (or, for the faint-hearted, wooden, look-alike horses) and kayaking are among the elements at your disposal in creating this venture.

- How many you use and how long you spend in preteaching them and on the actual game is up to you.

- The game or battle can also be as rudimentary or complex as you wish and have given your PSGs time for, starting with the **basic battle** of pitting two armies (or teams) against one another, each bidding to be the first to capture the other side's 'battle standard' and deliver it to the winning 'territory'.

11

- Your PSGs can be supplied with repeater marker pistols to knock out their enemies by shooting wet-colour pellets at them.

- In addition to small arms and rifle training consider including **cross-bow** and **archery courses** in which there is rising interest since we won those Olympic medals.

- **Clay pigeon** shoots are becoming big business because of corporate entertaining and this activity could be profitably included in the venture.

- For the actual adventure games you will need to have (or rent access to) 25+ acres of wooded country ideally with water running through it.

- Camouflaged combat clothing and face vizors are essential so have ample sets in different sizes available to **hire/buy.**

- Consider the issue of **Merit Certificates.**

- Of course, you have to break up all of this very rigorous activity with something more relaxing.

- If **Napoleon** was the first strategist (seeing all his combat as part of an overall pattern that would win him a war and improve his political position) it is in refighting his and other generals' tactical battles where the interest could lie for your PSGs.

- So, although all the **miniature soldiers** and the faithfully reproduced battle **'terrain'** do not come cheap, properly presented these (large) table-top battle games can provide riveting leisure breaks and discussion stimuli.

- The success of the venture rests entirely on your concept of your market and how you put your physical and cerebral elements together to form an irresistible package.

- Get it right, like perhaps shaping your ventures for the executive market (in which case don't forget the ladies) and you will make much money, for major companies use adventure and survival courses to test and train their executives.

- You will make even more money if you have an attractive **for-sale** display of equipment and games appropriate to the course. And selling anything of a specialist nature always opens up the possibility of **MAIL ORDER** (qv).

••• INFORMATION CHECK LIST

- 'Well, how much money?' you ask.

- The answer will rest on how good your package is and on what you are going to offer in the way of accommodation and nourishment.

- Don't be frightened to charge a good price for a really good package. See how others do it first.

- For example, HILTON HOTELS (0923 38877) charge £96 for a weekend (two nights, b&b) with one day spent on their Adventure Game. Their climbing/abseiling course comes in at much the same cost.

- MOTIVACTION (0438-86260) call their game Skirmish and charge £65 for a one-day battle for which you also get a barbecue lunch.

- MOTIVACTION began as a clay pigeon shoot operation (but will now lay on up to 30 other activities) and their one-day shoots go from £59 to £169 per person with food and drink varying from barbecues to lavish, according to price. Sleeping accommodation extra.

- Other indicators: HILTON charge £107.50 for a day's clay pigeon shooting with two nights, b&b; TRUST HOUSE FORTE (0345 - 500400) do it from £163, with dinner. You can get archery training for similar cost. THF also offer breaks with horse riding, climbing and kayaking.

- Somewhat higher up the tariff AIR FOYLE ESCAPADES (0582 - 419792) will charge around £500 for a weekend's clay pigeon shooting at Gleneagles Hotel. That's for shooting and b&b only, but you get there by executive jet and chauffeur-driven limousine!

- Another activity provider is GOWER'S CLYNE FARM ACTIVITY CENTRE, Mayals, near Swansea (0792 - 403333). For £1.50 per hour you can chance your mountaineering arm at their 60-metre long artificial traverse. Basically this is wall climbing around a concrete-framed, covered barn and the challenge has been designed by experts.

- Residentially for £180 per week you can also enjoy GOWER's kayaking, assault and obstacle coursing, archery, orienteering, windsurfing, pony trekking and camp craft.

- OUTWARD BOUND (0788 - 60423) are well-respected for their tough courses. Eight-days £285 or 20-days for £585; held in Wales, The Lake District and Scotland, etc.

- Phone the BRITISH ACTIVITY HOLIDAYS ASSOCIATION (0597 - 3902) for other activity operators and check your Sunday newspapers.

- MODEL SHOP (01 - 863 9788), wargaming

model and terrain specialists.

- Also contact MODEL MASTERS (0934 - 750885) for terrain.

- Read THE TIMES ATLAS OF THE SECOND WORLD WAR, pub. TIMES BOOKS, £27.50, for graphic coverage of all aspects.

- If you feel that this wide-ranging field of activity is for you then the obvious thing to do is to attend as many of the courses as your time and money will afford.

- Get the feel of the thing and be relentless in asking questions. Be alert to how you would organise **your** venture in this field.

- Contact THE SPORTS COUNCIL (01 - 778 8600) for general information and names and addresses of the organisations that govern the various activities and training required to qualify as an instructor.

- If you think it's all very exciting but you don't feel up to the physical aspects why not try and get hold of an expert? Try an ad in:

- THE GLOBE & LAUREL (01 - 583 6077), the journal of the Royal Marines;

- MARS & MINERVA, the journal of the SAS, or

- PEGASUS, the journal of the Parachute Regiment. Phone number for both of these is 0252 - 515891.

- Or read the quite extraordinary COMBAT, monthly, £1.20. This *!?*! magazine is raw but totally dedicated, calling itself 'The Bible of the

Martial Arts'. Information on personalities and an amazing array of courses and equipment.

- **Stop Press:** Contact SCALEMEAD ARMS CO (034 - 282 4433) for details of their range of wet-colour pellet (or paint ball) 'weaponry'.

• ANTIQUES APPRECIATION & RESTORATION

- BBC's Antiques Roadshow demonstrates just how much people love heritage and its artifacts and always want to know more about them.

- As something has to be at least 100 years old to qualify for the appellation **antique,** at which point prices sky-rocket, you may not be able to afford too many of the genuine articles; so unless you are very rich you will have to rely heavily on slides, photos and videos, together with conducted visits to any nearby houses and shops where the genuine article can be enjoyed and commented on (but also see **INFORMATION CHECK LIST**).

- Nevertheless, with ingenuity you will attract plenty of customers to these courses; plural naturally because you have various categories to choose from: furniture, carpets and rugs, glass, porcelain, silver and so on.

- Even more customers if you go in strongly on the renovation aspect since, following years of exporting the 'family silver', what we do have left here is even more precious.

- Obviously there are vast numbers of books about antiques but study of the sample publications and sources suggested below will get you started and help you decide on which of the specialty areas appeals and enable you to focus on the particular training necessary.

- Don't forget the elegant sale. Books will be snapped up by your PSGs; even humble but approved furniture polish, as well as the restoration tools and finishes.

••• INFORMATION CHECK LIST

- Choose from the following magazines and publications: ANTIQUE (twice yearly) £3; AN-TIQUE CLOCKS (monthly) £2.25; ANTIQUE COLLECTING (monthly) £2.25; ANTIQUE & COLLECTORS FAYRE (monthly) £1.25; THE ANTIQUE DEALERS & COLLECTORS GUIDE (monthly) £1.60; THE ANTIQUE COLLECTOR (monthly) £2. Most available from larger newsagents.

- ANTIQUE TRADES GAZETTE (01 - 930 4957) Subscription £35 p.a. brings you their 50 gazettes a year and includes, with much else, information on sales around the country.

- WORLD FURNITURE by HELENA HAYWARD pub 1965 by PAUL HAMLYN. Used as a reference by Sotheby's so although now out of print well worth taking the trouble to find, e.g. try Bookfinders' Service on 0424 - 754291.

- SOTHEBY'S CONCISE ENCYCLOPAEDIA OF FURNITURE, pub CONRAN OCTOPUS, £25.

- THE WHICH? GUIDE TO BUYING AN-TIQUES (0992 - 589031) is rather more than the title suggests, covering also care and restoration. Price £9.95.

- MILLER'S ANTIQUE PRICE GUIDE, by JUDITH & MARTIN MILLER, pub themselves, £16.95.

- BETTER THAN NEW, A PRACTICAL GUIDE TO RENOVATING FURNITURE, by A. JACKSON & D. DAY, pub BBC PUBLI-CATIONS, £4.75.

- BRITISH ANTIQUE FURNITURE RE-STORERS ASSOCIATION (01 - 603 5643).

- WEST DEAN COLLEGE OF ARTS (0243 - 63301) re their highly regarded restoration courses.

- THE VICTORIA & ALBERT MUSEUM (01 - 938 8500) will not only give information on restoration and courses but also on virtually anything else at all that you want to know about the vast and fascinating study of antiques.

- For an early and relaxed 'taste' speak to THF HOTELS (0345 - 500400) for information on their breaks, ANTIQUE HUNTS and ART & ANTIQUES weekend, from around £100-133 incl. breakfast and dinner, pp. for two nights.

- Also HILTON (0923 - 246464) and their ANTIQUES weekends, £103 pp, incl. breakfast and dinner, for two nights.

- Opportunities for other close looks at the sort of thing you could wind up running yourself will be found in courses advertised in the magazines mentioned, the Sunday papers and the glossies.

- Finally, consider coming to some arrangement with local antique dealers of repute to temporarily borrow (or hire) from them particular pieces to 'illustrate' your courses.

• AQUA GROOMING & OTHER THERAPIES

- Ideal for those who love swimming and want to put their own large, covered, heated pool to profitable year-round use.

- Aqua Grooming is based on some simple facts:

  - In water your body weight feels only a fraction of what it is on land.

  - This reduced gravity makes the heart's work easier.

  - Exercise in water is much safer than dry land activity because weak joints and tissues do not run the risk of stress to anything like the same extent.

- The net result is that exercising feels easier and thus much more enjoyable (and thus more **marketable** to a wider range of people and age groups).

- The fact is that a lot of people are unfit and feel uneasy enough about this to make a gesture towards getting fitter: jogging, aerobics, etc.

- But after a time they find, surprise surprise, that the old saying 'no gain without pain' is all too true, which is where Aqua Grooming comes into its own.

- Almost all conventional body slimming, toning and building exercises can be done in the water, some by hanging onto the pool rail.

- (Make the exercises even more enjoyable by doing them to **music.**)

21

- Remember that, because of the expensive training requirements in today's difficult labour market, employees are valuable corporate **assets.** Health and fitness courses for employees can therefore be readily sold to a growing number of companies.

- (Incidentally, swimming pools can be expensive to heat. It's well worth getting advice on how **alternative technology** can help. And if you are going that route you will quickly see how AT can lower **all** your energy costs.)

- Also in the water-is-great-for-you context, consider offering the numerous gentle, but effective, **herbal** bath treatments discussed in The Herb Book. With the addition of the proper herbs to the bath (of which there are several variations) many beneficial effects can be created: the skin may be softened, moisturised, scented, tightened and toned; relieved of excess oil and of itching; muscle aches eased away and other benefits achieved.

- A grooming-therapy operation that has both a theme and some unusual therapy machines is worth weighing.

- A prime candidate for specialisation concerns the problems with **backs.**

- Consider:

- One of the commonest causes of lost working days is a back problem; in the UK alone currently some 35,000,000 working days are lost to this complaint.

- Conservatively, it is said that 1 in 10 people suffer from their back. However, this figure may be absolute nonsense if you believe an American research study reported in GP magazine. Based on a series of 100 consecutive post-mortems performed on cadavers aged between 12 and 84, a back problem of some kind or another was discovered in **every case.**

- The American deduction that **everybody** over the age of 12 has something wrong with their back may be taking things too far, given the size of the sample. Nevertheless it must be absolutely the case that any effective, well-marketed back treatment course is going to make money, quite apart from the bonus that an awful lot of currently resigned sufferers will be helped.

- Which brings us back to Aqua Grooming and its therapeutic aspect:

- Whilst some back problems are caused by mental stress and can only be cured accordingly, controlled exercise in water has the medical world's seal of complete approval.

- Now for the machines: One is the **Back Machine.**

- This see-saw like creation enables the user to swing through an increasing arc until he is completely upside down (secured at the feet, of course) thus using gravity to stretch and soothe spine and muscles and sometimes even ease errant discs back into place.

- An even more delightful machine for back therapy, fitness training and sheer play is the Austrian invention, the **Aerotrim.**

- The user puts himself inside a large, tubular **universal joint** which reacts automatically to changes of movement and weight distribution resulting in three-dimensional rotation — every whichway can be achieved, even upside down.

23

- The promoters claim that the machine is so sophisticated that it can be used safely and beneficially by all age groups, even the advanced in years.

- Not cheap but a thrilling and unusual machine for your customers to enjoy.

- Hardly a machine perhaps but nevertheless very beneficial for back therapy is the **Back Chair,** distinguished because it has no back and makes you sit properly and comfortably.

- It could be used for lectures and even in dining rooms for those who wanted to try a correct sitting experience.

- If you were prepared to consider other wet therapy aspects there are two further treatments that might profitably be included in your thinking:

- Immersing the client in hot mineral **mud** which miraculously draws out aches and pains (**Pellosotherapy**).

- That involving sea water body spraying and seaweed powder baths for revitalisation, deep skin cleansing, muscle relaxation and toning (**Thalassotherapy**).

- Apart from these and the other treatments mentioned earlier, there are a raft of other back therapies ranging from physiotherapy to osteopathy together with an ever-widening range of **alternative therapies** coming into vogue all the time. How far you wish to tread down these paths must be for you to decide when constructing your back package.

- The more deeply you go into therapy, of course, the more qualified you or your colleagues will

24

have to be. But look at the size of the market!

- In any well-being situation there is always a customer demand for advice on what to eat and drink, which health books to read, etc.

- Having your own **Health Shop** therefore makes sense and could also be the source of a growing **MAIL ORDER** (qv) business for vitamins and other pills, machines, chairs and so on.

- Incidentally, talking about therapy, here are some statistics: Americans reckon that four **hugs** per day make for survival, eight HPD maintain equilibrium and with 12 HPD we **grow.**

- They also maintain that hugs are so vital that if starved of them you must get hugs unconventionally.

- One lady actually claims that she got her quota by asking people in a supermarket. She was never refused once she showed her doctor's prescription 'for hugs'.

- Is there a case for a **Hugging SEMINAR**? Should it be part of **PERSONAL DEVELOPMENT**?

- (We don't really know; we're still recovering after being thrown out of six supermarkets.)

••• INFORMATION CHECK LIST

- THE ALTERNATIVE TECHNOLOGY CENTRE (0654 - 2400) for advice on economical water heating.

- BACKSWING MACHINE (0525 - 383100) lightweight £230, heavy duty £280, both plus VAT.

- The AEROTRIM machine: contact HERMAN DITTRICH of CONTACTOS TRADING in Munich (010 4989 769 4052). Cost £2,000-£3,500 according to model.

- THE BACK STORE (01 - 741 5022) are back advisers who sell a variety of chairs and other clever aids to alleviate back problems.

- THE HERB BOOK, by JOHN LUST, pub BANTAM, £4.95.

- ULTRAHEALTH, by LESLIE KENTON, pub ARROW, £3.99, for hints on Pellosotherapy and Thalassotherapy.

- SEAWEED — A USER'S GUIDE by S SUREY-GENT & G MORRIS, pub WHITTET, £9.95.

- There are some excellent books on backs:

- BACK ATTACK, by DR EDWARD TARLOV & DAVID D'COSTA, pub LITTLE BROWN, £6.95.

- THE BACK BOOK: HEALING THE HURT IN YOUR LOWER BACK, by MAGGIE LETTVIN, pub SOUVENIR PRESS, £6.95.

- BEATING BACK PAIN, by DR JOHN TANNER, pub DORLING KINDERSLEY, £5.95.

- THE NATIONAL BACK PAIN ASSO-CIATION (01 - 977 5474) has over 50 branches and lays on professional talks and therapy classes.

- HERE'S HEALTH, monthly, 95p, one of many health magazines wherein you can find numerous courses to attend to get more insight into grooming and therapy aspects that appeal to you.

- An excellent US health magazine is SHAPE, monthly, £1.95, from bigger newsagents.

- THE ROYAL SOCIETY OF ARTS (0203 - 550707) will tell you how to qualify for their BASIC CERTIFICATE in the TEACHING OF EXERCISE TO MUSIC.

- The AQUATIC EXERCISE ASSOCIATION is run by RUTH SOVA, a professional fitness teacher working in water exercises. Write to her at the AEA, PO Box 497, PORT WASHINGTON, WISCONSIN, ZIP 53074, USA; or call her on 0101 - 414 3752503 to see how those energetic Americans approach this fascinating venture.

- Closer to home is SPLASHDANCE (0708 - 730431) who are developing a franchise in aqua aerobics. They make the point that you don't need to actually own your own pool (you can hire one from your local council, hotel or health club); however, you do need to be able to lay your hands on the £10,000 that they require for their franchise!

- Finally, if you're really serious (or just want a wonderful few days getting fit) why not see what water really can do for you? THE DANIEL HOTEL & SPA, Herzlia-on-Sea, Israel, 46769, is not cheap but offers a wide range of treatments including, inter alia, underwater massage, thalassotherapy (a bubbling bath in Dead Sea water which has a mineral content 10 times greater than other sea water) followed by pellosotherapy using Dead Sea mud. For details write or ring the DANIEL on 010 - 972 52 544444.

● BESPOKE

● In today's society there are many anomalies. One in particular confronts the person needing or demanding something **special:**

● That something for example may be a piece of furniture that must be a particular shape to fit an awkward corner; a piece of jewellery as a gift for a fussy or much-loved relative; some stained glass for a special window and so on (see fuller list).

● Here is a customer with the money to spend but all too often he confronts either the mass-produced that lacks specialness or the up-market that is both not what he really wants and is horrendously expensive.

● Such a customer, and there are more of them than you may think, is the target for the bespoke (= ordered to be made) craftsman who will undertake the commission of making an unique item for his customer.

● Although the cost of the item will be high (offering a handsome margin of profit) it will probably not be much different than the refined item referred to above, but, essentially for the customer, he has got **precisely** what he wants.

● What sort of artefacts? Expectably: carpets, ceramics, modern and reproduction furniture, fountain sculpture, knitwear, portraits in paint, sculpture or photography; rugs, stained glass, silver (bigger items are coming back into fashion), saddlery, shoes, shirts, suits, textiles, ornamental walking sticks and crooks, wallpaper and wigs for example.

- Perhaps not quite so obvious: The world is having a **memento-collecting** and **photo-snap** binge. Alas, most of this personally important memorabilia never actually gets the loving regard that it deserves because snaps wind up in seldom-opened albums, mementoes in the back of equally seldom-used drawers.

- Enter the **collage maker** who for no small fee will recreate the happy moments by artistically mounting the treasured objects into picture frames or by creating **three-dimensional** mementoes as interesting, eye-catching ornaments for niches or hangings for walls.

- Nothing unusual about **glass** artefacts but give this an appropriate twist by guaranteeing to use only **recycled glass.**

- Children and **toys** represent the happiest combinations; is there an even happier one by setting up a **bespoke toy** enterprise? A toy made either to the donor's idea or perhaps in an exact image of the **child's** own design?

- As we note elsewhere **war games** are addictive; the true addict will pay handsomely for soldiers and weapons and battle 'terrain' that are faithfully reproduced down to fine detail. **Metal** artefacts command a premium as the inevitable plastic finds its way into the picture.

- (There is always a market for the tacky: Full-sized suits of armour faithfully reproduced in glass reinforced plastic [GRP] come to mind [although okay we suppose if you have Hammer Films as a client]; and the other gee-whizz idea we've heard about concerns the fact that the **Louvre** has recently granted a licence to someone enabling them to reproduce as prints any of the museum's masterpieces — at whatever size is wanted! Dilate a Degas, miniaturise a Matisse?!)

- These lists are not exhaustive. Look around your area of choice to see what bespoke could sell.

- What are the **ground rules** governing this venture? Consider:

- Whilst impeccable workmanship is required to make the product, considerable skill is also called for in the technique of **dealing with** the customer so that he winds up yours for life after delivery of what he's ordered.

- Whilst a little bit of mystique helps, the customer has to be made to feel comfortable about what he is buying; it may be costly but not grossly extravagant.

- You have to find out by tactful reconnoitre that the customer really **does** need or want the item. Second thoughts can be fatal, especially if you have been drawn into doing work for which you are either not going to be paid or, if so, only after a lot of damaging hassle.

- You have to feel that you are going to be able to get on with your customer. He may well be discriminating (that's why he's come to you) but is he also evidently likely to be unfairly **difficult?** If so, you may be better off without him.

- The customer needs to accept that, with a complex item, getting to an agreement on the final design will probably take **time** (but you cost this in).

- For certain items it is essential that a detailed **drawing** is created which when agreed is signed by both parties. In the event of any hiccups this then can be referred to.

- After the drawing is agreed you confirm everything in writing, including the price and whether or not this includes VAT; how and when the bill is to be paid and the agreed delivery date.

- Upon acceptance of your **quotation** (and remember, in law you can be strictly held to its terms) you will receive whatever has been agreed by way of **deposit.** This can vary between 10 and 50% according to how much money you have to spend up front on materials, etc.

- Upon completion the work should always be signed or stamped in some way by the craftsman, not only because this shows that the maker is proud of his work but also because from the customer's angle, signed and dated pieces are going to be more valuable over time.

- The item should be photographed. Copies for you to show other customers; copies for your customer's insurance requirements.

- Very rough ideas on some bespoke selling prices: Jewellery can range from as little as £10 to the sky's-the-limit; furniture from hundreds of pounds for smaller pieces to around £2,000+ for larger; stained glass for between £30 and £100 per sq. metre; Jacquard weave textiles anything up to £50 per sq. metre subject to quantity; ceramics from £25 to £1,500 per piece.

- You do **not** have to be a skilled craftsman to make bespoke money. As many craftsmen are happier crafting than entrepreneuring you can consider being the manufacturer's agent: provider of space, greeter, office administrator, marketeer, organiser of exhibitions and promoter, to either one or more skilled craftsmen, perhaps a whole cooperative. In this case you work out financial details with each craftsman.

- In the early stages of such an enterprise, clearly each craftsman will have to produce various examples of his work for display in the **shop.**

- This can either be a spare room in your house that is readily accessible from the front door or, better, a clean, dry, well-heated outbuilding on your property.

- It will make initial cashflow sense for each craftsman to turn out items for casual sale but this would have to be carefully thought through as part of the business strategy bearing in mind that once bespoke orders start to roll in (and this will not take long if you market skilfully) the craftsmen will be flat to the boards and will not have much time for casual work.

••• INFORMATION CHECK LIST

- THE RURAL DEVELOPMENT COMMIS-SION (0722 - 336255) is your starting point for help in locating and funding suitable rural property; they also provide training and specialist and general business advice. However, as they operate only in England, for other areas you need to contact:

- THE WELSH DEVELOPMENT AGENCY (0222 - 222666).

- THE SCOTTISH DEVELOPMENT AGENCY (041 - 248 2700).

- THE NORTHERN IRELAND INDUSTRIAL DEVELOPMENT AGENCY (0232 - 233233).

- To find out further details of training available and to meet up with budding craftsmen/ entrepreneurs start by contacting your local polytechnic and art colleges.

- To get information on opportunities, courses and what's going on generally, read CRAFTS magazine, £3.25, pub six times yearly by the CRAFTS COUNCIL (01 - 930 4811).

- For a hard-nosed American look at craft money, marketing and management, consider THE CRAFTS REPORT, PO Box 1992, WILMINGTON, DE, 19899, USA. Cost $19.25 (surface) or $49.25 (air) for 12 monthly issues. Got your calculator?

- To see a sample commissioning service in action contact the CRAFTS COUNCIL (01 - 930 4811). They have slides of, for example, silversmiths' work. Or CONTEMPORARY APPLIED ARTS (01 - 836 6993) who also act as link between customer and craftsman.

- If you're going to get your goods before the trade and public you'll need the EXHIBITIONS AND CONFERENCES DIRECTORY from YORK PUBLISHING CO. (01 - 937 6636 or 01 - 278 4299).

- You can see the PARLANE recycled glass range at THE PERFECT GLASS SHOP (01 - 351 5342).

- Get a line on soldiers and war terrain at THE MODEL SHOP (01 - 863 9788).

• CALLIGRAPHY

- Most of us feel guilty about our own hand-writing; many of us would pay you to show us how to make it more beautiful.

- In some parts of the world calligraphy is a sublime art in its own right; e.g. because Muslims are forbidden the 'blasphemy' of doing figurative painting and sculpture — they believe that only God has the prerogative to give such form — all their artistic talent through the ages has had to concentrate on writing, spurred no doubt by their belief that, as the Koran contains the words of God Himself, writing must be beautiful.

- As well as on paper exquisite Muslim calligraphy has been expressed on papyrus, vellum, wool, silk, cotton, linen, brass, ceramic, stone, marble, wood and even on steel. At its finest this calligraphic art is quite dazzling in its beauty and artistic verve.

- In China, Japan and Korea calligraphy is also accorded the status of an art form.

- Showing others how to execute calligraphy is actually only one way to make money from it:

- A steady money-maker would be to produce in numbers **personalised** commemorative cards for Christmas, Birthday, 21st, Driving Test Pass, Conquering Fear of Computers, etc., because, if you stop to think about it, just a **few** common Christian names apply to large numbers of the populace.

- If you are doing birthday cards why not also add a list of some of the **famous people** born on the same day?

- Such cards would command a premium.

- As would offering a **coat of arms** service. Some people are entitled to armorial devices as authorised by the College of Heralds; most are not so entitled but there is nothing to stop you designing an **individual** coat of arms to personal order.

- A calligraphic artist has many other possible avenues to consider such as **graphic design, book illustration** and **design** and on a larger scale, **interior design.**

- These ideas will no doubt stimulate other money spinners of your own, e.g. why not sell to your PSGs handsomely framed examples of your own and other calligraphers' work? Whatever you do please bear in mind the **MAIL ORDER** (qv) possibilities.

••• INFORMATION CHECK LIST

- There are good and less-good books on this subject.

- DONALD JACKSON of THE CALLI-GRAPHY CENTRE (0600 - 4334) recommends:

- THE CALLIGRAPHER'S HANDBOOK, edited by HEATHER CHILD, pub A & C BLACK, £12.95.

- MORE THAN FINE WRITING (concerning the work of IRENE WELLINGTON), edited by HEATHER CHILD, pub PELHAM, £20.

- PEN LETTERING, by ANN CAMP, pub A & C BLACK, £3.95.

- The splendidly named SOCIETY OF SCRIBES & ILLUSTRATORS (01 - 748 9951) provides information on all aspects of calligraphy including training courses.

- Expect to pay in the order of £200 per week (probably including some meals but excluding accommodation) for instruction by top people.

- Talk to the CRAFTS COUNCIL (01 - 930 4811) to see if you can get grants.

• COMPUTERS FOR THE PANIC-STRUCK

- Before reading about this potential venture see our comments in **HIT LIST.** In short, our advice is that this is only for you if you are already fully computer-wise. On that basis:

- The title speaks for itself. The world is still full of people who have a nasty feeling that if their kids can work the things then they at least might try to understand the basics as well.

- And you may be surprised at the number of company senior executives who enrol; we are well into the era when one person in three will have a computer on their desk and the boss cannot escape because EIS looms. **Executive Information Systems** are developing that will enable top dogs to dip into their corporate database and extract and analyse key information.

- The senior managers who continue to boast of having 'never touched a keyboard' will be booked for an early bath.

- Insofar as you will be teaching people what **can** be learned elsewhere success will lie in **how** you do it.

- The 'panic' of this venture title arises from the fact that (particularly older) people think that, knowing absolutely nothing about computers, they are going to be made to look foolish, i.e. that teachers are going to assume some knowledge and ridicule them if they don't have it.

- Regrettably there are teachers around like this who encourage the image of mystery, perhaps hoping in some obscure way to increase their own status.

- Another panic is less logical: 'If teenagers can quickly become whizz-kids then conquering computers is something only the young can do.'

- The teachers who don't giggle over these concerns but accept their existence and overcome them with sympathy and care (and a twinkle in the eye) will get a lot of 'oldies' beating a path to their door — and a lot of grateful ones leaving to spread the word.

- And the word is — well, 'empathy'?

- Because one of the things you want to do is to 'disguise' your classroom; make the place look homely and comfy.

- As ever, don't overlook the very real prospects of selling computer books, magazines, and particularly hard- and soft-ware to your PSGs. What they're confident in they will probably buy or rent from you.

- After you have become a really proficient teacher then consider **computer consultancy** as a profitable sideline. Fees can vary between £100 to £300 per day. However, do find a market niche otherwise there's a minefield out there waiting for you, with hundreds of soft-ware programs and many different machines. Get your package together, say for new businesses who will need guidance for such basics as wordprocessing, accounts, etc. Thereafter expand your expertise and grow with your clients.

- Whilst we're on the subject of computers we can also talk about teaching **Keyboard Skills.**

- Some things it seems just won't go away. Just as the modern office and its technology was going to eliminate paper (more in demand now than ever before) so the demise of the typewriter was confidently predicted.

- This turned out to be only partly true because the typewriter's fighting back! The new generation go a long way towards computers but being less complex they are still a preferred option for many businesses. Add on the growing army of computers and you can readily see why keyboard competence is in demand by an even larger number and variety of people.

- Although the bigger typing schools seem wedded to the system of teaching by video in large classes, this can leave the slower student floundering and doesn't seem to produce a particularly high quality student, even amongst those who do 'pass'.

- As with your computer courses, smaller classes and more old-fashioned sympathetic mothering would garner a higher fee and a happier, more competent PSG.

- Get your PSGs to relax (plenty of laughs and cups of tea) and you're a long way further than half-way there.

••• INFORMATION CHECK LIST

- As this venture is only for the computer-wise you will already have preferred information and supply sources garnered from your own experience.

- You will also be aware that it makes sense to know about THE BRITISH COMPUTER SOCIETY (01 - 637 0471), an excellent standby for guidance on all matters and particularly if you find yourself facing difficulties with suppliers, litigation, etc. They offer advice to individuals.

- However

- If you are a company then advice on problems can be obtained from the COMPUTING SERVICES ASSOCIATION (01 - 405 2171).

- Even with experience and the best of advice you can still get it wrong. Therefore try to **rent** not lease or buy your machines for the first few months, on the basis that, say, 80% of the rent comes off the price if you buy. If there's a problem you sling them back and you're only out a modest amount and can start again, wiser but not much poorer.

- You know that it's a competitive world; once you have identified precisely what hard- and soft-ware you want bargain like hell on price. After all, you're a bulk buyer.

- On keyboard skills consider the video interactive TYPEQUICK TOUCH-TYPING COURSE (IBMs and compatibles), £69.95 (retail) from COMPRIX COURSEWARE (061 - 9269328).

- For students with weak hands or those suffering from repetitive strain injury (common to typists) consider introducing them to the MALTRON keyboard, ergonomically designed by an American print specialist who fed millions of words into a computer to come up with the most frequently used letters and then designed a new keyboard accordingly.

- Maltron say that it takes only a few hours to get used to it; the shaped keyboard comes with the conventional QWERTY style as a flick-of-a-switch alternative.

- And Maltron have other aids for handicapped people for whom the computer is often an important means of communication with family, friends and the outside world.

- There is also one for the single-handed keyboard operator (like accountants) who use the other hand for flicking through receipts as they enter the figures on the computer.

- Maltron keyboards cost from £175 for a BBC micro to £295 for IBM PC, plus VAT & delivery. Phone them on 01 - 398 3265.

- Maltron have also prepared several training manuals including one specifically for executives. It will get them up to 50wpm.

- Finally, as you expand you'll need competent help. Over in Hong Kong there's a high degree of computer savvy; there's an even higher degree of concern at the looming Chinese takeover. Consider reaching some of this talent through an ad in THE ASIAN WALL STREET JOURNAL (Advertising Dept., 01 - 334 0008).

• CULTS

- These have been with us for as long as man has found something and someone to worship. Here, however, we're interested in the secular.

- As we know, people have made and are making money out of cults surrounding Marilyn Monroe, Elvis Presley, James Dean, Dr Who, The Prisoner, Star Trek, Stingray and, at another extreme, Noel Coward. The list is virtually endless.

- Unlikely though it sounds, ex-President Nixon has become a cult figure. Could Reagan follow? Or has Spitting Image wiped him out?

- You will have your own ideas no doubt but, if not, to stimulate you why not acknowledge the British passion for **fancy dress.**

- For example, a cult seminar based on a wild west character, either real such as Wyatt Earpe, Doc Halliday or Jesse James, or fictional, such as the Lone Ranger or factional like Tom Mix and his roles.

- You could tap in on the widely-practised cowboy dress-up syndrome by inviting PSGs to appear in all their western finery, offering prizes for the most macho cowpoke and most winsome cowgirl.

- Six-shooter competitions, half-an-ox barbecues, etc, all going on in your version of a western goal or, more convivially, a bar; even a shoot-out in your own OK Corral.

- However, the best cults tend to take their wor-shipped one (and themselves) pretty seriously as well, exploring the moral, social, sometimes even the scientific impact on their lives of the cult.

45

- How you trade off tongue-in-cheek with a straight face probably determines the success of your venture.

- Don't overlook the boost to cult interest, and your bank balance, of in-house sales of cult memorabilia (see below).

••• INFORMATION CHECK LIST

- An example of a cult that has deservedly flourished over the years is centred round the brilliant TV series THE PRISONER, starring Patrick McGoohan. Contact

- THE PRISONER APPRECIATION SOCIETY "6 of 1", PO Box 60, HARROGATE, NORTH YORKS, HG1 2TP, subscription £12 per year includes their quarterly magazine.

- The Society holds various functions and once per year they have an annual convention at (where else?) the scene of the series, PORT-MEIRION (0766 - 770228). This is a total holiday village open all year round offering both hotel accommodation, from approx. £75 - £135 twin per night, and self-catering chalets, from approx. £100 to £495 per week, according to size and season.

- It also has THE PRISONER INFORMATION SERVICE and THE PRISONER SHOP both under the aegis of MAX HORA.

- Is there a more towering cult figure than ELVIS PRESLEY? At the ELVISLY YOURS (01 - 739 2001) emporium in London over 1000 different items of Elvis memorabilia are on offer. Business is evidently brilliant because MR SHAW the proprietor says that his is the biggest Elvis operation in the world outside America.

- The presentation of a successful cult operation depends largely on pure theatre so if this venture appeals some dramatic training could be important. You can almost certainly get this training in your local area. If not speak to:

- STAGECRAFT (01 - 483 2681) who run residential and non-residential courses in acting, directing, makeup and lighting etc. Charges vary from around £20 per day for non-residential to around £300 per six working-day week, residential.

- Having decided on your cult figure you and thereafter your customers will want to know every conceivable detail about the worshipped one; minutae is as important as the main event. You will be spending a lot of time in libraries and bookshops and wherever those researches lead you in tracking down the information.

- Naturally the ultimate in culting would be to cult in the actual house of the worshipped one. As this is pretty unlikely to be available, then does the **area** suggest a cult figure, e.g. SHERWOOD FOREST and ROBIN HOOD?

• DESIGN & DECORATION

- If you have creative design inclinations and want to train to a professional standard (or already possess such skills) there is evidently money to be made in several ways. Broadly by

- Practising the skill either as a manufacturer or consultant;

- Manufacturing and showing other people how to do it;

- Teaching by itself.

- It is the last two that we mainly deal with here.

- The market reveals some interesting figures:

- A four-day (no accommodation but lunch and coffee) course on **interior design** can fetch a fee in excess of £300.

- A three-week course on how to actually **become** an interior designer commands of the order of £1,300.

- Specialty teaching courses cost per day examples:
- Gilding   £40
- Curtain-making   £70
- Stencilling   £50
- Screen painting   £40
- Paint marbling &
  trompe-l'oeil
  (Fr = deception of the eye)   £60
- Paint ragging and dragging   £40

- As there are evidently course price variations your final charge will greatly depend not only on whether you offer accommodation but also how you actually **conduct** your courses; i.e.

- You will find that although PSGs will naturally want to be entertained, most of them are fiercely keen to learn. The right balance between jollity and concentration therefore is the winning atmosphere to aim at.

- Some unusual aspects to consider:

- Amongst the tales of boom and bust in the textiles business what is emerging is that customers increasingly want **individual designs.**

- Doing short runs however was a major problem until inevitably the computer was hauled in to lower the labour costs.

- Now the limited-edition or **commission weaver** is a fact of life, opening up exciting short-run design possibilities and therefore manufacture and/or teaching possibilities for you, e.g.

- A significant number of people have oriental carpets, rugs and kilims; **facsimiles** of these designs could be worked out on a computer and, via the software (see below), matching curtains, upholstery, table coverings, etc. could be produced. Yes, expensive and yes, profitable. (But, **no,** not for you unless you are computer-wise, see **HIT LIST**).

- The 18th century **print room** is making a comeback. Prints, engravings or mezzotints for example are cut into oblongs, ovals and octagons and pasted onto the walls of the room to be given the print room treatment. The effect is completed with elaborate 'frames' and 'hung' on 'chains' or 'ribbons' thus deceiving the eye and introducing a trompe-l'oeil element.

- The best print rooms depend more on imaginative layout rather than on the quality of the pictures chosen.

- Originating in the 17th Century, early **dummy boards** or 'silent companions' may have been conceived as a security measure: a life-like, man-shaped figure was cut out from wood, given foot support, back-lit and placed near windows to deter intruders.

- Before long the dummy boards attracted more artistic attention and urns, flower vases and animals, etc., featured as casual but attractive decorative stand-ups and firescreens in fashionable houses.

- Today you can again get them either hand-painted in period style or have a photograph of a favourite scene, person, or animal transformed into a painted dummy board.

- As design is the expression of imagination there is no limit to wit and inventiveness, e.g.

- The Japanese clothes designer **Issey Miyake,** in perfecting unique, sculptured metallic pleats and using them in his gold and silver thread dresses, raised the question of whether he was creating fashion or art;

- Another iconoclast, chair designer **Ron Arad,** also continues to raise the same question. Starting in 1981 with his Rover chairs (old leather car seats culled from scrap yards then mounted on tubular steel frames) he is still constructing comfortable, eye-arresting seats that wouldn't look out of place in the Tate.

- The range of things to **sell** to your PSGs will depend on which branch of design attracts you. Whatever that is, keep this important and legitimate added-earner well in mind.

- The world of good design is a magical world. Is it for you? You can start to find out by reading on.

••• INFORMATION CHECK LIST

- If no longer pre-eminent, a good starting point is the DESIGN COUNCIL (01 - 839 8000) which not only mounts a variety of exhibitions and provides a range of design information including a directory of design courses available around the country, but also produces

- DESIGN MAGAZINE, monthly, costing £29.74 per year.

- DESIGNERS JOURNAL is considered by some to be the country's leading magazine for professional interior designers. Ten issues per year, £2 each.

- CRAFTS MAGAZINE, every month, £3.25, and many of the glossies will point you to the courses you will want to consider. These range from taster to full-blown professional courses.

- Even more seriously you can get a MASTER OF ARTS DEGREE. Contact MA in ART & DESIGN, DEPT of VISUAL STUDIES, LEEDS POLYTECHNIC (0532 - 462935) for full information regarding the four institutions running the courses, which cost £600 but run to seven terms (two years plus one term).

- Read AN ILLUSTRATED HISTORY OF INTERIOR DECORATION, by MARIO PRAZ, pub THAMES & HUDSON, £45 (or from your reference library).

- PERIOD STYLE, by J & M MILLER, pub MITCHELL BEAZLEY, £19.95. How to create period effects with lighting, colours, flooring and furniture.

- THE COUNTRY HOME DECORATING BOOK, by MIRANDA INNES, pub DORLING KINDERSLEY, £14.95.

- NINETEENTH CENTURY DECORATION, by CHARLOTTE GERE, pub WEIDENFELD & NICOLSON, priced at a weighty £50 so maybe a reference library or bookshop peep first, eh?

- For a view on a period that continues to fascinate read RAGTIME TO WARTIME, THE BEST OF 'GOOD HOUSEKEEPING' 1922 - 1939, pub EBURY PRESS, £9.95.

- Read PAINTABILITY, by JOCASTA INNES, pub WEIDENFELD, £8.95. Breathtaking interior design effects with paint, including trompe-l'oeil.

- See THE DESIGN MUSEUM (01 - 407 6265) for a permanent reference collection, current design reviews and a half-dozen 'provocative' exhibitions per year.

- ROBERTSON NASH (051 - 2363699) do limited edition textiles working with an APPLE MACINTOSH 500AD computer and the MACINTOSH WEAVING PROGRAMME.

- Also computer-based are commission weavers C & J ANTICH (0484 - 435454).

- Speak to NICOLA WINGATE SAUL (01 - 821 1577) for information and a view of her print room work.

DESIGN & DECORATION

- See THE NATIONAL TRUST (01 - 222 9251) property at BLICKLING, NORFOLK for a view of their restored print room.

- FIVE FIVE SIX ANTIQUES (01 - 731 2016) stock dummy boards and also make to order.

- **ETIQUETTE**

- Whilst ethics or rules of conduct come down to us from the Greeks, the conventional rules of personal behaviour in polite society probably first emerged among the knights of southern **France** sometime in the 12th Century.

- Knightly chivalry demanded that they avenge the oppressed and defend the honour of ladies.

- However, the royal courts of **Edward III** and **Richard II** in the 14th Century provided the kind of luxurious, fashionable and sophisticated cultural centres in which etiquette began to flourish in Britain.

- The word 'etiquette' means a ticket or card and in former times a card of written directions and regulations to be observed was given to all those who attended court.

- Arguably the Victorians brought etiquette to its apogee but modern wars provide poor soil for etiquette and good manners to flourish; even common politeness suffered almost terminal damage in the indulgent 'me first' climate of the 1960s through almost to the present day.

- We say 'almost' because in fact there is now a backlash against yobbism and concern for more civilised behaviour is making a reappearance.

- Although very basic politeness is still the province of the French, it is to **America** that we turn to find that making a profitable business out of teaching people to be civilised to one another is on the increase.

- This may well have been sparked off with the appearance of new and aggressive chat shows, even a board game called Loudmouth, where success is geared to loutish aggro and plumbing the depths of bad taste.

- As with the Americans, many of us here would welcome the opportunity of a refresher course rediscovering lost refinement, perhaps because we realise that in an increasingly complex, competitive world the only defence against a return to the jungle lies in strengthening an awareness of the rules governing the way we deal with each other.

- (Of course, it may also well be that as people have become richer they simply want to be on safer ground when it comes to knowing which fork to use, which wine to serve, etc, when they are throwing their rather grand parties!)

- Just to remind you:

- **Etiquette** is the conventional code of acceptable behaviour within a particular group or class.

- For example, you **always** hand-write a thank-you note (in ink **not** biro) after receiving any major hospitality, **never** after a cocktail party or a funeral(!).

- **Good manners,** on the other hand, are barrier-breakers based upon consideration for others by adapting to make them feel more at ease.

- For example, after a stay at someone's house **do** ask the hostess if she would like you to strip your bed, but **don't** do it unless she says 'yes'. (Underblankets are not always designed for guests' eyes.)

- At random: **Nigel Dempster** the gossip columnist remembers a lapse of his own. 'In a hurry one

56

day I rushed into Harrods through the back door and a woman some distance behind berated me for not holding open the door for her. "Madam", I said, "I am not a doorman." "No" replied the ruffled lady, "but I had hoped you were a gentleman." '

- **Leslie Kark,** chairman of Lucie Clayton Grooming School, makes the point that 'Of course, it is the height of bad manners to dress sexually at any age or stage. Everyone tries to look attractive, but one should never go to someone's house dressed for bed and not board.'

- Perhaps it can all be summed up by **Anon:** 'The good host makes his guest feel at home; the good guest never behaves as if he is.'

- Consider also specialised etiquette courses for today's intending high-priced domestics: **butlers, housekeepers, chauffeurs,** etc.

- Apart from books on the subject (and there are many, covering etiquette all over the world) what else will you tastefully sell your PSGs? Whatever else, the list should certainly sooner or later include **your** book on etiquette, shouldn't it?

••• INFORMATION CHECK LIST

- To experience etiquette and good manners in action speak to THE HISTORIC HOUSES ASSOCIATION (01 - 730 9419) who will send you a list of stately home owners (many of them very grand indeed) who for a fee will entertain you in their own home.

- Before going it may be prudent to do a little revision:

- Read DEBRETT'S ETIQUETTE & MODERN MANNERS, pub PAN, £4.99. Also

- DEBRETT'S CORRECT FORM, pub FUTURA, £5.95.

- (In the pipeline: DEBRETT'S COMPANY DIRECTORS; essentially about top dogs but also covers COMPANY ETIQUETTE. Ring DEBRETT'S PEERAGE on 01 - 267 1699 for update.)

- GETTING IT RIGHT — A SURVIVAL GUIDE TO MODERN MANNERS, by LAURIE GRAHAM, pub CHATTO, £7.95.

- Possibly also read ENQUIRE WITHIN UPON EVERYTHING, by MOYRA BREMNER, pub CENTURY, £15.95. Another survival guide, this time to modern living.

- Consider joining THE POLITE SOCIETY (0782 - 614407) or write to the society's founder, the REV. IAN GREGORY, at 18 THE AVENUE, BASFORD, NEWCASTLE-UNDER-LYME, STAFFS, for ideas on how we are to improve our intrapersonal relationships.

- Ring the LUCIE CLAYTON GROOMING & MODELLING SCHOOL (01 - 581 0024) for details of LADY STYLE's (yes, that's her real name) monthly discussions on etiquette.

- There is a SCHOOL FOR BUTLERS (01 - 670 8424) run by the world-famous IVOR SPENCER, who is also President of the GUILD OF PROFESSIONAL TOASTMASTERS (01 - 670 5858) and an expert on etiquette if ever there was one. Held in London, Houston and Melbourne his courses produce both gentleman and lady **Butler/Administrators,** run for seven weeks and the London school cost is £2,500 + VAT.

- A snob, by definition, has an uncertain grasp of etiquette. Read BOOK OF TOTAL SNOB-BERY, by L JONES, pub NEW ENGLISH LIBRARY, £6.95.

• FAST READING, WRITING & RECALL

- A while back the received wisdom was that we were moving unstoppably towards a paperless society.

- Hollow laughter from those many, many of us faced with mounting piles of urgent paper that deep down we know we're never going to get around to reading unless we start at dawn and keep going into the indefinite future.

- As it's our own forecast that there are going to be more not less reading mountains ahead there is clearly a case for setting up fast reading classes.

- (Many people were baffled that **John F. Kennedy** could find time to both cope with the masses of paper that pass across the desk of a US President **and** have amorous liaisons with an astonishing number of eager young ladies. He was, of course, a formidably fast reader.)

- On the face of it the course has busy executive appeal but the field is almost certainly wider, with many different types of people being frustrated by even average reading speed ability.

- At the moment there do not appear to be many fast reading courses around and yet payment for training is excellent:

- A concentrated two-day 'laboratory' for five people will cost £1,000 plus.

- The experts we spoke to told us that during a two-day course the student would receive between eight and ten reading tests, each of greater difficulty, to monitor their progress and that they could almost guarantee that at the end students would scan faster and retain more information, with a perfectly probable overall improvement of 100%.

- These courses might naturally be linked with **Speedwriting.** This is not shorthand in the Pitman sense but an alphabetically based, easier-learnt system. Sample cost of class tuition approx. £735 for an eight-week course, 9 a.m. to 1 p.m. each day.

- In today's quickfire times the abilities to take it all in and take it all down carry premiums.

- Remember **W. J. Ennever?** Towards the end of the last century he invented **Pelmanism** and made a fortune out of teaching people easy **recall.**

- Today we can find no trace of Pelmanism, which seems strange given that a good memory would seem to us to be just as valuable today as ever.

- Basically humans are good at storing information but usually pretty poor at recalling or retrieving this information. This has been held by some experts to mean that if you have a 'bad' memory that you probably never properly took in the information in the first place.

- This in turn has been held to mean that the person with a poor memory also has poor concentration.

- Slow reading is reckoned to be one of the culprits because this allows the concentration to wander, so a memory course seems to fit naturally into this venture.

- Finally, consider what in-house sales you will make to your PSGs.

••• INFORMATION CHECK LIST

- SPEED READING, by BUZAN, pub DAVID & CHARLES, £9.95.

- SPEED READING — THE HOW-TO BOOK FOR EVERY BUSY MANAGER, EXECUTIVE AND PROFESSIONAL, by FINK, pub JOHN WILEY, £10.20.

- Contact NIGHTINGALE-CONANT (0101 - 708647 0300, or write to them at 7300 NORTH LEHIGH AVENUE, CHICAGO, ILL., zip 60648, USA) re their Catalogue Item No 463AD. Called READING DYNAMICS, this is a six audio cassette course on how to **'quadruple'** your reading speed!

- Ring GERNELLA COMMUNICATIONS LTD (01 - 799 2621) for fuller details of their FAST READING and WRITING laboratories.

- Ring LONDON COLLEGE OF BUSINESS (01 - 493 3401) for their SPEEDWRITING course details.

- A somewhat more economical way to get the flavour might be to buy INCREASED READING SPEED, an audio cassette costing £9.95 put out by ADVANCED LEARNING SYSTEMS (061 9268185).

- The same people also offer cassettes entitled POWER MEMORY, BETTER CONCENTRATION and UNLIMITED MENTAL ABILITY, all at £9.95 (if you order three cassettes you only pay for two).

- MAXIMISING MEMORY POWER: USING RECALL IN BUSINESS is a book by A BROWN, pub WILEY, £11.80.

- MASTER YOUR MEMORY, by BUZAN, pub DAVID & CHARLES, £5.95.

- MAKE THE MOST OF YOUR MEMORY, by ANSELL, pub NATIONAL EXTENSION COLL., £6.95.

- A book that has excited experts ever since it was published in 1968 is THE MIND OF A MNEMONIST, written by Russian psychologist A. R. LURIA following 30 years study of 'S', a memory artist capable of prodigious feats of recall far beyond the ordinary. Track down the book either through your library or a book-finding service.

- Contact MEMORY & CONCENTRATION STUDIES (061 - 4273513/4) for details of their correspondence course (£217.95) devised by renowned memory man, American DR BRUNO FURST, author of YOU CAN REMEMBER.

• FINANCIAL SPECULATION

- Underpinned by solid facts about how the global market works this course will better pull them in if it has spice: well-documented facts and stories about, for instance, the great 19th century robber-barons and gamblers (we reverently call them industrialists or financiers) and later moguls who go to make up the folk-lore of Money, e.g.

- **J Pierpont Morgan** (1837 - 1913) as daring as any and with a face that encapsulated Keenan Wynne and Walter Matthau. He parlayed rail-ways into a multi-billion dollar banking edifice. An astrology-addict (see **MYSTERIES**).

- 'The Commodore' **Cornelius Vanderbilt** (1794 - 1877), the ruthless competitor who killed off the opposition to his shipping lines by undercutting rates, before moving on to conquer the railways. He left $90,000,000 to his son William but rela-tively little to his wife and eight daughters, showing to the last his life-long contempt for women.

- **John D Rockefeller** (1839 - 1937), one of the most contradictory of all the great tycoons. A devout Baptist, from childhood Rockefeller made it an inflexible rule to give to charity. From a few cents a week then he wound up giving away a half-billion dollars in his long life. Perversely, he was a ruthless monopolist, controlling virtually all US oil supplies by 1882, and strike breaker, e.g. causing over 40 deaths when the militia were called in to break up a 1914 strike at one of his enterprises.

- And so on; personal tastes will dictate your own list of the great speculators, both ancient and modern.

- Back to nuts and bolts:

- Whilst we believe that money should be best used where you can control it (like in your own business), the fact is that many people either don't want to run an enterprise or are just plain fascinated by gambling on other people's organisations.

- However, all too often the newspapers tell stories of financial chicanery or mismanagement. So help your PSGs avoid the pitfalls by telling them about

- What **really** happens to their money when they take out that **PEP** or invest in those **Unit Trusts** (not forgetting the delicate aspect of **commissions** and **'charges'** that soak up cash before the residue actually gets to be invested!), and

- How to read **Balance Sheets,** debt-to-equity and price-earnings ratios, etc. (amazing still that people happily invest in all sorts of enterprises with over-geared and generally weak Balance Sheets);

- How the money-lending system works (it's called **banking,** by some);

- Options, futures, commodity trading, numbered accounts, merchant banking, takeovers, management buyouts, junk bonds and, importantly, the jargon used to describe all this activity, etc. It is a very large field (over **7,000** different securities are traded on the **London Stock Exchange** alone) so, apart from general background and spice, each course will probably have to be somewhat specialised.

- Don't overlook in-house sales to your PSGs. Mainly books probably but anything else?

••• INFORMATION CHECK LIST

- The STOCK EXCHANGE (01 - 588 2355) book-shop. On request they will send you a publications list of the dozens of books on offer. Choose your starter books from this list then, from their bibliographies, widen your reading according to the direction you wish to take.

- Whilst the FINANCIAL TIMES, daily 50p, is required reading there is a bemusing range of magazines. By all means take the well-known FT product, THE INVESTOR'S CHRONICLE, weekly £1.30, but also speak to their FINANCIAL TIMES BUSINESS INFOR-MATION LTD (01 - 405 6969 and 01 - 799 2002) for the FT list of other financial magazines and books.

- Contact LAMONT'S (01 - 629 4509) for a copy of their LAMONT'S GLOSSARY, £2.75, a guide for investors to financial terminology.

- By the time you have read your way through the results of the above research you will have both a reading study programme worked out and will have decided which courses interest you. However,

- Don't forget the spice we mentioned earlier — but be warned to avoid the **official** biographies of the master money-makers. These have usually been carefully sanitised to remove all the blood-and-guts chicanery, mistakes, liaisons and oomp-pah-pah that make them so fascinating; go for the books written by the people who hated or had a healthy cynicism for the subject!

- An off-beat book written by a character who doesn't always get his timing quite right but has some rivetting and unfashionable things to say about money and how to make it in the bad times: THE DOWNWAVE, by ROBERT BECKMAN, pub MILESTONE, £14.95. Also by the same author and publisher, INTO THE UPWAVE, £16.95.

- There is **software** around whose creators make the seductive proposition that you can successfully play the market using their product. We are sceptical but your PSGs might find them interesting. We will not quote them here (these programmes come and go all the time) but your magazines will give details.

- Finally, read anything you can get hold of written by the erudite and witty American economic guru, J K GALBRAITH. Many books, all gems of insight.

• GAMBLING

- Every gambling game or sport has some fascinating **rules** governing the probability of winning or losing.

- Although staggering amounts are gambled every day most punters amazingly seem to have no clue whatever about these rules and whether they are investing their money wisely or not (which probably explains why gambling has been described as a way of buying hope on credit).

- For instance, an unknowledgeable person who sees eight **heads** in a row come up when a coin is tossed is easily persuaded that a **tail** is more likely to occur on the ninth toss.

- Not so. The odds calculation will be quite uninfluenced by what has gone before and the chances of a head or a tail showing on the ninth remain exactly the same: **Evens.**

- To teach people how to gamble you have to have gambled yourself.

- However, take care! Do **not** gamble before **you** have learned the odds.

- And be wary of casinos; although the majority are straight, house games **give them a valuable percentage edge.**

- Only take with you the **cash** you are prepared to **lose.** When, as is probable, this happens, leave before you are tempted to get hooked on a credit line.

- When you can teach the subtleties of playing strategy and impart a sound knowledge of the odds you might make your PSGs winners.

- At worst you will ensure that they enjoy their gambling because even if they do lose they will know that they have had **'value for money'.**

- Spice your courses with anecdotes that you will cull from the many books you'll be reading if the bug gets you (e.g. When asked by the priest if he had some words of repentance for his wasted life, **Nick 'The Greek' Dandalos** said on his death bed 'Nope. The next best thing to gambling and winning is gambling and losing'.).

- As your gambling PSGs will likely be fairly competitive types it makes sense to give them plenty of opportunities to compete with one another by offering in-house games in as great a profusion as possible: chess, mahjong, bridge (which these days has become fiercely competitive), snooker, even humble darts, etc. (The only difficulty here might be getting them to go to bed at night.)

- Courses should be combined with visits to race tracks or casinos if you are not too remote.

- You can get special calculators and even software to 'help' get the odds right. Sell these to your PSGs strictly 'for fun', together with the huge range of books on gambling, access to which is at your disposal below.

••• INFORMATION CHECK LIST

- There are a lot of gambling games and sports and a very large number of books on each of them. Get the flavour economically with THE GAMBLER'S POCKET BOOK, by DAVID SPANIER, pub MITCHELL BEAZLEY, £4.95.

- The bibliography in Spanier's book will point you towards other books but to enjoy an Alladin's Cave of choice contact GAMBLER'S BOOK CLUB, (0101 - 702382 7555; or write to PO BOX 4115, LAS VEGAS, NEVADA, USA, zip 89127) who stock well over 1,000 titles (and also publish their own) and will promptly dispatch lists on any game and equally promptly dispatch your chosen volume(s).

- In the normal way we **try** only to quote books that are currently in print; however, although the following three are out of print, they each have something special to say and are well worth taking the trouble to track down, if necessary through book search agencies (see Yellow Pages under New & Secondhand Booksellers). Quote the ISBN number noted with each title.

- Self-evidently essential reading is HOW TO CHEAT AT CARDS AND CATCH YOUR FRIENDS DOING IT, by A. D. LIVING-STONE, pub MACMILLAN, SBN 333 15587 4. Ignore the slight jokiness of the title — this book is very much for real.

- Despite the well-known 'fact' that you can 'never beat the house' one man actually did! Read 13 AGAINST THE BANK, by NORMAN LEIGH, pub OXFORD UNIVERSITY PRESS, ISBN 0 19 424254 4 to find out how Leigh and his companions made his roulette system produce a healthy profit — but with less than healthy results. . .

- One of the very best books, not so much about poker as about the real high-roller poker players themselves and their bid to be World Champion, is THE BIGGEST GAME IN TOWN, by A ALVAREZ, pub FLAMINGO/FONTANA, ISBN 0 00 654075 9.

- THE CHANNEL FOUR BOOK OF RACING, by SEAN MAGEE, pub SIDGWICK & JACKSON, £15, a professional guide to horses, jockeys, form and betting.

- DGA SOFTWARE (061 - 330 0184) offer PROPUNTER, an 'expert' system which they say will tell you when to invest and when to keep your hand firmly in your pocket. Cost £57.50.

- The same people also offer other 'client advantage' racing services. Enquire.

- From the mail order people INNOVATIONS (0793 514666) you can buy the STARSHINE RACE TRACK COMPUTER 111, £14.95, to assess the relative chances of all horses in any race.

- To get a much closer look at the gambling industry consider attending one of the big boys' training schools. Speak to the organisation of your choice for details (but remember you'll only get into their schools if you measure up **and** they believe you are actually going to wind up working for them).

- THE BRITISH GAMING ACADEMY (01 - 287 5708) run casino dealer courses in blackjack, American roulette, Caribbean poker (a variation of stud poker), dice and punto banco (also known as Nevada baccarat). Single courses of eight 20-hour weeks can run to as much as £1,000 plus VAT for dice; £600 plus VAT for the six 20-hour weeks course on blackjack. However, there are some healthy price reductions on offer if you take more than one course. The Academy reckons to virtually guarantee a job to successful students.

- Licensed by The BRITISH GAMING BOARD the Academy makes the point that gambling is a

straight industry so they don't accept anybody with a bent record!

- Finally, two relaxing ways to have a closer look at gambling: MOTIVACTION (043 - 886 821) run what they call MULTIACTIVITY DAYS. Amongst the activities they offer the attractions of a MOBILE CASINO. LADBROKE THE BOOKMAKERS (01 - 863 5600) from time to time offer BIG RACE OCCASION breaks. Get details direct or from their HILTON HOTELS (0923 - 38877).

● GROWING THINGS

● In pondering your move into the country you will certainly have thought about growing things.

● It would be surprising if you hadn't; ever since some enterprising soul asked himself why he had to continually travel, compete and gamble to find his next meal, and then sat down to invent the mattock and the scratch plough so that he could till the soil; ever since in fact the founding of civilisation those many thousands of years ago in Mesopotamia man has beavered away growing things to feed himself, please his eyes and make money with the surplus.

● If all you are planning is to run a small vegetable patch for your own use, or grow a beautiful garden, then what follows need not detain you for here we are concerned with growing things for profit.

● We sound some early warning bells:

● Anyone thinking of going in for **conventional** agriculture should immediately proceed to lie down in a cool, dark room until the feeling goes away.

● The farmer these days lives in a twilight world, in the hands as he is of Brussels and Whitehall bureaucrats.

● An unhappy and not very profitable fate and so would yours be — if you went the conventional route (see **HIT LIST**). But there's no need, as we will demonstrate:

● Even in those halcyon days when the farmer knew what it was that he was required to grow and had a fair idea what he would be paid for growing it, he nevertheless always had one other problem: the **weather**.

- To grow anything **under cover** wasn't feasible given the huge spaces required for wheat, barley and so on.

- But it could be feasible for you because instead of creating such low-return, space-consuming commodities for the wholesale market, we suggest you both grow **higher-value** plants and then set up a **retail** selling project to get prime price for your produce.

- So, to defeat the weather (which will continue to be uphelpful even if the 'greenhouse effect' does turn out to be as real a threat as imagined), grow under cover, but only high-value crops. What these will be will depend on your market research (but read on for some ideas).

- As part of your selling package you will be able to offer **guarantees** of supplies, high quality and stable annual selling prices, all assurances that are essential to larger-scale buyers such as offices, supermarkets and other chains.

- As to the cover under which all this happens, light is vital so naturally you will need glass or heavy plastic greenhouse accommodation and straightaway we want to draw your attention to undercover growing by **hydroponics.** This is the science of growing plants in water, **without** soil, but supported in a neutral medium such as plastic, sand or gravel.

- No doubt it was inspired by nature's own hydroponics which can be seen at work in creating, for instance, that all-purpose vegetable, seaweed.

- Hydroponics will grow you almost anything, claim

its fervent supporters.

- To grow hydroponically the water has to have a carefully calculated addition of certain nutrients, minerals, etc.; the resultant solution is then fed to the plants automatically.

- It is even possible for hydroponic growing to be done entirely **organically**.

- Conservationists will be pleased to know that there is a significant degree of **recycling** not only of the water solution and nutrients but also of potash and alcohol which can be burnt for energy.

- Sufferers from back trouble will be pleased to know that you can comfortably tend and harvest your hydroponic plants by building the troughs at **waist level**.

- Research has shown that plants not only like being talked to but thrive in a **musical environment** (Handel's Water Music?).

- Summing it up, for the same capital costs per acre as would apply if bringing virgin soil under cultivation, you can grow valuable crops faster, more economically, more densely, much more profitably **and** independently of the weather.

- Also to a large extent of **you**. Some supervision is required certainly but with a computer doing most of the routine work hydroponic cultivation could allow you to get on and make money elsewhere, in which case you still have other ventures from this guide to choose from.

- (As we note in **HIT LIST,** however, computers must be considered with extreme caution).

- If growing hydroponically under cover appeals here are some ideas to stimulate your thinking and that tap directly into today's market:

- You have probably heard of the **'sick building syndrome'**. This expression refers to modern **office** buildings and their negative effect on the people working in them. Lethargy, flu-like fever, headache, chronic tiredness, irritated nose or eyes and skin rashes are some of the symptoms and are caused by things floating about in the office air, e.g. carbon monoxide and dioxide, benzene, formaldehyde and germs often bred in and then dispersed around by your friendly air-handling system.

- In all offices you will come across some of the offenders:

- Apart from germs you will almost certainly find harmful dust and odours from furniture coverings, polishes, cleaners, glues, correction fluids and thinners, carbonless copy paper, marker pens, wood preservatives and solvent-based paints. And that's not all:

- Depressingly, experts calculate that those working in a new building made of the new **synthetic** materials could be inhaling a daily chemical cocktail containing anything up to **300** toxic substances.

- SBS is causing sufficient official concern to prompt the setting up of international research to find out what can be done about it all. Glasgow's Macintosh School of Architecture has been mooted as the research base.

- Meanwhile, however, no less a source than **NASA** has confirmed that in some way not yet totally understood **plants** are surprisingly efficient at cleaning air of its harmful content.

- For example, the **Gerbera Daisy** and the **Chrysanthemum** are superior at removing benzene which has been linked to cancer; **Green Spider** plants are effective in disposing of carbon monoxide.

- Others at the top of the NASA hit parade: **Coconut Palm, Ficus Benjamina** and **Dracaena**.

- Also, says NASA, the more foliage the better the air cleaning achieved.

- The great herbalists of the past also saw benefits to be derived from plants like **Cedar** and **Coriander** which can improve concentration and therefore productivity in offices.

- One of the best health spas in the world is the **Dungl Centre** in Garsam-Kamp, Austria.

- There they restored ace driver **Niki Lauda** to World Champion after his near-fatal Grand Prix crash.

- This spa prides itself on its therapeutic environment and you may be interested to hear that floral decor is by way of hydroponic plants, thus also ensuring the ideal **humidity** levels for their guests.

- If in an expensive spa why not also in the office?

- The sales thrust to employers is clear: 'Air purifying, humidifying flowers and plants not only look great, they can help make your workforce feel great, stay well, work better.' Powerful selling factors in helping you set up a hydroponically-grown **plant supply** service for offices in nearby towns. (And why not for **homes,** too?)

- Once a basic supply service has been set up there will be other spin-offs such as flowers for **special occasions** (offices seem to spawn these) and sales to individuals of such specialties as **miniature gardens in bowls and bottles.**

- Let's face it — everybody loves flowers.

- Also profiting from today's sensible concern with improving health is the **herb** in its roles as flavouring, medicine and simply something pleasing to look at.

- Demand is rising particularly for fresh herbs.

- Your main income will be from selling the plants.

- There is, additionally, a steady call for the freshly-cut herbs themselves and for their seeds.

- Out of season the demand is for dried herbs but few people realise that these are a poor substitute and the better way to go is to sell them **deep frozen.** At a premium.

- Why not sell your herbs with **recipe suggestions** attached?

- A fresh herb **delivery service** to restaurants, pubs, bakeries and hotels would do well. And if you were to do this you might consider either making yourself, or bringing in and supplying the latest American idea of **liquid spices** featured in the New York Gourmet Show.

- Whilst herb-filled pillows and sachets are not exactly new on the market, something like herb-filled **key ring** tags or a **candle** that gave off a herby smell might take off for the more romantically inclined, or a herb-filled **teddy** to cuddle and de-stress with.

- Also not long in from America comes the profitable idea of growing and selling **edible flowers**.

- Big on menus in the US, Canada, Belgium, Switzerland and recently Japan, are such things as nasturtium, roses, pansies, roguette, viola, marigold.

- This all ties in with what we suggested above regarding herbs, e.g. borage, onion chive blossoms, basil, tarragon, angelica, dill, apple mint and pineapple sage and so on are all figuring in today's floral chef's thinking.

- As every housewife knows **salad** prices rocket during certain months.

- Very profitable, thank you, with under-cover, 12-month-a-year production.

- However, think wider. Think seriously of the other, more novel salad ideas; the cleverly named **Hedgerow** Salads, the herb **Winter Purslane** or **Miner's Salad, Lamb's Lettuce** and **American Land Cress** are some of the ideas appearing in the shrewder supermarkets. **Sorrel** and cultivated **dandelion** are being looked at for an early debut.

- In fact any type of plant that's tasty, decorative and high in nutrients.

- Aromatherapists and perfumers rely on **oil essences** from certain flowers. Perhaps this sort of production appeals to you? If so you'll be doing your bit for the balance of payments; most of these oils come in from abroad at the moment, e.g. **Rose Geranium** for scent is produced by **soilless culture** in Armenia on a large scale.

- Consider also the possibilities of growing

81

miniature 'exotics' such as **coconut, pineapple** and **banana trees**.

- If you are very, very bright indeed you might turn your attention to the idea of growing an entirely **new food**.

- Ranks had to spend rather a long time doing it but have come up with a microscopic relative of the mushroom, a fungal protein liquid fermentation which when mature and set is a food rich in protein and fibre; resembling it in texture and capable of being used just like meat, this astonishing product is being marketed as **Quorn** and made up into a variety of dishes. As rearing animals for meat has always been extremely wasteful and, because of the methane the unfortunate beasts produce, is now being seen as an environment problem, a product like Quorn seems set for a very bright future. Could you break the mould and come up with something as revolutionary?

- As more people turn to making their gardens beautiful they are more and more wanting 'instant' results. In the US, for instance, the number one bedding plant is the aptly-named **impatiens**, a large genus of herbaceous plants that earn their name because of the readiness with which the plants' seeds disperse and root. Could a sales range of **'instant'** plants be the market niche for you?

- Other possibilities for the future concern the cloning and growth in numbers of plants and trees by **micropropagation.** See below for follow-up.

- Now, what about space? Well for instance a half acre under cover may sound like a lot of plastic but in such an area you can grow over **500** varieties of herbs and flowers. By good planning the hydroponic grower can get **far more crop** from his space than by growing conventionally.

- If after all we've written you still want to try to make your money growing things under the open sky then so be it. In this case we only remind you of what **Dr Johnson** said: 'When two Englishmen meet their first talk is of the weather', and ask you to consider why this is so . . .

••• INFORMATION CHECK LIST

- The guru of HYDROPONICS is JAMES SHOLTO DOUGLAS. Read first his BEGINNER'S GUIDE TO HYDROPONICS, pub PELHAM BOOKS, £10.95 and then for a more recent and commercial approach, his ADVANCED GUIDE TO HYDROPONICS, pub also PELHAM, £17.95.

- For reasons of space we don't usually give addresses but as THE INTERNATIONAL SOCIETY OF SOILLESS CULTURE (ISOSC) is in Holland write to them at POST BOX 52, WAGENINGEN, NETHERLANDS. If you're in a hurry call 010 - 31 8370 13809. From them you will get comprehensive information together with guidance on further reading.

- Contact THE INSTITUTE OF HORTI-CULTURE RESEARCH (0903 - 716123). This station has done seminal research on hydroponics with particular reference to commercial exploitation.

- The FOOD & AGRICULTURE ORGANIS-ATION (FAO) (01 - 270 3000) is shortly producing an authoritative book on SOILLESS SUB-

STRATES, written by G W WINSOR. Contact FAO for publication date.

- For details of AUTOMATION BY COMPUTER CONTROL speak to ROBERT HARRIS-MAYES of COTHI ENGINEERING (055 - 85380) re their newly-created UNIVERSAL INTERFACE, a piece of hardware that plugs into your computer and acts as a link to all kinds of electronic equipment controlling temperature, liquid flow, etc.

- For reference to pollution and the SICK BUILDING SYNDROME (or 'indoor climate syndrome' as it's referred to in the book) read ULTRAHEALTH by LESLIE KENTON, pub ARROW, £3.99.

- You will obviously buy books concerning the specific plants that you intend to grow but one that is bound to be of interest is THE ROYAL HORTICULTURAL SOCIETY GAR-DENER'S ENCYCLOPAEDIA OF PLANTS AND FLOWERS, pub DORLING KINDERS-LEY, £25. Comprehensive, authoritative, 8,000 plant entries.

- The GARDENING from WHICH? GUIDE TO SUCCESSFUL PROPAGATION, £10.95, details the methods by which you will save money by creating plants from seeds, cuttings or by division. The CONSUMER'S ASSOCIATION telephone no. is 0992 - 589031.

- Read THE HERB BOOK, by JOHN LUST, pub BANTAM, £4.95.

- Contact THE HERB SOCIETY (01 - 222 3634) for information.

- Contact the NEW YORK DEPARTMENT OF

AGRICULTURE & MARKETS, No. 1, WINNER'S CIRCLE, CAPITOL PLAZA, ALBANY, NEW YORK, zip 12235, USA; tel: 010 - 518 45788, to track down the makers of 'LIQUID SPICES' as featured at the NEW YORK GOURMET SHOW.

- Contact THE ROYAL SOCIETY FOR NATURE CONSERVATION (0522 - 752326) for information on EDIBLE FLOWERS.

- DR PETER WILDE of ENGLISH FLORAL FRAGRANCES (0845 - 25690) is a pioneer in the development of harvesting fragrant oils from roses. He is investigating hydroponic growing which will produce 15 times the density of ROSES under glass. Other fragrant crops under consideration include FREESIA, LILY-OF-THE-VALLEY and NARCISSUS. Dr Wilde is keen to attract support to nurture this embryo industry into a major earner for Britain.

- D & D BRISTOW (PARTNERS) (0273 - 834685) are marketing a range of **exotic trees** and **plants**. They sell for £4.95 plus p&p **each**.

- For an update on research into **hardwood tree plantlets** contact DR ROGER LEAKEY, head of the tropical forestry team of the INSTITUTE OF TERRESTRIAL ECOLOGY (031 - 445 4343).

- For information on the progress of the FACTORY PLANT FARM MASS CLONING PROJECT contact PROF MALCOLM ELLIOTT at LEICESTER POLYTECHNIC (0533 - 551551).

- For what the market's up to read GROWER (01 - 405 0364), weekly, 75p.

- Put out by the BRITISH FOOD INFORMA-
TION SERVICE (01 - 720 7551) is FOOD
FOCUS 1. This is a comprehensive guide to
British agricultural and horticultural produce
giving a whole range of fascinating facts and
figures. £10 plus £1.50 p&p.

- For skills training information contact your local
AGRICULTURAL TRAINING BOARD'S
TRAINING ADVISER and/or the INSTI-
TUTE OF HORTICULTURE (01 - 834 4333).

- Finally, see **WINE & MALT WHISKY** for an
interesting slant on under-cover hydroponic
growing.

• INVENTING THINGS

- What's lacking but needed by a large enough number of people to make it worth your while to sit down and invent it?

- There's money to be had if you can produce the goods.

- A couple of points about creating things original:

- Many a good idea never sees the light of day because the inventor believes that, because **he** has thought of it, either it can't be any good or, if it is, then someone else has probably already done it.

- Fortunately not all inventors have been so timid else we'd still be dragging things around instead of carrying them on the wheel.

- The other point is that the British are the most inventive of nations, e.g. had Disraeli supported the efforts of the inventor Charles Babbage the UK and not the USA would have created the computer industry. As it is, however, 52% of all the world's major products successfully marketed since 1945 were invented in the UK. Yes. So why not yours?

- Incidentally the problems facing the inventor have not always been only those concerning burning the midnight oil, patents and manufacturing licences, hard going though all these undoubtedly are; there have been some star-crossed inventors who have had more terminal difficulties:

- The 4th Earl of Salisbury was the first to use cannon. He was also the first Englishman killed by a ball from one. . . .

- Henry Winstanley thought his 100 ft-high wooden polygon lighthouse would be an improvement on all others. It wasn't. The first storm washed the thing away, inventor inside. . . .

- Perillos of Athens, seeking a new way to execute criminals, invented a large brass container into which the hapless victim was to be locked whilst underneath a fire was lit. Perillos proudly presented the idea to his master, Phal'aris, who so admired the invention that he decided to try it out. The first victim baked to death in the hideous contraption was Perillos. . . .

- Some inventors fared better. Although Dr J B V Guillotin **was** beheaded by one, the actual inventor of the Terror's most gruesome symbol was another physician, but no relation, a Dr Joseph-Ignace Guillotin. He managed to keep his when all around. . . .

- From the macabre to the money and how to make it by inventing or improving upon the existing. You probably have ideas of your own but to prime the engine think on the following, all of which are to do with potentially large markets:

- **Pet Carrier & Home**

- It is not only difficult to buy things like kennels and carriers but when found they are either too cumbersome or expensive or both.

- The pet carrier/home we are talking about would:

  - be made of rigid **plastic**
  - be **small** enough to house a young animal as well as being **lockable** and **light** enough to carry the pet around in when travel-

ling, e.g. those numerous early-days visits to the vet

- have a removable, **clear plastic lid** so the animal could be observed at all times and interior cleaning is easy. (Anyone who has ever twisted themselves into a knot cleaning out a conventional kennel will appreciate this facility.)
- have **one side removable** so that as the animal grows a further section could be purchased and **bolted on**
- be offered in a range of **designer colours** with the maker's good, snappy **logo** displayed.

- In the UK alone it is estimated that there are some **12 million** dogs and cats. Whilst not all of them, unfortunately, are cared for as pets the market for anything useful in this field is clearly still vast.

- **Shaver Light**

- A small, torchlike light that could be clipped on to an electric shaver so that every elusive little hair would be seeable and shavable.

- And talking of shaving, what is needed is a means of glare-proofing **basin shaving lights** so that you can actually see what you are doing.

- Millions of men use shavers most days, and daily trillions of hairs escape the chop. Oh Lord, give us light!

- **Car Radio Recorder**

- Why has no one come up with a clip-on cassette recorder to tape those favourite programmes?

- Hundreds of radio programmes daily go out over millions of car radios.

- **Baby Breathing Monitor**

- Despite the fact that experts say a very young baby should never be left alone, they are — and sometimes they die. Considering the tragedy surrounding **cot deaths** it surely must be possible to create, for example, some simple, strap-onto-the-chest sound-reactive device to record a child's breathing.

- It would incorporate a shrill warning signal, the receiver located in the parents' bedroom (or even worn by them) to alert them of the baby's faulty breathing.

- Many precious young lives on the line — cot death syndrome claims over **1,700 babies** a year.

- **Baldness Cure**

- A drug that is used for heart conditions has been discovered in America to promote hair growth on previously balding heads.

- Apparently, the medics figured, this was because the drug stimulated **increased blood circulation.**

- Only one snag: it can cost around £1,000 to get the course of treatment from the hair clinics.

- If stimulation of blood activity in the bald areas is the answer, why then not sell a cure based on **liniment?**

- As any athlete knows, liniment cures bruising and stiffness by stimulating the blood flow to the affected areas.

- As few baldies would want to smell like a Rugby League changing room the answer might be to come up with a sweet-smelling or **odourless** liniment.

- Many, many millions of balding males go around worrying about their condition. (Maybe it's worrying about it makes it happen?). They're all potential customers.

- (Perhaps an even more effective cure would be to apply hirudo medicinalis. Not all that long ago doctors used to cure certain conditions with these, again on the principle of increasing the rate of blood circulation. However, as hirudo medicinalis is the humble **leech** it may be either a little late or a little early for this one. But **is** it?)

- **Throwaway Paint Brushes**

- Millions of paint brushes are bought annually.

- Cleaning the darned things is messy and time-consuming but has to be done because they are relatively expensive.

- However, it **isn't** always done, so, bingo, there goes another brush in the bin.

- Not only have you lost the money but, maddeningly, you probably cannot finish the job either.

- Why not a super-cheap **plastic brush** that you buy in 10-packs, use once and throw away?

- Or cheap heads that could be clipped to a **durable** handle?

- No substitute obviously for the fine hair brushes needed on certain finishes but more than adequate for most other work.

- The right substitute at the right price could have a similar impact to the biro replacing the fountain pen.

- **Some Other Ideas**

- How about a small multi-purpose **side table?**

- Sounds a little low key? Not if you consider what our side table should do and, if successful, how many people would buy it.

- **It should accommodate: your tea or coffee cup and saucer, cigarettes and ashtray (optional), newspapers/magazines, a novel and dictionary, work papers, a radio or cassette, TV remote controls, notebooks, pens, scissors, tissues, a snack tray.**

- It should have its own foldaway **reading light.**

- It should be on **wheels** that can be **locked** when the table is positioned.

- The designer who comes up with something good looking and compact to fulfill the above specifications will probably do well through **MAIL ORDER** (qv), not to mention the fact that every worthwhile furniture store would show keen interest.

- Talking of **witty furniture** consider the multi-function requirements to meet precisely what we are advocating in this guide: work in the home. A very basic example is

- The Scandinavian filing cabinet (16″ × 21″ × 27″) that with a hinged flap becomes a desk (20″ × 21″ × 27″).

- Yes, we **know** it's dead simple but that didn't

deter the inventor who we may assume is happily laughing all the way to the bank.

- Are there other examples that you can think of? The market is widening.

- For further stimulation look at the brilliantly simple, effective work of **Antii Nurmesniemi.** For example, his four-coloured **nesting tables** are masterpieces of to-the-bone thinking.

- And the **Mutaro** for an intelligent concept of a **bedside table/breakfast trolley.**

- Another market much on the move is in the **Infirmity Field** where, not before time, intelligent thought is being given to the very real needs of the disabled.

- Look at the inventions to be found in the Boots The Chemist catalogue on this and see if that sparks some ideas.

- Some more needs at random:

- **Electric wires** are a curse, both unsightly and hampering; e.g. your vacuum cleaner will not roll where you want it because the *!* wire gets in the way of the wheels. (Ironically, one of the world's greatest electrical geniuses, **Nikola Tesla** [1856-1943], claimed that, because the earth itself was a conductor, it was not necessary to have wires **at all.** And in 1900 he made it happen — by lighting 200 lamps **without wires** from 25 miles away! He proved that we **could** have a wireless world but maybe wire manufacturers didn't think **that** was his best idea. . .). Meanwhile we're stuck with wires. Any ideas as to how we can 'lose' them?

- **Umbrellas** are another incubus; expensive, bulky

and very losable. An idea we heard was to create a pocket-friendly **inflatable brolly.** Could you make this work?

- Maybe more of a fresh design needed here rather than a pure invention as such but can someone tell us why **TV and video recorder stands** are apparently made only for contortionists? We don't understand videos any more than you probably do, so why is the exasperation compounded by the video being sited so low down that we have to get the nose and eyes level with the floor in order to try and solve the problem? (All that dust can't do the video itself much good, either.)

- Anything to do with solving **car** problems will certainly make money. When will you or someone invent a device to keep the constantly changing position of the sun out of our eyes (current **car vizors** certainly don't)? Also there is a need to stop our expensive petrol being stolen. This problem calls either for a yob-proof **petrol tank cap** or, better, a device to stop **syphoning** taking place.

- **Dressing** is a problem for the elderly and handicapped. Even if you're fit and able it can be a time-consuming affair. Either way there surely is a case for the invention of clothing that still looks good but that can be put on easily and **quickly.**

- As we note elsewhere, **computers and learning about them** are a very real problem to the layman. **Anything** you can do to alleviate this will make much money. Remember: the computer-wise will not address the difficulty because, for them, natch, it simply doesn't exist. However, looked at with an objective eye, it surely does. To the layman computers remain an enigma.

- If you are skilled or prepared to train to become so, you may well be drawn towards **making up** your own inventions, at least in the early stages.

- On the other hand, if you are quite sure you cannot make yourself you have three options:
  - **subcontract** the work out
  - link up with a **craftsman/partner** or
  - **employ** your own craftsmen

- No 1 is the best option to begin with.

- Nos 2 and 3 should only be considered after you have established your market (and even then No 3 with great caution because of the **overhead.**)

- Manufacturing can have its pitfalls. Consider using a **consultant** (your Local Enterprise Agency will help find one) to guide you.

- Whichever way you go you do need to take the trouble to become a reasonably good **draughtsman** to be able to both properly make, or show how to make, your invention and, if it is a flat pack kit, to be able to illustrate with clarity how the buyer is to assemble it.

- Once you have a prototype you will then go for advice.

- You will be told that obtaining **patents** is a fairly costly and time-consuming business, depending on the degree of protection you want and in which countries.

- The alternative is to approach the sort of organisation mentioned below who will assess your invention and, if they reckon it, guide you through the formalities and advise on whether you should make and market yourself or license the whole thing out, in which case they will negotiate royalties for you.

- Be well aware beforehand, however, that such firms do not go in for fantasy; they're in it for the money. But then so are you, aren't you?

- A reminder that the invention process is usually slow and potentially expensive.

- John Logie Baird took years inventing mechanical TV and it took more years of electronic research before the BBC finally got TV to air in 1936-7, by which time they'd decided to use someone else's system, anyway.

- Be wise and have a basic **bread-and-butter earner** whilst hatching your masterpiece. As to which ask yourself:

- Has anyone else thought of it?
- Does it really work?
- Is there a readily perceivable market? *
- Have I kept my mouth shut so a patent application will work?
- Can I get research and development funds, e.g will the government help?
- How much profit could it make for me?

- As you've gathered, inventing things has its ups and downs, its swings and its roundabouts. We mentioned earlier the painful fate of the inventor Perillos, put to death in his own invention. Well, you'll be pleased to hear that Nemesis was keeping a close eye on the whole affair and evidently decided that Perillos had, after all, been rather harshly treated by his master, Phal'aris. This tyrant was in due course himself toppled from power — and baked to death in Perillos's very own invention. . . .

- Is there a moral to all this?

- Probably: Make Money Not Misery.

••• INFORMATION CHECK LIST

- Contact OSCAR WOOLLENS (01 - 435 0101) for information on the furniture and designs of ANTII NURMESNIEMI.

- INTERLÜBKE (01 - 858 3325) for information on the MUTARO bedside trolley with drop leaf, perhaps on show at HARRODS (01 - 730 1234).

- Check with the DESIGN CENTRE (01 - 839 8000). Many of their exhibitions display ingenius and inventive artefacts and design.

- For a free copy of HEALTHCARE IN THE HOME contact your local BOOTS THE CHEMIST.

- Contact the SOCIETY OF METAPHYSICIANS (0424 - 751577) who publish books on NIKOLA TESLA. You might be interested in their other publications also.

- Track down a copy of A BETTER MOUSE-TRAP, by PETER BISSEL, pub WORDBASE PUBLICATIONS.

- Your local POLYTECHNIC AGENCY or CHAMBER OF COMMERCE to help link with a craftsman/partner.

- Contact THE INSTITUTE OF INVENTORS AND PATENTEES (01 - 242 7812) for sympathetic advice and help in this esoteric field. Subscription £30 p.a. gets you right into the discovery business, with meetings of inventors and demonstrations of their wares; the Institute also provides a focus for those seeking to take up inventions. Included in annual sub are four issues of FUTURE & THE INVENTOR and six issues of NEW PATENTS BULLETIN, a synopsis of what's been newly patented.

- INVENTERPRISE LTD (01 - 485 7611) is run by inventors who in addition to marketing their own discoveries will offer a full range of services to the inventor, right the way from objective assessment, through drawings, models and patents up to license, manufacture and marketing.

- Another organisation which will both protect and help the inventor is the ASSOCIATION OF INVENTION MANAGERS (AIM). Their code of conduct calls for innovation managers to, inter alia, ensure that there is no conflict of interest and that they do not leak an inventor's idea. Under the aegis of THE INSTITUTE OF INVENTORS AND PATENTEES (see above).

- Finally, contact BRITISH TECHNOLOGY GROUP (01 - 403 6666) if you are an inventive academic. BTG's publication PATENTING: THE OPPORTUNITES AND PITFALLS shows how publication of ideas can invalidate patenting.

• KITCHEN FACTORY

- The UK food market is reckoned to generate some £34 billion a year so, even though you may not as yet be an accomplished cook, a chunk of this cash mountain could be yours if you're prepared to apply some energy and research to finding your niche in the market.

- However, read no further if you just love cooking and vaguely feel that you might make some money from cooking in a small way. Cooking as a working 'hobby' is a very enjoyable, labour-intensive way of making little or no money.

- Remember, a fair chef with a good business brain will leave for dead a brilliant cook with no financial nous.

- Your first questions will be: What are you going to make and for whom? The bigger opportunity lies in supplying the **wholesale trade** and a broad strategy for that market will look something like this:

- Let's assume you already have some idea (if not, read on for a couple of our thoughts) of what the market needs and that the local start-up market looks big enough. Excellent but don't get carried away. Instead make up plenty of free **samples,** remembering that eye appeal is nearly as vital as tastiness.

- Naturally you'll have to tell prospects what the price will be for your product so rule of thumb: **selling price** = wholesale cost of ingredients × 3 **less** any trade discount you then have to give.

- Take the samples to local food stores (not supermarkets; you aren't big enough for **them** yet), wine bars and restaurants to get their general reaction.

- They may or may not care for your offering but that's not the main point:

- Because you have taken the trouble to prepare and cost an item for their consideration they will know you are for real and will tell you what it is they are **actually** looking for.

- Always do the selling/market research **in person**.

- Once your research has revealed what is in demand and the market price your major decision then will be based on whether or not there's going to be enough **profit** in it.

- Once this strategy has revealed the Big Picture you can turn to the details, the tactics.

- Whilst **thinking** big, start **small**.

- Do not up-front over-commit yourself on deliveries. Commercial bulk cooking is a tricky business and you have to work out your own personal techniques, as far as possible without the panic that unrealistic deadlines entail.

- Save labour and **mechanise** as quickly as possible but don't risk money on machines until you know that you are ready for them and that they'll do the job.

- Although expensive, an Aga or Rayburn cooker will also heat your water and some of your radiators so look closely at these early on.

- Setting up your kitchen is going to cost plenty so buy good quality **second-hand** goods where possible to preserve precious cash.

- See your local Industrial Development Officer

to check if there are council or other **grants** that can assist you.

- Do not underprice your product. Value your own labour at **market rates**.

- Concentrate if possible on supplying the **top end** of the market where margins are fatter.

- Contrariwise, and only if you are running a range of foods, see if you can do one line that, although excellent, is sold at absolutely **minimal** profit.

- Strictly allocate this line as part of your **marketing budget**, otherwise you will distort your ordinary trading figures.

- **Rent** don't buy your motor delivery transport until you have settled on the size you need.

- To begin with employ **cash 'casuals',** i.e. local occasional help. Do not commit to the burden of either regular part-time or full-time employees.

- Get on top of **costs** from Day One.

- If you're computer-wise (if not see **HIT LIST**) base your pricing system on a **home computer programme** which has overheads built in, which stores prices of all stock ingredients and can print out the cost of any recipe at the touch of the keys. Alternatively, use a religiously-kept-up-to-date **card index system**.

- **Buying** is obviously of critical importance. Do leave yourself adequate time to sift, compare and bargain for the best quality at the right price, which will also mean that as you grow you buy direct, saving that middleman-profit.

- However, unless you suddenly come across a

101

great bargain, don't overstock and tie up capital.

- **Packaging** is expensive. It has to be strong enough to take the bumps and also must look attractive if it is going to compete.

- Unless you are talented in this area (in which case start by asking yourself what **you'd** expect the pack to look like on the shelf) employ a professional pack designer.

- Your **Environmental Health Officer** will only be an ogre if he is called in, or calls upon you, **after** you have begun operations.

- See him early on and do not be surprised if he comes up with a better and/or cheaper way of setting up your cooking and storage areas than you had envisaged.

- There is only one rule about **operational space:** there is never enough. Plan ahead for when your products really take off.

- To stimulate your thinking here's a couple of ideas that you might consider and the market should be ready for:

- **Chip-Smoked Foods**

- Why can't you readily buy properly smoked foods instead of the shrink-wrapped, artificially flavoured and dyed offerings to be found in most food shops?

- Sadly, the answer may be that, of its nature, food smoking is a smoky business and, just as the chore of emptying tea leaves led to the pathetic tea bag, so the food scientists have been encouraged to produce the so-called chemically **'smoked'** foods — which are a travesty.

- Anyway, if you perceive that there could be a demand for real smoked foods in your area consider meeting that demand because to do chip-smoked foods properly is not difficult.

- To experiment economically buy a basic **kettle barbecue** with a minimum cooking area of not less than 18″ diameter and with a pull-over lid to completely enclose the product.

- Water-soak half-a-dozen handfuls of **hickory chips** (never use soft woods for smoking) for at least an hour, if not overnight, then get your charcoal up to maximum heat and sprinkle with the soaked chips (a handful at a time).

- Pop the product on the barbecue and close the lid so that the food is totally enveloped in the smoky heat.

- From time to time add more of the soaked chips and allow approx. 20 minutes per pound cooking time, according to the density of the flesh; e.g. 20 min per lb for a sirloin side.

- Absolutely ambrosial hot but for selling allow to naturally cool before, if appropriate, slicing on a proper **slicing machine** (for cost control).

- Particularly effective with sirloin of beef but there's an obvious range of other meats, fish, cheese, even vegetables, that work.

- The kettle barbecue will see you through the early stages of a commercial operation but it will have to be replaced by a more professional one as demand grows.

- As a means of both making extra money and publicising the products your advertising could offer a complete **barbecue service** for social and business gatherings, including crockery, cutlery, drinks and glasses, through to waiters.

- **Ayran**

- A delicious and refreshing, thick, health drink which is very quick in the making.

- It's the Turkish version of the Indian yoghurt drink Lassi.

- Into a blender put a handful of ice cubes, 4 oz thick goat's milk yoghurt, 2 oz iced water and a dash of salt. Blend until ice is crushed. Serve with a dash of cumin sprinkled on top.

- This basic drink is white but, following the marketing of yoghurt, ayran can be flavoured and coloured, with the addition of various fruits or other tastes that you think might sell.

- Once someone markets this seriously it will catch on with adults and children of all ages, just like yoghurt with its £300m per annum sales (Ayran Bars?).

- Some other ideas:

- Although not exactly up-market, if you are tuned into **children's food** likes and dislikes, this could be a starter idea before you go on to more ambitious things. As midday meals are not always supplied in schools and busy parents themselves are often short of time, consider supplying healthy, tasty food for school children. If the idea appeals use the two-box system for each youngster: you deliver the food in one container and pick up the empty container used the day before.

- Do you see an opening for **Edible Gifts**?

- **Vegetarianism** will increase in line with growing concern for ourselves, the environment and the animals themselves. Does this sort of cooking turn you on?

- Over 50 years ago **Dr William Hay** developed the **Hay System** which has been vindicated as the ideal wholefood diet advocated today by leading nutritionalists. Hay based his System on the fact that, as the body uses acids to digest proteins and alkalis to digest starches, mixing the two will lead to impaired digestion and worse. Perhaps a range of foods based on Hay's methods could work.

- Clearly concern with healthy eating is here to stay; is the timing right for the next kick-on, **'Sports Cuisine'?** A keen sportsman himself, **Dr Robert Haas** has developed his eating ideas from the time when he was facing a lifetime of medication due to faulty blood pressure. As he was responsible for bringing world champion tennis player Martina Navratilova to her peak his philosophy of food clearly works.

- When searching for your second-hand equipment you will come across a lot of perfectly good **freezers.** To help your early-days cashflow (and if you have spare space) consider buying a number of freezers, cleaning them up and renting out their space to caterers, food dealers, hotels, etc., who all, from time to time, face the need for extra freezer capacity to cope with major functions, breakdowns, bulk buying and so on.

- Those who find this section of interest will probably have some particular dish(es), drinks or snacks of their own in mind. It is worth noting that our best and most inventive ideas usually concern things that we **know** are good but cannot be easily obtained. What do **you** love to eat or drink that you cannot readily go out and buy?

- If, despite your interest in the **KITCHEN FACTORY** you feel that your cooking skills are not up to it, then you may consider employing a local well-referenced cook but, as we have warned elsewhere, you are more secure if you are actually doing the job yourself.

- There certainly will be cookery courses to attend in your locality but don't go in for expensive Cordon Bleu, good though that is. Stick to the basics in training because commercial cooking with its special techniques and machinery has to be very largely learned the hard way — by **doing it.**

- Think on the title of this section and run your business like a well thought-out production line.

- This way you not only maximise your precious time but will also ensure consistency and high quality in the product, the essentials that, with the right price and unfailingly prompt delivery, will underwrite your success.

- In your thoughts on this venture please do not overlook the possibilities of **MAIL ORDER** (qv).

- One day you will be so expert and successful that while others are cooking for you in your kitchen factory you will have time to run your own profitable cookery seminar. Maybe this could include **MICROWAVE COOKERY** (qv).

- And why not, then, write your own **cookery book(s)** as well?

- There's a steady market that never fades.

••• INFORMATION CHECK LIST

- Even if you think that you've already spotted your niche give yourself benefit from some of the huge amounts of research done for the food market. Top analysts EUROMONITOR (01 - 251 8024) will let you have a copy of their current INDEX showing what research is going on. They have produced such titles as THE EATING OUT SURVEY; UK FOOD MARKETS; CONVENIENCE & PREPARED FOODS; THE MICROWAVABLE FOODS MARKET and HEALTHY FOODS & HEALTHY EATING, to name only a small selection but as you may not want to buy each survey (they can cost from a few hundred to over two thousand pounds each) you should be able to track them down at the SCIENCE REFERENCE LIBRARY, part of the BRITISH LIBRARY (it's a big and changing organisation but start with 01 - 323 7454) or possibly at your large reference library. Wherever you find them you may read up but not photocopy.

- Read the professional magazines: CATERING, monthly, £2.50; FOOD & DRINK (0705 - 862541), monthly, is the magazine reaching the restaurant and licensed trade and the CATERER & HOTELKEEPER is another self-explanatory trade bible, weekly, 85p.

- Also contact FOOD TRADE PRESS (0959 - 63944) for a list of their range of titles on food manufacture.

- For a compendium of trade information refer to the FOOD TRADES DIRECTORY (01 - 439 0335) but as it costs something of the order of £90 check it at a reference library first.

- SMOKING FOOD AT HOME, by MAGGIE

BLACK, pub DAVID & CHARLES, £8.95. Due to be reprinted.

- EDIBLE GIFTS, by CLAIRE CLIFTON & MARTINA NICOLLS, pub BODLEY HEAD (now out of print so quote ISBN 0 370 304455 4). How to make, gift pack, wrap and sell delicacies, particularly for celebratory occasions.

- THE VEGETARIAN EPICURE, by ANNA THOMAS, pub PENGUIN, £3.95. A classic — one of the really outstanding cook-books of any type.

- FOOD COMBINING FOR HEALTH, by DORIS GRANT & JEAN JOICE, pub THORSONS PUBLISHERS, £5.99, re the Hay System.

- EAT TO WIN, by DR ROBERT HAAS, pub PENGUIN. ISBN 0 670 803 43 X pb; or 014 0075 95 X, hb.

- DELIA SMITH'S COMPLETE ILLUSTRATED COOKERY COURSE, by DELIA SMITH, pub BBC, £17.95. The TV cook's classic, particularly interesting for her advice on new types of food.

- THE READER'S DIGEST COMPLETE GUIDE TO COOKERY, by ANNE WILLAN, pub DORLING KINDERSLEY, £19.95. Strong on how to choose, store, preserve and freeze ordinary and exotic ingredients.

- PROFESSIONAL CHEF'S GUIDE TO KITCHEN MANAGEMENT, by FULLER & KNIGHT, pub VAN NOST RHEINHOLD, £24.50.

- APPROACH TO FOOD COSTINGS, by R KOTAS, pub HUTCHINSON, £3.95.

- Put out by the FOOD FROM BRITAIN information service (01 - 720 2144) is FOOD FOCUS 1,
a comprehensive guide to British agricultural and
horticultural produce, giving a whole range of
fascinating facts and figures on nearly 100 british
food products, £10 plus £1.50 pp. It accompanies
FOOD FOCUS 2, same price (or £19.99 plus
£2.50 pp for the set) which lists over 1,000
different companies offering over 1,500 local
specialty foods, from smoked salmon to condi-
ments, tea, fruit, meat and cheeses. Serving ideas
and regional menus feature.

- By all means approach CITY & GUILDS of
LONDON INSTITUTE (01 - 278 2468) or the
HOTEL & CATERING TRAINING BOARD
(01 - 579 2400) for details of their training courses
but as we have said you may be better off
getting minimal training (if you really feel you
need it) and then developing in your own instinc-
tive way from there.

- The GOOD HOUSEKEEPING INSTITUTE (01
- 439 5000) puts out a fairly up-to-date list of
cookery courses available throughout the UK.

- You will find useful the booklet COMMON
SENSE ABOUT FOODCARE IN THE KIT-
CHEN, from the FOOD & DRINK FEDERA-
TION (01 - 836 2460). Ask them for details of
their other publications.

- Well before you commence serious production
contact your local council to check on any legislation that will affect you (Weights & Measures,
Labelling, Food Acts, etc.)

• LANGUAGES

- Extraordinary in so many ways, man is seen at his most unique in his ability to communicate by the conventional system of spoken and written symbols that we call language.

- Broadly, languages are 'split' into eight geographical areas (where the language spoken is classified genetically as descended from a common ancestral language): Europe, South Asia, North Asia, Southwest Asia, East Asia, Southeast Asia, Africa and the Americas.

- However, in our idiosyncratic way we have managed to create 4,000 local language variations since we've been here.

- Although many of these tongues are now 'dead' there are still plenty left and it is beginning to dawn on the Briton that an increasing number of important foreign customers are getting increasingly fed up with his single-tongue complacency.

- Kicking and screaming maybe but the numbers who will be seeking language instruction are growing very rapidly, e.g. 82% of company directors do not have a second language and many are reluctantly concluding that they have to do something about this. Perhaps they might take comfort from the fact that not all Britons are solo-tongued; our greatest linguist has mastery of no less than **54** languages at his command!

- As the peace and quiet of the country provides an ideal setting to show other people how to do things, providing a language course or courses is something for you to consider.

- Apart from deciding what language(s) to teach

there are some other decisions, e.g.:

- Is your teaching to be geared to industry or the private sector? There's money in the former **but** courses do have to be skilfully constructed to be time-effective for the executive and stop him becoming bored and resentful. For example, it has been established that to avoid brain melt-down an executive cannot take the four-week, 30-hour per week courses required for average proficiency, straight off; work every other week is considered the general answer but courses are increasingly being tailored to cope with individual complexities.

- If industry, then which end? Many firms are realising that they have to language-train **everybody** who may come in contact with a foreigner: receptionists, gatemen, secretaries, security guards, etc, as well as the executives.

- Will you teach by class or one-to-one? One-to-one commands around three times the fee to be had from class work, which itself can be about £300 per week per student.

- What level of proficiency will you offer? CBI research indicates that for most non-technical situations only about 700 words are needed for a level of spoken fluency and awareness of what's going on.

- What part will computers, software and videos play in your teaching? (See **HIT LIST**).

- As firms swallow the language pill they tend to designate a particular person to oversee the training, thus making your marketing target more readily identifiable.

- Some senior executives are wondering, if they

have to 'lose' staff for language training, why the staff can't at the **same time** be trained to do their basic job better. **Dual-skill** training (originated in Germany) is here. Could you take advantage? e.g. train the telephonist in a second language **and** how to become a better telephone communicator as well (see **TELEPHONE DYSPHORIA**).

- Language-learning 'cold turkey' has arrived: there are courses where the student is totally 'isolated' from, indeed forbidden to speak, his own language at all!

- And it gets tougher: We've just heard of a firm of accountants which will reject without ado **any** job applicant who does not have at least one foreign language.

- And tougher: Manchester Business School will only grant an MBA to graduates who have a working knowledge of two foreign languages.

- However, it's not only we insular Brits who are suffering in this language explosion: That most language-proud nation the French are to make it mandatory for all children over eight years old to learn English.

- Which raises the point that world-wide £6 billion is spent on the teaching of English, £1 billion of that in the UK alone. Perhaps therefore your very own tongue could be your contribution to this venture heading? Apart from foreigners there are many UK resident/immigrants who still struggle with our language.

- Any reference to language should recognise one other statistic: Some hundreds of thousands of people around the world speak **Esperanto,** the most successful of all 'artificial' languages, designed in 1887 by a Pole as a medium for all persons of all nations. It is spoken in over 80 countries and over 30,000 books have been published in it. After all, is Esperanto the future. . .?

- Finally, no involvement with languages should ignore the commercial possibilities of a translation service. As such a service has to offer a complete menu, the hardest up-front task might be tracking down the range of interpreters you need. These are mainly independent freelancers who do the job for a fee, sending the finished work back to you down their computer telephone line. See **WRITING.**

••• INFORMATION CHECK LIST

- For an appraisal of the corporate sector market for language tuition read LANGUAGES IN BRITISH BUSINESS: AN ANALYSIS OF CURRENT NEEDS, by STEPHEN HAGEN, pub NEWCASTLE-UPON-TYNE POLY-TECHNIC PRODUCTS and by mail order from CILT (qv), £17.95 + £1.80 p&p.

- Get advice from CILT aka the CENTRE FOR INFORMATION ON LANGUAGE TEACH-ING & RESEARCH (01 - 486 8221) who have, inter alia, a contacts list of people who specialise in languages for business people.

- More guidance available from the INSTITUTE OF LINGUISTS (01 - 359 7445) who publish THE LINGUIST journal four times a year, subscription £15.50, and give advice on assessment programmes and training routines.

- Other sources of information:

114

- LANGUAGE EXPORT CENTRES (01 - 934 0888) are very much into dual-skill training. They treat language training and guidance as part and parcel of the export effort and will give details of local teaching sources, as will

- BRITISH INSTITUTE OF MANAGEMENT (0536 - 204222) and

- Local CHAMBERS OF COMMERCE, UNIVERSITIES and POLYTECHNICS.

- From the wide range of **private language schools** many experts choose BERLITZ (01 - 580 6482) and its own direct teaching method as the best, but even so let your fingers do the walking for an initial look at prices.

- **Correspondence courses** abound. Get names from the COUNCIL FOR THE ACCREDITATION OF CORRESPONDENCE COLLEGES (01 - 935 5391).

- With justification the BBC has always claimed leadership in English language teaching but it is perhaps rather less well-known that they are into other languages and that they pioneer interactive teaching methods as well. Details from BBC CONTINUING EDUCATION SERVICES (01 - 991 8031) who will also give you a list of **residential courses** based on BBC language series.

- Sister organisation BBC ENTERPRISES (01 - 576 0361) offer training videos in four European languages. At £149 each however you may want to look at the preview tape first, cost £15.

- The ESPERANTO CENTRE (01 - 727 7821) has information about its artificial language, runs (very modestly priced at £15-£25) correspondence courses and will put you in touch with other centres. There is a LONDON ESPERANTO CLUB (no phone) that meets and holds classes once per week.

- If the translation service idea appeals then you'll need to be on the lists of the ASSOCIATION OF TRANSLATION COMPANIES (01 - 821 6560). Their service helps clients to quickly find the right translation company to handle their work. Free ATC handbook lists all members, their languages and other specialities.

- Whilst you're mulling over this contact THE CENTRAL BUREAU (01 - 486 5101) and get a copy of their paperback STUDY HOLIDAYS, £5.50 + p&p. This lists over 600 organisations offering language courses in 25 European countries. Could there be a pleasanter way to further investigate this venture heading? (But you have been warned: Watch out for the 'cold turkey' courses. . . .)

• LAUGHTER

- Have many of us perhaps forgotten how to laugh, and the **therapeutic** value of laughing?

- Did you know, for instance, that one minute's laughter is the equivalent of a 45-minute session of relaxation?

- More important still, how many of us realise that laughing can actually **save life**?

- For laughter, you see, positively affects every organ in the body: inter alia, blood circulation is stimulated but blood pressure is reduced; muscles are toned up, tissue growth and healing are promoted and endorphines (the body's natural pain killers and soothers) are released into the bloodstream.

- As a powerful weapon against the killer cancer, laughter is being used in America to show patients how to help themselves by rediscovering the **pleasure principle.**

- In some hospitals there are **laughter rooms** where funny books and comedy films help patients learn to laugh again instead of dwelling on problems that otherwise might overwhelm them.

- As is often the case, we don't actually discover something, we **rediscover** what history has known for some time: Although remembered now for his 16th century satirical masterpieces, Pantagruel and Gargantua, **Rabelais** was also a distinguished doctor, clever enough to realise e.g. that patients with syphilis had little hope of surviving the only treatment available, mercury ointment (ouch!), so he resorted to laughter therapy instead.

117

- Even earlier, in the 13th century, a **Dr Henri de Mondeville** used laughter to rehabilitate his patients after operations.

- An Indian doctor, **D. Chopra,** believes that it is the diagnosis, not the disease, that does the damage! An extraordinary view, but, if correct, the ancients we mentioned above must have known something that, until recently, has been lost on the medical profession at large.

- Today the French are urging people to make laughter part of their daily keep-fit routine. They reckon a laugh is as good as a trot around the block, hence they dub laughter **stationary jogging.**

- The Spaniards have a rather taciturn image but they are smart enough to attract many million tourists a year to their shores — and shrewd enough too to realise that in such crowded conditions laughter can solve a lot of problems.

- Since the early 1980s the Madrid-based firm of Animatur has been training hotel staff in, amongst other things, the delicate art of making their customers laugh.

- There is little doubt that a laughter course would be well booked from its inception but serious planning would be needed to make it work.

- Points to consider:

- **Decor:** Light, sunny colours; well but not garishly lit rooms with homely, comfortable furniture; plenty of framed, amusing cartoons on the walls.

- **Atmosphere:** Light-hearted, with some music, even pop, where appropriate. All connected with the project should have a naturally sunny, pleasing attitude and genuinely be able to smile and laugh easily.

- (But no-one, particularly the **host/hostess,** should for a moment feel that they have to crack jokes all the time. Anything more calculated to have your PSGs catching the earliest train home would be difficult to imagine.)

- The **talks** themselves would combine both fact and carefully-structured-beforehand laughs, amply illustrated with slides, films, videos and tapes.

- A few potential topics:

- **What** is laughter?

- **Why** should we laugh? Which leads to

- **How** laughter benefits us and those around us.

- **What** can we do to increase our ability to laugh, to hone our sense of the **ridiculous,** and in particular, to learn how to laugh at **ourselves**?

- Is **pomposity** the biggest laugh of all? W C Fields made a fortune out of it!

- As any laughter is good for us, **Why** is **sick humour** frowned upon? Groucho Marx made a fortune out of this.

- **Why** laughter is provoked differently in different countries.

- An analysis of the **great comedians.**

- **Why** do **women** smile more than men? Yes, they **do**; up to 50% more, according to a Dr Argyle of Oxford University. He thinks it is because ladies have a more positive, trusting approach to life.

- **When** is laughter appropriate? And conversely?

- **Laughter** as a **business-clincher.**

- People who laugh plenty in the **office** are probably more effective, productive workers than the po-faced. So thinks another scientific boffin, Dr John Chesney, a psychologist working with Central Nottingham Health Authority.

- Laughter in **love.** Is it great — or a drooper?

- Such questions and points might form part of the outline structure, backed up by selected guest speakers who could throw some serious or comic light on this absorbing subject.

- Ample opportunity for add-on sales of books, cartoons, tapes, films, cassettes, etc., etc.

- Finally, did the 18th century wit **de Beaumarchais** say something profound when he stated: 'I force myself to laugh at everything for fear of being compelled to weep'?

••• INFORMATION CHECK LIST

- SMILE THERAPY, by LIZ HODGKINSON, pub MACDONALD OPTIMA, £4.95. Not, we have to say, absolutely rivetting but in its rather serious way exposes you to the idea. More important is

- ANATOMY OF AN ILLNESS, by NORMAN COUSINS, pub BANTAM, £3.95. Although now, surprisingly, out of print, do try to find a copy quoting ISBN 0 553 17363 4, because it tells how a patient used his powers of courage and **laughter** to beat an 'incurable' **illness**.

- COUSINS has also produced six audio cassettes, MIND OVER ILLNESS, No. 510 in the NIGHT-INGALE-CONANT catalogue. Contact them on 0101 - 708 6470300, or write to them at 7300 LEHIGH AVENUE, CHICAGO, ILL., zip 60648, USA.

- PRIMAL HEALTH, by MICHEL ODENT, pub CENTURY HUTCHINSON, £4.95. Odent, a medic much concerned with creating the ideal environment for **childbirth,** refers to the importance of laughter in this context.

- Read also anything by DEEPAK CHOPRA, the guru of AYURVEDA ('Knowledge of Life'), an ancient form of Indian therapy that holds that man is part of the stream of nature and must balance life as **nature** demands: 'If you want to have a good time on this earth choose experiences that make you happy.' Read, e.g. Chopra's QUANTUM HEALING, pub BANTAM, £5.99.

- Everyone thinks they laugh at different situations but there is probably something approaching a common funny bone:

- LAUGHTER IN THE AIR, by BARRY TOOK, pub ROBSON BOOKS, £3.95. An informal study of **British radio comedy**.

- Another valuable source of laughter material is PRESENT LAUGHTER, by ALAN COREN, pub ROBSON, £8.95; a 500-page selection of his idea of the 20th century's greatest **comic writing,** from Wodehouse to Woody Allen.

- That droll man CLEMENT FREUD contributes

NO-ONE ELSE HAS COMPLAINED, pub ELM TREE, £6.95. The restaurant as war zone!

- Surely also on the list of great laughter-mongers are Tommy Handley, Laurel & Hardy, John Cleese, Clive James, Batman, Dad's Army . . . . But you will have your own list, no doubt. (Interestingly, the French, when asked to vote on who made them laugh the most, came out overwhelmingly in favour of a **politician** . . . .)

- Our very own favourites will never be known to the world; those anonymous college students and their panic-struck view of history as set out in **exam papers**:

- 'In the first book of the Bible — Guinesses — Adam and Eve were created from an apple tree.'

- 'Pharaoh forced the Hebrew slaves to make bread without straw.'

- 'Later, Moses led them to the Red Sea, where they made unleavened bread which is bread without ingredients.'

- 'The Greeks invented three kinds of column: Corinthian, Doric and Ironic.'

- 'During the Middle Ages everyone was middle-aged.'

- 'The Magna Carta provided that no free man should be hanged twice for the same offence.'

- 'Sir Francis Drake circumcised the world with a 100ft clipper.'

- 'Shakespeare is famous only because of his plays. He lived at Windsor with his merry wives, writing tragedies, comedies and errors.'

- Maybe after all this you think your presentation could do with some polishing. If so, contact JACKSONS LANE (01 - 340 5226) and OVAL HOUSE (01 - 735 2786) for details of their stand-up **cabaret and improvisation workshops**.

- Oh, and by the way, did you hear the one about why the sun never set on the British Empire? 'Because,' wrote the exam student triumphantly, 'the British Empire is in the east and the sun sets in the west.'

- Possibly depressed at the prospect of endless daylight it is unsurprising that Victoria was not amused and so (according to our priceless student) 'the longest Queen died, which was the final event that ended her reign.'

• MAIL ORDER

- To qualify for the MO treatment the **ideal** would be that your product or service is highly **desirable, unique,** and can **only** be bought from you. This of course is a highly unlikely combination but the closer you can get to it the better.

- There are other basics to be respected:

- Arriving at the right **selling price.** Your calculations will be based on actual cost to you of the product, plus the cost of packaging materials, labour and other overheads necessary to get it to the customer.

- When all of this is added together you should multiply the result by a **minimum** of three to arrive at the retail price, plus VAT if applicable.

- You then have to use your keenest judgement to assess whether the market will bear that price.

- If the cost arrived at is so high as to make the product or service a non-runner, do your sums again to see where you can economise. If the end price is still too great the best advice you can get is forget the whole exercise if this means going below the three-to-one formula.

- On the other hand, if the cost arrived at is on any view too low then, without getting too greedy, be quick to apply a multiple of four, five or perhaps even higher if you believe the customer will still willingly pay.

- Before we explain why the markup must be a minimum of three times let's dispose of one case that can be treated slightly differently.

- If you are selling a very **high-priced item** and

the number of pounds of profit per item times the projected number to be sold is going to equal or exceed at least three times your total overhead costs (phone, depreciation of equipment, vehicles, insurance, salaries, etc) then you can afford to consider this 'alternative' formula.

- So why three times cost? Although you are selling direct and cutting out the middle man and store profit percentages, you have to replace their function by organising and paying for the selling yourself and coping with the costs of individually handling and dispatching each item.

- You must budget for between 35% and 45% of selling price to cover the costs of handling and making your sales connections. You may find on one line this percentage proves far too high and it should therefore be adjusted downward **if** you are only selling one line and intend to continue that way. Once you have tested it on a number of lines, however, you will find it's uncannily accurate because you **will** make mistakes and your successes have got to carry the cost of those mistakes.

- Before you begin you must have done sufficient research to give yourself some broad idea of the likely demand.

- You are required to get the product to your customer within 28 days unless you specify otherwise so if you make a nonsense of your **stock in hand** and can't whistle up supplies quickly enough you must, penultimate disaster, return the cheque and, ultimate disaster, that customer is almost certainly not going to buy from you again; a pair of commercial catastrophes too awful to contemplate.

- You should not be going into MO unless you

expect a volume of business and to handle that volume you might **computerise** (but only if you are computer-wise; see **HIT LIST**), well ahead of time to familiarise yourself with, and prove out, the machine and your chosen software to keep track of it all.

- Your computer will not only record enquiries and orders but put all of this information into a form that can go on future **mailing lists** which, as they grow, become another asset that you both use and **rent out.** Additionally your machine will, inter alia, deal with management and annual accounts systems.

- However, if you are not on top of computers don't run the risk of them getting on top of you. Instead you'll have to have a very, very good, constantly up-dated card index system and manually kept books.

- Please have a minimum of **two telephone lines,** one of which is **never** used for outgoing calls but kept clear for enquiries and orders from, particularly, the impulse buyer with his credit card. The phone that is always engaged exasperates customers and discourages sales.

- Equally off-putting are poor telephone manners (see **TELEPHONE DYSPHORIA**).

- Whoever answers the phone must leave the customer feeling he really has made the right buying decision.

- A part of your **MARKETING PLAN** (qv) may be to advertise in the **media** so consider the following:

- Before writing any ads ensure that they are decent, legal, honest and truthful by reading **The British Code of Advertising Practice.**

- Media choice is tricky and mistakes expensive.

- However, don't be a cheapskate. Be prepared to pay the going rate to get into the marketplace which means:

- However 'different' your product or service, only get into publications that carry ads for similar products, so far as this is possible.

- And at least to begin with advertise in a similar way to other traders in a similar business, again so far as this is possible.

- Better still to begin with use several different ads in several publications and code each one so that you can judge responses effectively.

- Lacking an acceptable response rate, say after three or four insertions, do not assume your product is no good. **Switch** the ad to another publication.

- Do not automatically assume that an expensive display ad will do a better job than the humble classified.

- 'The more you tell the more you sell'. Use enough words but

- Use them (and boldly) to tell about the product or service and the problems it solves for the customer **not** irrelevancies.

- Irrelevancies can include too much copy about **you.**

- One of the early decisions you must make is whether you will sell **off-the-page** (respondents must send their money with the order) or **by enquiry** (respondents first ask for fuller particulars). You will naturally get a heavier response (although not necessarily heavier sales) from the latter.

- Which you choose is largely dependent on the product/service you are selling: Simple = off-the-page; Complex = by enquiry.

- By enquiry involves the customer receiving a **sales letter** and/or **brochure.**

- Do not overspend on the brochure but do ensure that the contents are clear and expand on the advertisement, telling the potential customer everything he reasonably needs to know to make his buying decision.

- Only send details requested; a deluge of other material only irritates people.

- The best ads will succinctly outline the product's/service's positive and interesting points and benefits. The best brochures will do the same in greater detail.

- You may decide however that **direct mail** is preferable to ads. Cost will depend on the quality of brochure, etc.

- When the reply letters start rolling in **record immediately on opening** the customer's full details and requirements. Any delay and you could get swamped and lose track, which will certainly mean losing customers.

- Record the name of the publication in which the customer saw the ad to help your future **media preference** decisions, or if you have used varying direct mail shots note the differences of response.

- Even if payment is by **cheque** dispatch the goods

at earliest. The percentage of bounced cheques in MO is negligible (experts reckon on less than 1%).

- Be certain of the safe arrival of your goods by paying close heed to quality **packaging.** For bulky items it may be worth employing a package design company.

- And consider **promotion** — see that your logo is well displayed on the packaging.

- Organise your dispatch system. The 'now-where-did-I-put-that?' system isn't; it's an invitation to chaos.

- You don't have to dispatch every day, therefore in the early stages you will perhaps not need full-time help. Use cash casuals say once or twice a week if you can't physically do the job yourself.

- Keep a **Proof of Posting** book that the Post Office will stamp.

- Store all letters of enquiry as hard evidence of customer lists in case you want to **sell** these lists or the business.

- To test topicality of bought-in customer direct mail lists have your own envelopes over-printed with a **return-to-sender** address to keep track of gone-aways.

- For this venture you are of course in 'partnership' with the Post Office. You may perhaps be surprised at how highly organised they are. The information packs are excellent and their wholesale deals attractive. Whatever else you do, carefully consider their Freepost and Freephone deals. The less trouble and expense to the customer the more you will sell.

- You have to have the right product/service for Mail Order to work for you. But then you will — if you have been properly using this guide.

••• INFORMATION CHECK LIST

- You may feel the need for some market research. Here you run into something of a Catch 22. Whilst your LOCAL ENTERPRISE AGENCY will tell you about the generous grants available, research can still be expensive, more so if you are unsure of what the market actually **is** (a common problem for very innovative products/ services). However, the researchers EURO-MONITOR (01 - 251 8024) have published MAIL ORDER: HOME SHOPPING IN THE 1980s (ISBN 086 338124 3) which, if you don't want to spend £180, may be viewable at the SCIENCE REFERENCE LIBRARY, part of the BRITISH LIBRARY (start phone no 01 - 323 7454) or maybe at your local large reference library.

- If you have a clear enough view of your market then you will also know more or less the media you want to advertise in but do check BRITISH RATE & DATA. BRAD is the monthly media bible and lists pretty well every publication with advertising rates and deadlines. Ring the publisher on 01 - 975 9759 to get a copy (expensive) or find a big library that has BRAD regularly and might spare you one of their older numbers.

- For a copy of THE BRITISH CODE OF AD-VERTISING PRACTICE contact the ADVER-TISING STANDARDS AUTHORITY (01 - 580 5555).

- If you've decided on Direct Mail then you'll need lists so contact the BRITISH LIST BROKERS ASSOCIATION (0272 - 666900) to get started on this trail.

- As with advertising, the more clearly you 'see' your market the easier it is for media and list brokers to help.

- We suggested earlier that the POST OFFICE is your partner. They **do** try hard and have information and back-up which will guide you towards other information sources. Speak to them either locally or centrally (01 - 245 7031). Just say that you're thinking of going into Mail Order. . . .

- Read DO YOUR OWN ADVERTISING, by ALASTAIR CROMPTON, pub HUTCHINSON BUSINESS, £6.95, covers media and direct mail.

- PRACTICAL GUIDE FOR ORGANISING YOUR OWN MAIL ORDER BUSINESS, written and published by L FORSHAW PUB-LISHERS, £3.95, and

- SELL IT BY MAIL: MAKING YOUR PRO-DUCT THE ONE THEY BUY, pub WILEY, at a hefty £21.35, so try your reference library first.

- For 'off-the-page' sales you may need to join the National Newspapers Mail Order Protection Scheme (MOPS). Details 071 - 404 6806/9.

- Finally, Mail Order is an industry that has created its own specialist professionals; if you feel in need of advertising and media guidance seek out well-referenced agencies with a proven track record in Direct Response, the trade jargon for MO. The right agency can also make significant media-buying savings.

- **MASTER DRIVING**

- The motor car has come a long way since Otto, Benz and Daimler got the horseless carriage show on the road in the '70s and '80s of the last century.

- Alas, whilst cars have improved, too many people's ability to properly drive the things certainly hasn't, as the multi-crash horror stories demonstrate. According to the Driving Instructors Association the problem may lie in the fact that testing is by rote, whereas driving is a life skill.

- As quite a lot of more sensible drivers do actually want to stay alive on the road a course that helps them to do that by improving their driving and, critically, their speed of reaction and skill in dangerous situations, should be considered.

- Although advanced driving training is far from boring there are, in addition, other ways to go: e.g. Teach
  - how to take avoiding action in a car under **criminal attack**
  - **skid control**
  - the proper use of **four wheel drive** vehicles (some very rough terrain essential)
  - **bus, articulated lorry** and even **racing car** driving
  - **rally** driving
  - **mechanical courses** for **ladies**

- Indeed a **he-man** course entirely directed at the lady customer could have a strong market appeal. (Did you know, for instance, that a lady both runs and is on the board of Brands Hatch racing circuit?)

- A spin-off would be to have **sub-agencies** for your own preferred car and 4WD vehicles.

- Students are likely to seriously consider buying the make of vehicle that they have trained on and that you recommend.

- In this respect do think about unusual, value-for-money vehicles. We know they're unfashionable at the moment but we believe that the day of the cheap but effective **Eastern European** vehicles will soon dawn, once the penny drops and buyers conclude that paying vast amounts for trendy, over-hyped machines no longer makes total sense.

- For positive cashflow in the initial phase these specialised courses could be backed up by offering one-week **crammer** courses for the basic driving test. Such courses garner good fees; with accommodation, around £300+ for a five-day course.

- One million people a year pass the driving test but another million don't. (One lady only passed on her **47th attempt**.)

- Consider teaching master driving, first aid and **ETIQUETTE** (qv) to would-be chauffeurs. 'Morning, guv' doesn't quite do when greeting a captain of industry or peer of the realm.

- People are naturally obsessed by cars. Could you have a display of old ones to add yet more interest?

- Drivers are always buying bits and pieces for their vehicles. Your attractively laid-out **accessories shop** will ensure that you get a healthy slice of this profitable impulse buying.

••• INFORMATION CHECK LIST

- To be a driving instructor you have to be DEPARTMENT OF TRANSPORT approved. If you go to a specialist organisation such as THE DRIVING CENTRE (061 - 428 7658) they will charge approx. £280 plus VAT for their five-day course of training which is followed by three written exams. If you pass you then go to an appropriate DoT exam centre for their written and practical exams. Your four-year driving instructor registration fee is £100. The whole process including waiting time, etc., will take about four months.

- Contact the DRIVING INSTRUCTORS ASSOCIATION (01 - 660 3333) for fuller details, particularly of their skid control technology, **Slide Car** and **Astatic Skidmaster**.

- THE INSTITUTE OF ADVANCED MOTORISTS (01 - 994 4403) offers 'skill with responsibility' tuition to a high standard which covers the syllabus used by the Police Driving Schools. Being an IAM member is probably an essential. However, as your PSGs will expect you to be an absolute ace then you should also go for membership of

- THE HIGH PERFORMANCE CLUB: this involves passing a rigorous test organised by the HIGH PERFORMANCE COURSE (01 - 568 1313); a half-day assessment, if necessary a half or full day's tuition, before the HP assessment itself that last two days. The HP people emphasise that the process is only for highly skilled drivers. Cost per half-day £106 and £626 for the two-day assessment.

- DRIVING MANAGEMENT (06285 - 27387) run a very professional series of specialist driving

135

courses ranging from advanced and high performance (from around £200+ per day) through anti-hijack techniques (£1,610 for four-day course) to WOMEN MOBILE SECURITY courses (around £40 per day). Contact them for fuller details.

- BILL GWYNNE RALLY SCHOOL (0295 - 251201) provide one-day rally driving courses from around £125 per person.

- Consider joining the ALL WHEEL DRIVE CLUB (0761 - 71159), subscription £15 p.a. includes their six times a year magazine ALL WHEEL DRIVER.

- ROUGH TERRAIN TRAINING (0327 - 61886) provide 4WD courses from £200 plus VAT per day for a single pupil (£950 plus VAT for a five-day course, ex accommodation) but corporate groups come in at around £70 plus VAT per day per head; clay pigeon shooting and catering available. RTT are founders of the OFF ROAD TRAINING ASSOCIATION (same phone number).

- Read SUPERDRIVER by ex-champion driver SIR JOHN WHITMORE, £5.95, from your local RAC shop or from RAC MOTORING SERVICES (01 - 686 2525). Sir John can be paraphased as saying that the only thing stopping you becoming a superdriver is — you.

- Read RUNNING YOUR OWN DRIVING SCHOOL, by NIGEL STACEY, pub KOGAN PAGE, £5.95.

- THE DRIVING TEST: ESSENTIAL INFORMATION, by BRIAN STRATTON, pub FIRST TIME DRIVING (0634 - 362744), £3.95 and LEARNER DRIVER, a video-based tuition system from FOURMOST TRAINING (0977 - 600117) costing £19.95. Both could be of interest to your PSGs when you get going.

- To get the flavour try a HILTON (0923 - 38877) SKID CONTROL weekend break. £82.50 pp, two nights B&B. Their MOTOR RACING costs around £120 pp, two nights B&B.

- MOTIVACTION (043 - 886821) offer RACING DRIVER days at around a hefty £225 per person.

• MICROWAVE MAGIC

- Our favourite microwave recipe is Choc-Rum and Raisin **icecream.** Yes, that's right; you can cook icecream in this magical engine which has revolutionised our busy, two partners-working-full-time household over the last eight years. (We only use the cooker for baking bread and the occasional roast.) It can change your life too.

- Microwaves as an energy source were discovered by the British in 1940 but the Americans developed them in the 1950s and since then it seems that the microwave oven has been used by the housewife to heat the teapot while the kettle boils, warm hand towels and even dry tights, whilst its main culinary purpose — for the domestic **and** commercial caterer — has been only to reheat or cook chilled or frozen ready-prepared meals.

- What we have not heard enough about is that the microwave is a machine for cooking entire meals in **from scratch.**

- It does take a little time to get used to: Cooking times are a lot faster which means you have to be better prepared before starting. However, this is its great advantage over conventional cookers. And when you're in business for yourself every minute of the day has to be used profitably. Save time in the kitchen but not at the expense of tasty, nutritious meals and you will have more time for catching up on the paperwork or for leisure.

- Less water and fats are used than in conventional processes therefore more nutrients are retained and the flavour of fresh foods is not destroyed.

139

- You needn't worry about listeria poisoning if you use a microwave properly.

- French onion soup, steamed salmon and maltaise sauce, double-saucing chocolate pudding. . . . Recipes abound.

- Domestic machines usually are of only 600-700 watts and do **not** save time over conventional cooking methods. Many two-person households erroneously buy a smaller machine; what counts is that cooking times are extended by quantities, so cooking or reheating a meal for two takes much longer than for one person. The serious health risks concerning food heated or cooked by a microwave oven need not concern users of the commercial machines (see below) because their much higher power ensures food is cooked and bacteria destroyed if used correctly.

- Our message is this: If you are to be safe, a success and master of the microwave you must use a **commercial** machine of at least 1330 watts, with variable power settings. Consider one with dual emission for more even cooking of double quantities and with a drop-down door to hold plates and dishes on whilst you check and stir the food to ensure thorough cooking.

- There are companies who will rent you a machine short-term while you try your hand. They will then extend rentals for a year or more, which means you can update easily; try till you find the one that best suits your requirements.

- Fear is the biggest problem to conquer. The speed with which the microwaves cook is amazing. However, a little patience is all that is required to overcome this problem. Cook for shorter times, rest and test, then cook on — in seconds.

- As with other forms of cooking, it is essential that food is thoroughly cooked by getting it to a high temperature, which destroys bacteria.

- So, when first starting, get a microwave heat probe to test the cooking. It is essential that all the food reaches at least 70° (preferably 80°) to kill any bacteria. And by using your high-powered commercial machine to prepare meals from raw ingredients you avoid any potential health hazards that arise when chilled or frozen prepared meals are inadequately reheated.

- Where is the business in **MICROWAVE MAGIC?** For a start, teach yourself and then teach others, not only house persons but professional chefs as well. (Consider in due course writing your own commercial oven cookbooks.) Even leading schools **do not** teach cooking-in-microwave-ovens; they occasionally do a few hours' demonstration on how to use the domestic versions to defrost or heat food, considering that microwaves do not produce good-tasting food. Nonsense! We know of a leading restaurateur who cooks most of his meals at home in his microwave.

- Many a leading chef has had no formal training, so don't let your own inexperience worry you. All cooking, at the end of the day, is trial and error until you know your equipment and the recipes.

- The commercial power microwave is an eye-opener; consider the profitable add-on of selling, leasing, or renting them to your PSGs.

• INFORMATION CHECK LIST

- The best cookbooks, albeit for a domestic microwave, come from THE AUSTRALIAN WOMEN'S WEEKLY HOME LIBRARY series, called MICROWAVE COOKBOOK 1 & 2. If the beautiful colour photography doesn't have you rushing out to get a machine and fresh ingredients then don't read on. Available from bookshops, £4.95 each, or contact J. B. FAIRFAX PRESS LTD on 0933 402330. With your variable power setting microwave you will be able to cook-to-recipe then experiment at higher settings, thereby reducing the time taken.

- Commercial microwave suppliers will be found in your Yellow Pages. Ring around until you find someone local willing to do a short rental.

- To test for cold spots and to ensure that the food is cooked correctly — the core of the item being cooked must reach at least 70°C — buy a MICROWAVE PROBE and MICROWAVE CHECK (which tests for microwave leakages from the door) — both available through RDM TEST EQUIPMENT (0920 - 871231), £12-£100, depending on model.

- In the research time at our disposal we were amazingly unable to find any schools where you can learn on commercial machines (which means there's a gap in the market for you to fill). However, TRICIA BARKER runs the BEACONSFIELD MICROWAVE SCHOOL (0494 -676409) offering 1–14 days demonstrations on domestic machines, at £19.95 per day including lunch. You can attend as frequently as you wish to suit yourself. Instruction is by demonstration only, not hands-on.

- PAMELA SPARROW runs similar courses at her specially-designed home kitchen in Bingley, West Yorks (0274 - 569570), £17 per day including lunch, or three evenings over three-weeks for

142

£26. Accommodation available at hotel nearby. Classes restricted to 10-12.

- Check your LOCAL AUTHORITY'S CLASSES OF FURTHER EDUCATION. Maybe **you** can find a commercial machine course.

- The INSTITUTE OF HOME ECONOMICS (01 - 404 5532) can give you a list of freelance teachers.

- If you have problems while experimenting, help is available from the OXO MICROWAVE AD-VISORY SERVICE (0345 - 58180) between 11-4 weekdays. They also have free leaflets.

- GOOD HOUSEKEEPING INSTITUTE (01 - 439 5000) charge £1.50 for their excellent laminated card MICROWAVE KNOW-HOW. Get it and stick it on a wall near your microwave oven for easy reference.

- If you can't find a teacher or school nearby then get TV cook GLYNN CHRISTIAN'S 90-minute video, £8.99 including p&p, by phoning 01 - 760 9051 during working hours.

- Special microwave utensils available from your supermarket, good hardware stores or direct from LAKELAND PLASTICS (09662 - 88100) or MICRO CUISINE LTD (0454 - 323653). Rigid plasticware is good for short cooking periods but anything requiring a longer time (3 minutes or more) in the commercial machines should be cooked in glassware like ANCHOR HOCKING, from major department stores or specialist catering firms.

- When you are confident and ready to start making money from your commercial microwave read THE MICROWAVABLE FOODS MARKET report from EUROMONITOR (01 - 251 8024). Check it at the SCIENCE REFERENCE LIBRARY, part of the BRITISH LIBRARY (start with 01 - 323 7454) as it is expensive.

- Whilst at the library check out A GUIDE TO MICROWAVE CATERING, by LEWIS NAPLETON, pub NORTHWOOD PUBLICATIONS, ISBN 7198 26411.

• **MOBILE PROFESSIONAL**

- Using the home only as your **base** this idea steals a march on the competition:

- Because of pressure of work and distance, country dwellers and business people often find it difficult to make time to visit a professional, important though such a visit may be.

- This venture therefore concerns those many situations where **on-the-spot** personal consultation, inspection and treatment could be provided.

- By equipping a suitable van with all that's needed you can be completely mobile because today every significant piece of office equipment is made in portable form so that even when visiting a client you can easily be reached and can contact other clients or your base.

- Having all your files with you in your mobile office means business can proceed smoothly, although you are offering a Rolls-Royce service by spending much of your time personally advising clients on the spot — their spot.

- To be even more effective the travelling office could house a secretarial colleague, perhaps a spouse.

- More and more people are working from home but are tied there. A well-advertised, quality visiting professional service therefore would garner above-average fees.

- In particular this idea would suit **accountants** or **book-keepers** because it would save the client the hassle of delivering and temporarily losing the use of his books and papers of account for regular management accounting and year-end audits.

- On-the-spot typing, copying, fax and printing services, etc., could all profitably be made available to clients.

- This venture could also be for you if you are into, e.g. **beauty, hair, health care, alternative healing, chiropody, counselling,** etc. Indeed, wherever a skill that is in demand can be taken **to** the customer.

••• INFORMATION CHECK LIST

- It is becoming more and more possible now to **flexi-rent** equipment.

- You will have to press suppliers but with persistence you will find those that will give you this option.

- The advantage for a start-up is clear: if the equipment doesn't suit you swop it instantly and without penalty for something that does. (Compare this to the hassle involved in a leasing contract to see what we mean.)

- Such flexi-deals can be negotiated so as to rebate to you most of the rent if you decide to buy later.

- Contact WHAT TO BUY FOR BUSINESS (01 - 730 0403) for lists of their current and back issues to pinpoint their reports on the equipment that interests you. As back issues cost a hefty £19.75 each to non-subscribers it may pay to consider joining; cost £69.50 for 10 magazines and a reduced price of £7.50 for back numbers. (Sadly, we, with many others, sometimes find their advice confusing, but until somebody comes

146

up with a better format this magazine is pretty well all we have.)

- As most of us under-estimate the amount of space we need consider this in connection with your vehicle and, again, seriously think of flexi-renting for your initial period.

• MUSIC

- It comes down to us from ancient times, embellished by the Greeks, the Jews and the Church. Its first great age flowered in the Renaissance. Today music continues to stir a deep and powerful response in all of us.

- What is even more to the point is that increasing numbers of people don't just want to listen to it — they and their children want to **make** music.

- By way of sheet publishing, broadcasting, live music and performance and recording etc the music market in the UK alone is worth in excess of £2 billion p.a.

- To show what can be achieved by teaching music take the experience of two music teachers, the **Johnstons.**

- Initially they and their colleagues were teaching from private homes.

- With talent and organisation they became so successful that they were able to attract **Business Expansion Scheme investment** backing enabling them to acquire a sizeable country mansion into which to expand what has become a flourishing £250,000 plus p.a. turnover business.

- Proceeding via booking the Royal Festival Hall for one of their concerts and founding the National Children's Wind Orchestra charity, the Johnstons have found business so good that it has already outgrown their premises.

- A report indicated that they might be considering some form of franchise.

- When weighing this venture don't think only classical. Jazz too has an enormous and dedicated following.

- Sell, rent, new or second-hand, instruments to PSGs from your own **music shop.** Do not, please, overlook the fact either that, full of enthusiasm, some people take up music but don't last the course. So if selling build in a **buy-back** (at a discount) option. It's a confidence booster.

- Finally, consider selling **music tapes** to read, write, work or think with. See below.

••• INFORMATION CHECK LIST

- For background: EUROMONITOR (01 - 251 8024) do in-depth research and their UK MUSIC INDUSTRY costs £235 but you may be able to read it at the SCIENCE REFERENCE LIBRARY, part of the BRITISH LIBRARY (start phone no. 01 - 323 7454) or it may be available at larger local reference libraries.

- It is recommended but not essential to have qualifications. GETTING JOBS IN MUSIC, pub CASSELL (01 - 222 7676), £3.95, sets out to lift the fog but meantime contact

- THE ROYAL ACADEMY OF MUSIC (01 - 935 5461) regarding their exam (cost £85) to become an LRAM (LICENTIATE of the ROYAL ACADEMY of MUSIC). You may only sit this test after reaching Grade Eight proficiency.

- From your local polytechnic or university get details of their course required to get a DIPLOMA OF EDUCATION.

- If your taste inclines to jazz contact the GUILD-HALL SCHOOL OF MUSIC & DRAMA (01 -

628 2571) or the JOHNNY DANKWORTH SCHOOL (0908 - 582 522) for details of their offerings.

- The INCORPORATED SOCIETY OF MUSICIANS (01 - 629 4413) can offer information regarding a good private teacher in your locality; expect to pay £10-£15 per hour.

- The MUSIC RETAILERS ASSOCIATION (01 - 994 7592) will help you on the instrument sales aspect.

- A book that could help you make up your mind about your instrument(s) is MUSIC, pub DORLING KINDERSLEY, £6.95, which describes every kind of instrument, its history and the nature of its sound. It also gives details of makers and even noted performers.

- Recommended magazines include: JAZZ JOURNAL INTERNATIONAL, monthly, £1.50; THE MUSIC TIMES, monthly, £1.40; CLASSICAL MUSIC, fortnightly, £1.20 and the MUSIC TEACHER, monthly, £1.25.

- Mr & Mrs DAVID JOHNSTON run MUSIC-ALE (0582 - 713048) from their mansion. Talk to them about music lessons (private tuition around £75 for 10 half-hour courses) and franchise possibilities.

- Contact NIGHTINGALE-CONANT (0101 - 708 647 0300) or at 7300 NORTH LEHIGH AVENUE, CHICAGO, ILL., USA, zip 60648, re their SOUND SUPPORT ONE, catalogue no. 425AD, six audio cassettes of 'scientifically composed music and sound patterns that can stimulate the brain to attain the optimal brain-wave state for accomplishing a given task.' That's what they say!

- **MYSTERIES**

- What fascinates people they will always pay to find out more about — and that which is hidden, the **occult,** concerns fascinating goings-on beyond the range of ordinary knowledge.

- Despite a good deal of professed cynicism the probability is that there are relatively few totally committed non-believers in the occult and for good reason:

- Since his very earliest days in existence man has been sharply aware that he is a puny thing and needs all the protection and help he can get in a cruelly unforgiving, unpredictable world, e.g.

- Imaginary gods (viz, for the Greeks it was Gaia, for the Anglo-Saxons it was Erce) 'controlling' the weather, crops, procreation et al, have been propitiated through the ages.

- Indeed it is difficult to see how the great religions could have become established unless, deep down, man had always acknowledged that somewhere out there was some unknown, unknowable power that controlled his destiny.

- There are reckoned to be about 250,000 occultists (or **witches,** or **pagans** as they are sometimes called) in the UK.

- In general terms
  - 85% are between 20 and 40 years old
  - 75% reject **satanism**
  - 75% believe in **reincarnation**
  - nearly all think they get a raw deal from the media!

- This last may not be too surprising because occultism (said to be concerned more with predicting and inducing events rather than explaining them) has attracted the charlatan as well as those who appear to have genuine para-normal abilities.

- For example, the Russian spiritualist **Helena Blavatsky,** founder of the **Theosophical Society,** claimed that, as many of her followers still believe, she had extraordinary **psychic** powers. However, in 1885 after an investigation by London's Society for Psychical Research, she was accused of creating fictitious spiritualist phenomena and declared a fraud.

- Another last century practitioner **David Home** baffled fans, sceptics and European royalty alike with phenomena ranging from temperature drops, floating tables and personal levitation to personal elongation(!).

- In his case, however, and despite the closest of scrutiny, Home never was proved to be fraudulent.

- More recently **Jeane Dixon,** an American clairvoyant, accurately predicted through her crystal ball electoral victories and defeats, even the deaths of Marilyn Monroe and the Kennedy brothers.

- And, of course, there is **Uri Geller** . . .

- Not the least bemusing fact to emerge from any study of the mysteries is man's near-genius in finding things, elements and abstracts to be mysterious about.

- He has found significance and divination
    - by the inspection of the entrails of sacrificial animals (**haruspicy**);
    - by the study of water (**hydromancy**);

- by the examination of smoke and fire (**pyromancy**);
- by agonising over the patterns made by bits of earth thrown about (**geomancy**);
- by grappling with the omens revealed by analysing dreams (**oneiromancy**);
- (in the hope that they might have something useful to say) by talking to the dead (**necromancy**);
- (and thus encouraged he has even gone the whole hog) by communing with God Himself (**theosophy**).

- How far down this rune-strewn path you want to take yourself and your PSGs must be a matter of personal inclination but to ponder on we offer below a small sample from the long list of mysteries:

- **Astrology**

- Used by the Babylonians to understand their own destinies, the seminal text book **Tetrabiblos** was written by the Alexandrian **Ptolemy** in the second century AD.

- Later the Arabs refined our knowledge of **planetary motion.**

- Many famous people such as **Copernicus, Newton, Einstein** and **Ronald Reagan** have had a deep interest in, and have been influenced by, astrology. The financier **J P Morgan** was a believer and is quoted as saying 'Millionaires don't use astrology, billionaires do!'

- (Some infamous people, too. Knowing how strongly swayed **Hitler** was by his astrologer, the British employed their own, **Louis de Wohl,** to predict what astrological advice Hitler was receiving during the last war.)

155

- The ancient Greeks were the first to perceive a connection between astrology and **plant life.**

- Because each astrological sign is held to govern a particular part of the body, any plant used as medicine for that part of the body could be linked to the sign ruling it, e.g. Aries rules garlic, which is great for the liver and gall bladder, Taurus governs lovage, which can be beneficial for stomach ailments.

- We note that however sceptical people may **say** they are about astrology, almost everyone knows their birth sign and papers and magazines would hardly devote the space they do to them if their readers didn't study horoscopes.

- Some people even consciously shape their persona to their birth sign's image (the dour and hard-working Capricorn, the witty social butterfly Gemini, and so on) and some even go so far as to pick their pet (cat or dog) through astro-logical match-pairing. (Gerbils are too small to have their sign read!)

- **The Conception Theory of Astrology**

- This theory makes the revolutionary claim that the emergence-from-the-womb birth sign is irre-levant and that all calculations should start from the time of **conception,** as best this can be known. The theory is that **then** the parents' characters are fused into the embryo and it is therefore the influence of the heavenly bodies in their particu-lar positions at **that** particular time that is signifi-cant, not their positions nine months **after** the child has been in being.

- To conventional astrology the conception theory is of course a bombshell and therefore might be profitably explored, for everybody's birth sign would have to be replaced by one approximately **nine months earlier.** There would be something of an upheaval in the persona stakes: the earthy Capricorn could be a fiery Aries, the airy Gemini an earthy Virgo and so on!

- **Chinese Astrology**

- Whereas Western astrology is based on the **solar calendar,** the Chinese put their astrological faith in the **moon** as the decisive body. Roosters, Dogs, Tigers and Rats, etc., take the place of our zodiac signs.

- **Yin,** the dark, passive, female principle of the universe, and **Yang,** the bright, active, male principle of the universe, also have powerful roles to play.

- Although attempts are made to make Eastern and Western astrology appear compatible this is almost certainly not the case and the two forms should be taken as separate one from the other.

- Finally, it is only fair to point out that astrology is thought, erroneously, to be about predicting the future, whereas serious astrologers claim to do no more than indicate trends which may be avoided, or promoted, by taking the appropriate action.

- **Cartomancy**

- Divination through the medium of ordinary **playing cards,** when these are shuffled and revealed according to arcane formula.

- **Crystal Gazing or Scrying**

- Just before a vision the rock crystal ball should mist up from within. However, the ball may be

157

nothing more than a convenient object for the **clairvoyant** (clear-sighted) to focus upon in order to harness concentration and intuition before revealing all.

- Very ancient; said to work best when the sun is at its northernmost declination.

- **Dowsing**

- Introduced from Germany in the 16th century. The word may originate from the German 'denton' = to declare or interpret.

- Truly remarkable results continue to be obtained by dowsers. Some are so attuned that, without even visiting the site and waving their forked hazel, rowan or willow twig around, they can sense from **correspondence** and **survey maps** alone whether or not water or minerals, etc., are present.

- Dowsers frown upon the term 'divining rod', claiming that divination is **not** part of their process.

- Has even been successfully used to locate dead bodies!

- **Feng Shui**

- Feng Shui in Chinese means 'wind and water' and is claimed to be the mystical link between man and his environment, ancient ways and modern life.

- It interprets the language articulated by natural forms and phenomena, by man-made buildings and symbols and by the continual workings of the universe, including moon phases and star alignments.

158

- It is claimed to be the key to understanding the silent dialogue between man and nature, whispered through a cosmic breath or spirit called **ch'i.**

- This term means a life force or energy that ripples water, creates mountains, breathes life into plants, trees and humans and propels man along life's course.

- Man feels and is affected by ch'i even though he may not know it.

- If ch'i is misinterpreted man's life and luck may falter.

- It is said that the film star **Bruce Lee** died because he ignored bad ch'i — the Feng Shui signals that told him he lived in an unlucky house.

- Feng Shui experts fill the need to intuit, decode and interpret our environment, using psychic antennae to pick up messages and signals from the surroundings. The rituals can be complex or simple.

- Some simple Feng Shui remedies include putting red ribbons on doors with knocking knobs and putting chalk under a bed to cure backache.

- **Plants** can indicate good Feng Shui. Where they thrive round or in a house or office so will the human occupiers.

- Major international corporations including Jardine's, Chase Manhattan Bank and Wall Street Journal employ Feng Shui experts in their offices to auspiciously position each employee's desk to ensure contentment, thus higher productivity and greater prosperity.

- **Graphology or Chirography**

- Inferring character based on a subject's **hand-writing,** e.g. large writing is a sign of ambition, small is an indication of pedantry.

- As handwriting is unique to each individual and is a combination of both the conscious and un-conscious many believe it is a particularly reliable guide.

- Because of this it is now widely used as a tool in **personnel selection.**

- It is also used to trace criminals and even (is there some connection here?) by parents to check the suitability of their son/daughter's pros-pective marriage partner.

- **I Ching or Yi Ching**

- This is the title of a Chinese book of wisdom dating back to 1000 BC, although the underlying system may go back much earlier, to the emperor **Fu Hsi** who reigned in 2400 BC and got his inspiration from the patterns on the back of a tortoise.

- (There is the suggestion that the book was either written or edited by **Confuscius.** If so, someone's got their dates confused as the 72-year-old sage died in 479 BC. He was also strongly opposed to such esoterica).

- The English translation is **Book of Changes** and it is very complex. Simplistically, however, the book guides fortune-tellers regarding the meaning of **patterns** created when coins, cards, dice or, more traditionally, sticks are randomly thrown on to a surface marked with eight groups of three lines and 64 groups of six lines.

160

- I Ching also attempts to explain, inter alia, the complementary interaction of Yin and Yang from which all things spring, and it stresses the connection between nature and man's destiny.

- Forget all the other mysteries: I Ching is a lifetime's study all by itself!

- **Iridology**

- To many of us the every-day diagnosis, prognosis and cure of ailments is still, despite all the modern technology, something of a mystery.

- Iridology is an intuitive system of diagnosing a subject's present and future state of mental and physical well-being or otherwise by close microscopic study and photography of the **iris of the eye.**

- There is a strong speculative aura surrounding iridology and whether it fits into these mysteries or perhaps better into **alternative therapy** is for you to decide.

- **Oneiromancy**

- Divination by the interpretation of **dreams** and based on the very ancient belief that dreams are messages sent to the soul by gods or the dead, most usually as warnings. This mystery had some very eminent followers, **Freud** and **Jung** amongst them.

- The dreams of which oneiromancy is made take place during periods of **REM (Rapid Eye Movement)** which only happens for part of the time that we are asleep.

- Woken during a REM period the subject's recall is vividly clear and detailed, not so if woken during non-REM periods.

- Modern thinking is trying to remove dreams from their guilt-ridden Freudian provenance and make us see dreaming as healthy, fantasy play-time. Evidently the ancients would not have approved.

- **Palmistry or Chiromancy or Chirosophy**

- Palmistry has been with us since times of great antiquity and although something of a fairground joke perhaps deserves to be taken seriously; certainly **Jung** thought this.

- Whether or not he agreed with the ancients that pigmentation spots indicated a pact with the Devil is not, as far as we know, on record.

- The shape, flexibility, lines and mounds on a **hand** are unique to each individual and over time the palmists have constructed a persuasive set of rules as to what hands can tell about their owner and his past and future.

- **Pespedisology or Podomancy**

- Did you realise what a complex extremity is the **foot**?

- 26 bones are connected to 38 muscles by no less than 56 ligaments! With so much going on it ought to be able to tell us something . . .

- Pespedisology is anchored to the speculation that character can be read from the mounds and contours of the sole.

- Strictly from the **brain's** point of view, the body's most important bits are the eyes, tongue, lips, hands and feet as prime relayers of information, so maybe feet reading can provide the diviner with similar information as is held possible by the study of the hands in **Palmistry.**

- **Phrenology**

- Reading character and mental potential by studying the shape and features of the **skull.**

- Much used by Freud as a guide to his obsession regarding the unconscious.

- Phrenology was first propounded by one **Dr F J H Gall** (1758 - 1828).

- He based his theory on his claimed discovery of 26 organs within the brain, each of which was responsible for a particular faculty; the better these organs worked the larger they were and the more they affected the shape of the skull, maintained Gall.

- Unfortunately, 20th century scientists like their knowledge to be based on proven research and fact. Perceiving neither in Dr Gall's theory they have dismissed it as rubbish. But . . . ?

- **Physiognomy or Siang Mien**

- Divination of character from the **features** of face or **form** of body, e.g. large ears point to a broad grasp of affairs and so on.

- **Aristotle** was an early proponent, using animals for his analogy, e.g. leonine features indicated great courage and strength, etc.

- Scientists are predictably sceptical but nevertheless admit that certain facial and bodily characteristics **do** correlate to psychological function.

- There is an even more arcane divination called **Metoscopy,** which is based on the **lines** of the brow and **moles** on the body.

- In some opaque way this means of divination appears to have connections with astrology, as the lines and moles are believed by adherents to be the 'stars of the body'.

- **Sortes or Bibliomancy**

- From the Latin sors, sortis = change or first.

- This divination involves opening a **learned book** (such as the **Bible**) at **random** and the passage you touch by chance with your fingers is the oracular response to the question that led you to ask the book in the first place.

- Oracles by nature of course can be deeply obscure and ambiguous (hence Delphic) but there are records of some spectacularly accurate responses, e.g.:

- **Lord Falkland** was a close favourite of the star-crossed king, **Charles I.** Seeking to amuse his patron one day Falkland suggested this kind of augury and Charles lit upon IV, 615-620, the gist of which is that 'evil wars would break out and the king lose his life.'

- The embarrassed Falkland, in a misguided attempt to laugh off this chilling news, said he would show the king how ridiculously the book would foretell the next fate and going to it chanced upon XI, 153-181.

- This, alas, was the lament of Evander for the untimely death of his son Pallas.

- The rest is indeed history: Very shortly after-wards, in 1641, the Civil War broke out; King Charles later mourned the death of his noble young favourite, for Falkland was slain at Newbury in 1643. Charles, of course, lost his head on the 30th January 1649.

164

- **Tarot**

- India, Arabia and China share, or fight for, the right to the origination of this mystery.

- The diviner uses the pack's 78 **cards** (or topically 54) to reveal the past, present and future of the subject.

- The picture cards carry symbols that date back to the Egyptians and are amongst the oldest known to us, e.g. the Sun, the Moon, the Lovers, the Devil, and the Tree of Life.

- The pack is split into four suits: Wands, Cups, Swords and Pentacles and each suit has an underlying theme.

- There are several systems for laying out the cards, each one of which moderates and influences its neighbours.

- Despite the conventions governing the laying of cards the Tarot reader must still use much intuition.

- **Telethesia**

- The direct **perception** of and divination from **distant occurrences** or **objects** that is not effected by the recognised senses.

- This remarkable ability could be described as clairvoyance; it also takes us into the highly complex field of **parapsychology** and **ESP.** But why not? After all, the mysteries are everywhere . . . .

••• INFORMATION CHECK LIST

- We would fill this entire guide if we attempted to offer a bibliography on this enormous subject. However, you will be able to find what you want from the following sources:

- An emporium called THE SORCERER'S APPRENTICE (0532 - 753835) claims to stock 3,000 psychic/occult items.

- MYSTERIES (01 - 240 3688) is a bookshop specialising in a range of occult and paranormal material.

- Similarly WATKINS BOOKS (01 - 836 2182).

- For the really arcane you may have to prowl the vastnesses of THE BRITISH LIBRARY (01 - 636 1544).

- For a source closer to hand your local library will get you started, and also try

- Your local W H SMITH bookshop to see if it carries a rack entitled MYTHOLOGY & FOR-TUNE TELLING.

- Details of practitioners are to be found in many glossy magazines. For those wanting their pet's horoscope forecast, contact PRETENTIOUS PETS (01 - 937 2575). Costs £9.95 for one pet; or £12 for a pet-and-owner compatability horo-scope. In either case, have ready the time of birth (if possible), date and place.

- Also read PSYCHIC NEWS, weekly, 22p, and THE SPIRITUALIST GAZETTE, monthly 20p.

- Lastly, we do know of an actual witch. Her

166

name is DOT GRIFFITHS, although she is better known to her **coven** (meetings every Tuesday) as MADAME MORGANA, high priestess of Buckinghamshire for many years and teacher of **Wicca** (witchcraft). She operates in Milton Keyes close to the Open Univeristy and if you are serious about meeting her no doubt you will be able to do so by local enquiry.

• NOSTALGIA

- The British have been accused of being a nostalgic nation, something in us always sentimentally pining for some earlier time or period of the past.

- Perhaps with our long history this is not surprising, particularly as we are fortunate to be still well-endowed with museums and stately homes to feed the yearning.

- However, the nostalgia aspect that we want you to consider as a money-maker concerns an altogether tighter focus on history: accurately (re)constructing your home as an exact replica of a home from the past, down to the fine details.

- Creating and **running** a home just as it would have been at the moment in time of its building and first occupation, or some appropriately later and suitably nostalgic date of your choice.

- (Stately homes do not fulfill this function; what you see are either lifeless rooms frozen in time or how people live today's life in old surroundings.)

- To work profitably this nostalgic **theatre** has to be done as totally as possible.

- As well as the closest attention to the decor (and don't forget the appropriate lighting as it would have been, e.g. gas light, candles), all concerned have to dress themselves accurately to period (no modern watches, jewellery, etc) and the food and drink offered must be the appropriate cuisine for the time and the region. The further back in time you decide to go the more climate, economic conditions, even religion would have affected the choice of food and the method of cooking it.

- Something of what we mean is to be found at **Dennis Severs's** house in Spitalfields, London.

- This American entrepreneur has created a **'theatre of the imagination'.**

- The straw scattered outside the front door heralds the time-warp to be found within, where Severs has recreated the history of a refugee family of Huguenots from the 17th to the early 20th Century.

- Each of the 10 rooms is cluttered and decorated in the style of a different period in the family's history.

- But this is no inert waxworks of a place; **special effects** evoke a sense of present occupation:

- In the basement doors slam; elsewhere you can hear voices speaking French; you negotiate round an overturned chair; warm yourself at a roaring grate; catch the smell of roasting meat.

- At Mr Severs's Christmas Party, the turkey, the trimmings, mince pies and all, come from the ancient oven and you enjoy the background sounds of muffled sleigh-bells and carol singers just outside the shuttered windows.

- Who suggested nostalgia doesn't pay? Mr Severs charges a handsome £25 per person for his three-hour tour (eight per tour).

- And **Dickens's Old Curiosity Shop** in London has witnessed a phenomenal increase in visitors rising from 150,000 a year to 275,000 a year at the last count.

- A whole town (**Llandrindod** in Wales) actually turns **itself** over to nostalgia in the summer. For a week it largely clothes itself and behaves as in the last century in its **Victorian Festival.**

- Whilst you're boning up on all the off-beat minutae of your locale's history of the chosen era, you will also be accumulating information for the second leg of this venture; for, in addition to enjoying your house, your PSGs will want to get out and about with you to explore what you have discovered in your research.

- Whilst talks, sight-seeing tours, rural walks of interest, local lore, customs and industries are the stuff of which this aspect is made, it will be the particular enthusiasm, even **idiosyncrasy,** with which you put it all across that will make it live and sparkle.

- Spice your information with plenty of anecdotes and of course **know** your subject backward (no two PSGs will ever be exactly alike and they can come up with some deeply amazing questions. . .).

- Find discreet opportunities to sell items of interest to your visitors and, as they will have an above-average interest in the past, consider catering for this also by e.g. running a **genealogical trace service.**

- You knew that people visit historic sites in large numbers but did you know **how** large? According to the British Tourist Authority over **150,000,000 visits per year** are now being recorded!

●●● INFORMATION CHECK LIST

- DENNIS SEVERS'S HUGUENOT HOUSE (01

171

- 247 4013). According to season, he can be booked up for three weeks ahead.

- Nearby is another quite extraordinary, 'frozen', monument, a synagogue that was simply **abandoned** in the middle of full activity, lock, stock and barrel, some years ago: the RODINSKY ROOM, open only on certain days; contact the SPITALFIELDS TRUST (01 - 247 0971) for details.

- Whilst in London visit the DICKENS'S OLD CURIOSITY SHOP (01 - 405 9891).

- Further afield and perhaps not quite so dramatic is THE GEORGIAN HOUSE in Edinburgh, home of a Scots grandee. Contact the NATIONAL TRUST FOR SCOTLAND (031 - 226 5922).

- In nearby Glasgow there is the rather forbiddingly named TENEMENT HOUSE (041 - 333 0183), a time capsule of the Edwardian era.

- There's another GEORGIAN HOUSE in Bristol, once home of an 18th Century sugar tycoon. Contact 0272 - 299771.

- FLAMBARDS TRIPLE THEME PARK(!) in Cornwall (0326 - 573404) offers the CHEMIST SHOP TIME CAPSULE, the down-to-the-last-detail, actual shop of a chemist who died in 1909. There is also a 'Victorian' village.

- See the REMINISCENCE CENTRE at Black-heath (01 - 318 9105), a successful AGE EX-CHANGE experiment in exposing the elderly and the very young to the past.

- To learn how to properly do the job of a GUIDE consider going for a BLUE BADGE course.

These are operated by tourist boards in conjunction with local authorities.

- If you go that route consider contacting the GUILD OF GUIDE LECTURERS (01 - 839 7438).

- You may be interested to see the THEATRE MUSEUM. For opening hours ring 01 - 836 7624; for research enquiries ring 01 - 836 9858.

- Indeed why not consider doing the job in style by polishing up your acting ability? Contact STAGECRAFT (01 - 483 2681) regarding their courses.

- SOCIETY OF GENEALOGISTS (01 - 251 8799).

- Read FOOD IN ENGLAND, by DOROTHY HARTLEY, pub MACDONALD, ISBN 0356 0069069 hb, or ISBN 0708826962 pb, a survey of English food and cooking methods throughout the ages.

- The NATIONAL TRUST BOOK OF FORGOTTEN HOUSEHOLD CRAFTS, by JOHN SEYMOUR, pub DORLING KINDERSLEY, £12.95.

- The METROPOLE HOTEL (0597 - 2881), LLANDRINDOD WELLS, offers 'A VICTORIAN EXPERIENCE' break for the town's VICTORIAN FESTIVAL.

- For tips on period detail and useful house history see the **Architectural Salvage** section of **RECYLING;** also **SPECIAL EFFECTS & ACQUIRING YOUR COUNTRY PROPERTY.**

- Once you're under way you'll want to know

how to keep your precious house intact; visitors can knock it about a bit. Contact the NATIONAL TRUST (01 - 222 9251) for details of their video KEEPING HOUSE, by SHEILA STAINTON. This lady has the responsibility for 190 of the Trusts' historic houses.

- To get the flavour:

- HILTON (0923 - 38877) offer two-night COUNTRY RETREAT breaks from £95 to £140 pp, breakfast and dinner;

- For more sumptuous country mansion time-benders consider STAPLEFORD PARK (057 - 284522), in Leicestershire; the antique book publishers Mr & Mrs Miller's CHILSTON PARK (0622 - 859803) in Kent; or TULLOCH LODGE (03397 - 55406) in Aberdeenshire. At a price, all hold out the prospect of comfort as in another age.

• PAINTING, DRAWING & SCULPTURE

- Every-day communication with one another we undertake almost without thinking, yet ask people with no experience to communicate by painting, drawing or sculpting something and the majority will freeze solid. Those that do try will most times produce crude stereotypes.

- This need not be: experts believe that almost anyone can express themselves artistically; it is not simply a question of tuition but more importantly of developing a **new way of seeing.**

- In painting there are at least nine different media with which to work: acrylic, ink, oil, watercolour and so on; wishing to draw you may choose also from at least nine media: chalk, charcoal, crayon, pencil, etc; with sculpture there is a minimum range of 10 media: stone, metal, concrete and glass fibre being amongst them.

- Evidently there are very many choices and following your own personal inclination, whilst paying keen regard to what the market is most looking for, will provide the key.

- Ever since the first painful efforts in his stone-age cave man has yearned to express himself artistically and this is just as true today; the market comprises those frustrated people who are willing to come to you to learn how to do something positive about it.

- Once you have mastered the skills, or gathered around you skilled teachers, the first challenge is a marketing one; thereafter your success will flow from getting across the same message as we are sending to you through this guide: 'Yes, you **can** do it!' and cheerfully, enthusiastically demonstrating that this message is true.

175

- Amongst your PSGs you are bound to get some with real talent. Consider setting up and promoting an **art gallery** to show their work and sell it on commission to other students and visitors.

- Apart from the obvious extra income from selling basics like **brushes** and **easels** etc, think about **framing** and **correspondence course** possibilities.

- When you are very proficient another eventual money spin-off could arise from advising potential art purchasers, such as business organisations, on their requirements both for decoration and investment. You will need to know your artists and their product but here you make the purchase then sell onto the client with your mark-up added.

••• INFORMATION CHECK LIST

- There are countless books, the best of which you will get to after you have chosen your niche. However, the single most important book you must track down and read if you are serious about this venture is DRAWING ON THE RIGHT SIDE OF THE BRAIN, by the American artist and teacher BETTY EDWARDS, pub FONTANA COLLINS, £8.99. She has proved that the student's breakthrough comes when he can shift his brain from analytic to spatial processing. Her book shows how the shift can be learned. 'If you can ride a bicycle you can draw,' she says, in effect. The book also has an impressive **bibliography.**

- Your local art college for information on courses but also read

- The annual STUDENT BOOK, pub MAC-MILLAN, £8.95, for diploma/degree courses on your chosen subject.

176

• PERSONAL DEVELOPMENT

- This concerns personal awareness and the need many people feel to improve and develop themselves and their relationships with others. How all this is to be achieved can be something of a puzzle but modern thinkers are helping us get closer to the answers.

- The eminent American sociologist **G H Mead** suggested that the individual's conception of himself and of how he appears to others is a product of **social interaction**.

- Mead emphasised the constant tension between the pressures of social conformity on the one hand and the impulse to assert **individuality** on the other.

- He distinguished two components of self: the **Me** and the **I**. The **Me,** maintained Mead, is the social component and is the impression we **think** we make on other people whose opinion matters to us.

- We gather these impressions by putting ourselves in the place of these others.

- The individual's reference groups are therefore critically important for the development of **Me**.

- The **I** is the individual component and consists of the **actual responses** of the individual to the perceived attitude of others.

- **I** represents the creative, spontaneous, uncertain elements in self and is **unpredictable,** so people's actions are never fully socially determined.

- Across the whole spectrum of our lives we are

faced with the compelling need to resolve the challenge posed by the constant tension between **Me** and **I.**

- Any significant imbalance will pose problems and create confusion.

- Personal Development endeavours to resolve these threats to well-being and contentment by, inter alia, persuading us to honestly examine our deepest feelings about our ambitions for ourselves and, bearing **Me** and **I** in mind, how these can be achieved and self-fulfilment enjoyed.

- There exist development courses that for very good fees indeed will teach you how to become a better salesman, manager, shop assistant or whatever.

- Whilst in these courses students have to submit to certain personal discipline and analysis, by their nature most such courses have a rather materialistic bias.

- The PD course that you might consider would be more geared to the student attaining peace of mind by learning to be in charge of his life and, with that self-confidence, enjoy the making of correct decisions about his **whole** existence, not only about his job and making more money.

- Such peace of mind comes from, inter alia, freedom from fear; health and energy; loving relationships (do you laugh with your loved ones?); worthy goals and values and a high degree of self-knowledge/understanding/honesty, leading to control of one's affairs and self-fulfilment.

- In short, being who you want to be and on comfortable terms with yourself and your environment.

- Naturally, all of this involves some concentration and thought but it has been said that the reason some people are confused and unhappy is that although the conscious and subconscious human minds are the most powerful tools on earth, perhaps in the universe, they don't know how to use them. If you don't know how to run your mind it is rather like having the latest computer but no instruction manual.

- (Perhaps this explains why most of us only put to use 5 or 10% of our mental power. Even Einstein, it's said, used no more than 20 or 30% of his mind.)

- A good Personal Development course represents the instruction manual.

- We believe that in deciding on the most effective PD course to use two things are of the first importance: how much intelligent study and reflection has gone into preparing the course and how understandably is the result presented?

- In making our recommendation below we noted that its creator claims to have spent over 30,000 hours studying to put his course together; as a presenter he is attractively uncomplicated and communicates his propositions with considerable impact.

- To run PD courses successfully naturally requires that you first subject yourself to the chosen course with commitment and rigour and believe in its philosophy and goals. Then you will enjoy interpreting your knowledge and insight for the many PSGs you will attract.

- Enjoy? Oh yes, because PD's aim is to lead

each PSG towards becoming **'The finest Me I can be'**.

- Profitable and very worthwhile; some may think that an unbeatable combination.

- **nb** A PD course represents a very rich mental diet for your students. In no circumstances try and cram too much into your sessions or your listeners will before long start to show signs of cerebral melt-down!

- The PD bibliography is very extensive, as you will discover once you begin your research. However, it should not take an undue length of time to compile your preferred list then stock and sell these books to your PSGs.

••• INFORMATION CHECK LIST

- BRIAN TRACY has been so successful with his courses that he now commands large fees for personally conducting them. To meet this challenge he has produced a series of audio and video tapes which can be bought or hired (e.g. a full set of audio tapes for his PHOENIX PERSONAL DEVELOPMENT COURSE costs £79 plus VAT).

- Contact THE TRAINING COLLEGE (0382 - 29292) re BRIAN TRACY LEARNING SYSTEMS and for both their information pack and the name and phone number of the Tracy representative near you. You will then get information on the routine for attending their PD **SEMINARS** which cost around £95 plus VAT per person per day. The info pack will also give details of other PD offerings; some of these will only be obtainable from NIGHTINGALE-

CONANT (0101 - 708 647 0300, or write to them at 7300 NORTH LEHIGH AVENUE, CHICAGO, ILLINOIS, USA, zip 60648).

- There are of course others in the Personal Development field; a good look through the health and glossy magazines will tell you what's on offer.

- You can get from COTTON TRADERS (061 - 926 8185) their ADVANCED LEARNING SYSTEM tapes (£9.95 each), such as SELF-ESTEEM, POSITIVE SELF-IMAGE; RELAX-ATION, STRESS MANAGEMENT and SELF-CONFIDENCE, ERASING DOUBT.

- The BBC too has a number of training videos on such subjects as MANAGING CHANGE. These range from £99 upward and you can get their list by ringing 01 576 0361.

- However, our recommendation remains that for a look at a comprehensive course your best starting point is TRACY. If you decide that route do try and arrange to get a copy of the bibliography upon which the PHOENIX course is based. This will guide you to much instructive and fascinating reading.

● PHOTOGRAPHY

● The very first photograph was taken by a gentleman called **Niépce** in 1826.

● His equipment was a little larger than today's compact, instant miracles; Niépce needed a whole, darkened room and eight hours to complete his exposure onto a pewter plate.

● One hundred and sixty-four years of research and development later we face a confusing avalanche of technology ranging from the point-and-click camera to the one-roll-throwaway; even cameras that don't need film, on to machines that can record the earth's minutest details from way out in space.

● Approximately **three-quarters of a billion pounds** are spent annually in the UK on buying new cameras.

● And the short step from camera to **camcorders** has been taken by increasing numbers of enthusiasts who have created yet another multi-million pound industry that as yet may just be in its infancy.

● However, many enthusiasts (and they **are** enthusiasts — the UK boasts two cameras per family in half of the country's homes) are now looking for something more than the bland results of their own unaided efforts. You can show them how to take more rewarding and artistic pictures.

● Evidently, this is a very wide-ranging creative form so you should consult your instincts and decide early on which of the many possibilities really interests you.

● There is an embarrassment of riches but to begin

with you can try making a broad, albeit arbitrary, distinction between photography as a medium of **art** and photography as a medium of the **descriptive process.**

- Success as a teacher in either will depend not only on your photographic skill but on how well you communicate. However, it's worth reminding yourself that although some very serious money has been and will be made with photographic art, the more commercial descriptive process holds out readier rewards if you want to pump up your positive cashflow by doing photographic work outside the classroom. A few examples where both still and video pictures could be sold:

- Increasingly **estate agents** are finding that their own amateur efforts are not good enough and that professional photographs of property help sales and, with really expensive property, a video recording can get potential buyers anxious to view in person.

- The buying and selling of **boats** also frequently involves big money and is another area where a video of the vessel could help clinch a sale.

- Although you may not earn very high fees per job, a properly organised, volume business will produce a steady second income whilst your teaching business grows.

- **Weddings** are a natural and where the bride's father really goes to town the fees for stills and videos run well into four figures.

- Still on the family front, consider that in most families one or more will be members of a **sports team.** Recording the heroics could be more income for you.

- Increasingly, **commercial events** are being re-corded both for the satisfaction of the participants and for promotional purposes.

- Properly marketed your skills will be of interest to **authors** and **publishers.**

- More specialised certainly but **advertising** work is very remunerative.

- Even more specialised is the world of **fashion** where very high fees are achievable.

- If you become involved with fashion you will sooner or later get opportunities of working profitably with **pop groups.**

- If you come to live in a reasonably affluent area consider **make-overs.** These represent a growth industry involving taking 'before' pictures of the client, who is then made up to look 'a million dollars' by a skilled make-up artist, before finally being portrait-photographed to provide a series of amazing-but-true 'after' pictures.

- Whilst you might think that make-overs are strictly for aspiring model girls, experience shows that the clients are men and women of all ages and from all walks of life. Why do they do it? Well, one client's reasons: 'Whenever I'm depressed I look at my pictures and cheer myself up'!

- Somebody once remarked that everybody wants to be on TV. That's not going to happen for most of us but there's clearly a very deep need to ensure that posterity has something to re-member us by.

- Your own imagination will take you on from

185

here. Thereafter it's marketing energy that counts.

- As ever, what equipment **you** use and recommend will find little sales resistance amongst your PSGs. Ensure your sales counter reaps the benefit.

- Finally, when you have established an income and developed your own unique style you might **then** consider cultivating the media, art galleries and publishers to get sales for your more **artistic** work.

••• INFORMATION CHECK LIST

- The 'no-film' camera is the CANON ION. You plug it into a TV set whereupon the camera's two-inch disc immediately transmits the picture(s) on to the screen. Useful where instant pictures are a plus (weddings, property viewings, etc). The disc will hold up to 50 pictures. The camera costs several hundred pounds but the price is expected to fall as other manufacturers bring their versions to market.

- EUROMONITOR CONSULTANCY (01 - 251 8024) have produced a survey entitled UK CAMCORDER MARKET TRENDS, OPPORTUNITIES, PROSPECTS TO 1991, which, apart from its intrinsic interest, also looks at the market for photographic products. Pricey at over £1000 but see if you can track it down at your local large reference library or the SCIENTIFIC LIBRARY division of the BRITISH LIBRARY (start phone no. 01 - 323 7454).

- Contact your local art school or polytechnic for details of foundation courses.

- The more dedicated may want to follow up with a vocational course at an institution recognised by the BRITISH INSTITUTE OF PROFESSIONAL PHOTOGRAPHY (0920 - 464011) who will give you full details of the courses and of their magazine THE PHOTOGRAPHER, monthly, £1.80.

- It may sound forbidding to get information from a trade union but nevertheless the ASSOCIATION OF CINEMATOGRAPH TELEVISION & ALLIED TECHNICIANS, or ACTT (01 - 437 8506) are the people to talk to for details of recognised courses on moving-picture camera training.

- If you're really aiming for the top then you'll be on the trail of a **Fellowship** of the ROYAL PHOTOGRAPHIC SOCIETY (0225 - 462841). Speak to them also about their magazine THE PHOTOGRAPHIC JOURNAL, monthly, £3.75.

- THE ASSOCIATION OF FASHION, ADVERTISING & EDITORIAL PHOTOGRAPHERS (01 - 608 1441) is for you if your talent and taste take you in their direction. Their list of professionals is consulted when work is around. Ask them about their magazine IMAGE, monthly, £24 per annum.

- Some useful books:

- STARTING YOUR OWN PHOTOGRAPHY BUSINESS, by SCHWARZ, pub FOCAL PRESS, £22.50, so maybe check it at your reference library first.

- PROMOTING YOURSELF AS A PHOTOGRAPHER, by ROSEN, pub AMPHOTO, £13.50.

- GETTING JOBS IN PHOTOGRAPHY, pub CASSELL (01 - 222 7676), £3.95, sets out details of skills training and qualifications available.

- To get insight into techniques and highly artistic success study the work not only of BAILEY, LITCHFIELD, and SNOWDON; seek out also the photocraft of e.g. ANSEL ADAMS, GJON MILI, H. CARTIER-BRESSON, IRVING PENN, W. EUGENE SMITH, WILLIAM GARNET, MARIE COSINDAS and HIRO. Unique stylists all.

- When in London see the MUSEUM OF THE MOVING IMAGE (01 - 928 3535); from early Chinese shadow play to TV by satellite.

- How much can you **earn** teaching photography to others? Quite a lot, judging from the fees charged by the respected professional JORGE LEWINSKI and his wife. Their 10-week (3-4 days a week) course costs around £3,000. Theirs is a comprehensive course and at the successful termination of it they issue a certificate and you should be well advanced towards an under-standing of what separates the professional from the point-and-shooter. Ring 01 - 672 2664 for details.

- In conjunction with the Midland Bank, the RAPID RESULTS COLLEGE (01 - 947 2211) do SUCCESSFUL PHOTOGRAPHY/THE BUSINESS START-UP PROGRAMME. Contact them for details.

- The NEW YORK INSTITUTE OF PHOTO-GRAPHY (0800 - 282120) offer a professional course by correspondence. Worth mentioning because they 'guarantee you will earn money or your fees **returned'**.

- You may want to find out more re **make-overs.** Contact THE PICTURE HOUSE (0539 - 821791); prices range from £250 to £1,000.

- It seems we often mention the big hotel chains and their weekend 'taster' breaks but they do seem very well worked out, with first-class professionals to guide you. Speak to HILTON (0923 - 246464) re their PHOTOGRAPHY breaks, from £90, or scan the glossies for other short starter courses.

• RECYCLING

- Why do Britons throw away more money than almost anyone else in Europe?

- Of the tens of millions of tonnes of **domestic waste** slung out each year well over 50% can be recycled; only a pitiful 2% is.

- Of the near half-billion tonnes of industrial and agricultural waste the proportion saved for re-use is probably even less.

- Given the negative effects on the environment, the criminal waste of energy and of money, these figures are deeply depressing.

- As to our question the answer is that there has been neither enough hard information nor facilities made available to enable people to take positive action.

- However, things are beginning to change for the better and there is no doubt that a mighty **recycling industry** is in the making. It could present opportunities for you. Consider the following:

- **Recycled Paper-making**

- Whilst the original writing material, papyrus, was used by the Egyptians over 5000 years ago, modern paper-making derives from the Chinese and came about 3000 years later.

- Little could those ancients have foreseen the global industry which has arisen since nor the potentially deadly consequences that that growth threatens today.

- Worries grow with the increasing sound of the world's forests (essential for our oxygen supply) crashing to the ground on their way to the pulping and saw mill.

- We in the UK alone are responsible for 90,000,000 trees (of which only 10% come from Britain) being felled annually, partly to meet our incessant and frequently wasteful demand for paper and board.

- Bearing in mind that a mature tree can take between 20 and 40 years to grow and that only about 25% of current paper and board demand is met by **recycled product,** the problem is clear enough: the forests are disappearing — fast. Friends of the Earth reckon forest loss is now 100 acres per minute. Recycling more paper will help reduce this.

- Plainly, therefore, in taking up recycled paper-making as an occupation (vocation?) you will also be doing your important bit to help save the planet.

- Not only will you help preserve precious trees but recall also that recycled paper uses only about **50% of the energy** required to make the new stuff.

- Financially this need be no marginal activity either because there are relatively few hand-made paper workshops in Britain.

- As well as for such things as toilet paper and office stationery supplies, there is demand, e.g., for unusual writing paper, wrapping paper and cards.

- Some makers go so far as to add **plants** such as daffodils, dandelions, pansies, roses, reeds and grasses, even red cabbage(!) to their product giving it a colourful and exotic finish for which premium prices are commanded.

- Like all start-ups you have to put in plenty of up-front effort, particularly in tracking down sources of supply.

- Green consciousness is spreading through town halls and this problem is getting easier to solve but

- As well as getting material from waste companies, you may have to organise, e.g., neighbourhood collection-schemes to keep stocks rolling in.

- Which brings us to another cost-attractive way into the recycling business — running your very own licensed

- **Waste Dump**

- Before you fall about laughing consider a noble precedent for using some of your land in this way:

- **Lord** and **Lady Guernsey** have a stately home near Coventry. They have turned part of the estate into a dump that handles 400 lorry-loads a day.

- Lord Guernsey explains that the dump is a long way from his house but says that even if it were nearer he'd put up with it because 'it's a very good site'.

- What! More financially rewarding than opening his house to visitors? **'Oh lord, yes! In a different league,'** he said.

- His Lordship did not volunteer any clue on the profits, but, e.g., Shanks & McEwan are a straightforward waste disposal plc. This company has increased profits in 10 years from £2m to £350m per annum.

- In the parliamentary debate on the Control of Pollution (Amendment) Act 1989 to combat the illegal fly-tipping of waste on unauthorised sites, it was revealed that the cost of disposing of waste **in a proper manner** was about £200 per tonne.

- The Act now provides for **very heavy** fines for fly-tipping, so encouraging the use of more orthodox methods.

- These will soon include the activities of **registered disposal firms** who will **collect** and dispose of waste (another opportunity).

- All over the country councils are running out of their own space for waste tips so getting a licence for a suitable site should not be unduly difficult.

- Predictions are that the cost of dumping will climb steadily; provided you run a legal, well-organised dump this means climbing profits for you bolstered by new tax relief measures.

- After some vigorous initial marketing (and in these green days you need not lack for media coverage) you will find a growing flow of commercial, industrial and agricultural customers coming your way. The domestic market will need prodding but ordinary householders **will** come if your set-up is well-promoted, organised and accessible.

- The main challenge is to get customers to stop putting all their rubbish together which renders it useless. You may have to therefore be much involved initiating the use of neighbourhood bulk containers for separating waste.

- But as your tin, bottle and plastic (now more readily re-usable) banks burgeon and your paper mountains etc grow there are still other opportunities to exploit:

- Instal magnets to separate aluminium from steel cans — then crush the product to make delivery to the mills more economic.

- Why not also **treat** waste for its by-products? e.g., using a machine called a **Digester** you can obtain 150 profitable cubic metres of **methane gas** from a tonne of suitable waste such as vegetable matter.

- The methane you package and sell will not only help your bank balance it will also help the environment, to which methane is by no means very friendly.

- (There is no end to people's ingenuity: one lady designer made a lot of money converting tyre inner tubes into rucksacks, selling at £40 a time. Might some similarly unregarded but plentiful waste objects inspire you?)

- There is another reason why you must actively encourage domestic customers: they will not only bring their refuse but also their **junk.**

- Properly organised, sorted and set out one man's junk becomes another man's little jewel.

- However, junk need not be the end of your interest in recycling because another branch concerns:

- **Architectural Salvage**

- A business that can make a lot of money, that requires plenty of covered and open storage —

and a fair amount of patience.

- Its claim for your consideration rests upon the fact that more people are now prepared to pay higher prices for genuine artefacts from the past to enable them to sympathetically restore their period properties and thus increase the aesthetic and financial value.

- The patience we mentioned comes into play when you know that the few quid you paid for those old stair balusters, tiles, cast iron baths, Belfast sinks, high level cisterns, Edwardian wash-hand basins, brass taps, old bricks, bits of timber, flooring and cornices etc, etc, will be marked up by **very many times** once the right buyer walks into view. And he will, once the word gets around that **your** salvage yard has the goods.

- However, actually getting started in the salvage game also needs some patience because the goodies, apart from such things as exterior adornments like garden furniture and statuary, tend to come mainly from (and, essentially **before**) the demolition of old properties which means getting in with your local building, demolition, skip-hire and transport contractors. Track them down in the pubs they use.

- A further successful neighbour to salvage and recycling arises from other people's **clangers,** errors made by people decorating and furnishing their homes.

- One lady does extremely well from buying and reselling, inter alia, new sofas that were too big, curtains and materials vetoed by the decorators' clients because they were the wrong colour. She also sells slightly shop-soiled and used-at-exhibition goods and so on.

- The name of her game is summed up by the name of her shop (see below).

- Some energy required to track down the goods from manufacturers, decorators and stores but the profit margins are attractive.

- Other mistakes that could feature alongside the above in a dry, but suitably shabby, showroom are the **seconds** or **imperfects** turned out with some regularity by the nation's factories.

- There are now books available giving lists as to where this bounty can be tracked down.

- Further recycling can be elegantly and profitably achieved if you can spot **tomorrow's antiques** (as you probably know, the word is widely abused; strictly, 'antique' should only be used to describe something at least 100 years old, so, more accurately, **nostalgic collectables**) before or at about the time they become desirable.

- Objects as bizarrely different as slot machines (a 1905 example has been sold for £50,000), cigarette lighters, comics, even dolls (one has been sold for over £90,000) and teddy bears are all having their day.

- It may be too late to expect to make serious money out of **them** but our recommended books are required reading so that you can see if the idea appeals.

- For example, one author reckons that cycling, aviation, gramophones, things to do with the railways, painted tin containers, the Wild West, even — wait for it — redundant robots, have the right collectability aura.

- (Come to think of it, how redundant can a

197

robot be? Could surely take the dog for a walk?)

- **J & M Miller** are backing Art Deco pottery, anything sporting, particularly fishing and golf equipment, pens and pop memorabilia.

- Someone else even believes 1960s plastic toys are due for a run!

- Other amazing items going for amazing prices include venerable vacuum cleaners, vacuum flasks, mixer-blenders, typewriters, Anglepoise lamps and even 1970s stereo units.

- **Kitchenalia** — breadboards, potato ricers, storage tins, etc — is flourishing too.

- Even **Ephemera** — scraps of paper, letters, bills, etc from the past can make money.

- When you manage to accumulate your artifacts don't overlook the potential positive cashflow that can arise from **hiring out** durable items to film and television companies, even for posh social occasions and so on.

- And ponder the export market. One trader in kitchenalia sends 95% of her goodies to the USA and Australia.

- Final thought: Consider hiring a village hall and organising your own **auctions.** This will not only make money but, by bringing yourself into the business mainstream of your locality, people will know who to come to when they have **interesting situations.** And you will know who to go to if it's necessary to get help or consents to profit from those.

••• INFORMATION CHECK LIST for Recycled Paper-Making

- As we have mentioned, hand paper-making is as yet not a big industry so, whilst this means greater opportunities for you, it also means that you have some ferreting ahead of you to find training courses. Your best starting point is DIVISION 24 of the CITY & GUILDS of LONDON INSTITUTE (01 - 580 3050, ext. 3558) who will tell you what facilities they have near you for training in PAPER & BOARD MAKING.

- Depending on your dedication you can gain CERTIFICATES 1 & 2 before going on to becoming a LICENTIATE of the Guild.

- Private information is available, e.g., JANE MANSFIELD is a successful recycled paper-maker working in Wales with her own factory and sales point; from time to time she gives talks and demonstrations. Speak to her on 0559 - 370088 for details.

- Otherwise it is a question of scanning craft magazines or the glossies.

- As courses appear to be thin on the ground so with magazines. However, a trade journal well worth reading would be PAPER FOCUS (09277 - 61555), monthly, £6, because this deals with the various types of paper and the people who buy it. Also contact

- BRUNTON BUSINESS PUBLICATIONS (025672 - 8569) who publish WASTE PAPER NEWS INTERNATIONAL, fortnightly, £35 p.a.

- Relevant is RECYCLED PAPER/PAPER RECYCLING, pub WASTE WATCH, £2.50. Con-

199

tact them at 26, Bedford Square, London, WC1B 3HU.

- Contact FRIENDS OF THE EARTH (01 - 490 1555) who are naturally into recycling in a big way. Get information and their street-by-street guide for your locality's paper collection facilities and their book RECYCLING POLICY: ONCE IS NOT ENOUGH, £2.00.

- Make contact with refuse-managers CSAWS (0222 -397241) for inside information on paper recycling.

- Your local library should be productive of books on paper-making. Meanwhile try the following:

- PAPER: HOW IT IS MADE, by PERRINS, pub FABER, £5.95.

- RECYCLED PAPER-MAKING, by PAT BROWN, pub PNL PUBLISHING, £2.50.

- PAPER BASICS: FORESTRY, MANUFAC-TURE, SELECTION, PURCHASING, MATHEMATICS and METRICS and (wait for it) RECYCLING, by SALTMAN, pub VAN NOST REINHOLD, £14.95.

- Finally get in touch with the INDEPENDENT WASTE PAPER PROCESSORS ASSOCI-ATION (IWPPA) (0327 - 703223) to see what help they can give you to source supplies in your locality.

●●● INFORMATION CHECK LIST for Waste Dump

- Contact the Cardiff-based COMMUNITY

SUPPORT ANTI-WASTE SCHEME (CSAWS) on 0222 - 397241. This is claimed to be the largest community-based refuse management organisation in the UK with profitable activities covering the whole spectrum. Their junk reclamation is of particular interest.

- Cardiff is the Friends of the Earth's UK 2000 RECYCLING CITY. Their experience leads them to believe that 98% of rubbish will be recovered by the turn of the century.

- All councils are now actively concerned in waste and recycling. Contact your local people for advice and information in your area.

- THE NATIONAL ASSOCIATION OF WASTE DISPOSAL CONTRACTORS (01 - 353 1961); they also publish NAWDC NEWS six times a year.

- If you're serious about this venture consider doing some work with one of the reclamation bodies to get first-hand experience. Contact local collection groups and FRIENDS OF THE EARTH (01 - 490 1555) to see what leads they can give you. Also get from them their RECYCLE IT guide for your area to lead you to sources of waste supply.

- Speak to IWPPA (see above), the ALUMINIUM CAN RECYCLING ASSOCIATION (021 - 633 4656) and BRITISH STEEL TINPLATE (0792 - 310011) for information on their end of the recycling market.

- Read WASTE & RECYCLING, by B JAMES, pub WAYLAND, £7.50.

••• INFORMATION CHECK LIST for Architectural Salvage

- Where better to start consideration of this aspect of recycling than by looking at the operations already up and running? Get a copy of the DIRECTORY OF ARCHITECTURAL SALVAGE COMPANIES, pub MORGAN GRAMPIAN (01 - 855 7777), £3.75, to see who is nearest to you. (Calculate probable buy-in cost then compare that with their selling price!)

- Also by MORGAN GRAMPIAN is BUILDING REFURBISHMENT magazine, 10 times a year, around £32 p.a. They point out that nearly 60% of all building work concerns refurbishment, repair and maintenance.

- Read also TRADITIONAL HOMES magazine, monthly, £1.70.

- THE BARGAIN RENOVATOR'S GUIDE TO LONDON, pub ATTICA PRESS (01 - 609 0061), bi-annual, £2.20; whilst mainly concerned with prices and availability in the capital will nevertheless give you further insight into the market.

- These three books will interest the dedicated: HISTORIC HOME OWNERS COMPANION, by MATTHEW SAUNDERS, pub BATSFORD, £14.95, gives advice to the restorer; PERIOD DETAIL: A SOURCEBOOK FOR HOUSE RESTORATION, by J & M MILLER, pub MITCHELL BEAZLEY, also £14.95, bears on design and structure from the 16th to the 19th centuries, and THE HOUSE RESTORER'S GUIDE, by HUGH LANDER, pub DAVID & CHARLES, £16.

- For their amazing historical know-how, store of

202

artefacts and photographs of the past contact the LONDON ARCHITECTURAL STUDY COLLECTION at ENGLISH HERITAGE (01 - 734 6010).

- They may be able to point you towards the local councils that have conservation and salvage stores.

- For more information regarding older buildings see **ACQUIRING YOUR COUNTRY PROPERTY INFORMATION CHECK LIST:** also **SPECIAL EFFECTS INFORMATION CHECK LIST.**

- Not every one is hooked on the deep past. Contact THE THIRTIES SOCIETY (01 - 381 9797) to see what they can tell you about their particular obsession that might be of interest to you.

- Contact the NATIONAL FEDERATION OF DEMOLITION CONTRACTORS (01 - 404 4020) to find out who is knocking down what near you.

••• INFORMATION CHECK LIST for Other People's Clangers

- Run by ALEXA RUGGE-PRICE is the Fulham Road shop called MISTAKES (01 - 736 2108).

- You can track down factory seconds by consulting FACTORY SHOP GUIDES (01 - 622 3722) for UK, upwards of £2.25 each + pp.

••• INFORMATION CHECK LIST for Tomorrow's Antiques

- The PHILLIPS GUIDE TO TOMORROW'S ANTIQUES, by PETER JOHNSON, pub WEIDENFELD & NICOLSON, £14.95.

- MILLER's COLLECTABLES PRICE GUIDE, pub MILLERS PUBLICATIONS, £12.95.

- The 20th CENTURY ANTIQUES: HOW TO BUY INEXPENSIVELY TODAY THE ANTIQUES OF TOMORROW, by TONY CURTIS, pub HEADLINE, £14.95.

••• INFORMATION CHECK LIST on Kitchenalia

- ANN LINGARD is the expert who runs ROPE WALK ANTIQUES (0797 - 223486). She has 10,000 sq ft devoted to Kitchenalia and other bygones.

••• INFORMATION CHECK LIST on Ephemera

- Read COLLECTING PRINTED EPHEMERA, by MAURICE RICKARDS, pub PHAIDON-CHRISTIE'S, £25, so see if you can locate this at your nearest large reference library.

- If you get hooked then think about joining the EPHEMERA SOCIETY (01 - 387 7723). Annual subscription including their reference handbook and quarterly magazine THE EPHEMERIST is £10 for country members.

• SEMINARS

- Conferences and seminars are growing at around **20%** per year so think seriously of running them yourself. Properly done they're winners; and going this route could mean that you can sensibly consider taking on a larger and more comfortable house with more spacious grounds than might be feasible otherwise.

- The outline proposition is that you select a subject or series of subjects that you have mastered and take Paying Student Guests (PSGs) into your home and teach these skills to them either in outline or in depth, via courses varying from a few hours in duration to several weeks.

- These skills may well have been learned for instance by already running some successful business from your country home.

- The seminar proposal is based upon the fact that we live in a thirsty age and the thirst is for more knowledge, a widening of horizons.

- A really significant percentage of the population, retired, young, employed, unemployed, rich, poor, wants or badly needs to learn some new skill or to develop some latent talent; to express themselves more fully or simply to earn a better living.

- Many have ample resources to pay for this learning themselves.

- For others their companies or the government will pay.

- Knowledge is a growth industry. If you doubt this look around.

- As your seminar will be in the countryside you offer your customer a number of extra attractions:

- The journey to get to you (yes, despite the traffic, most people still love to travel);

- The pleasure of a new and totally different environment (the view and the hospitality have to be of a good-to-high standard but, remember, you will be enjoying the view too);

- The delight of meeting new people.

- The thrill and glow of satisfaction flowing from whatever they learn from you.

- The knack that you will learn from experience is to make each seminar into a mildly disciplined house-party, with the briskly cheerful learning periods contrasting with the chatty informality of meal times and thoughtful periods when your student guests are just left to enjoy either one another or a solitary hour to themselves.

- As we indicated above, it is clearly going to help if you yourself are already an expert in some desirable field of activity but if not you still have two other options:

- Select a subject (perhaps from this guide's list of ventures) that would give you pleasure to master and teach and go right out and get the training to make you proficient. (Yes, you **can** do it! You can do anything if you want it **enough.**)

- However, if you can't hype yourself up to be sufficiently confident to begin with, then hire someone else to do the teaching for you whilst you concentrate on being host to your PSGs.

- Although maybe the tougher route to follow

206

there are good reasons to choose to do the teaching yourself:

- Not only will you be in total control of your operation, you will also save the overhead of a key member of your new organisation.

- Importantly, also you will be the focus of the admiration and gratitude of your students. The pride and satisfaction flowing from this will, to many entrepreneurs, be nearly as rewarding as the profits.

- And, remember, you don't have to have a 30-room mansion.

- Seminars can be run profitably with as few as six students; the ideal for close contact is probably a dozen.

- More is fine as you grow but obviously you will need extra, paid, assistance.

- Consider beforehand that running seminars in your own home is taking you into the front line of the **people business** so be clear that you will enjoy being **on parade,** binding the talks, demonstrations, discussions and so on into a really enjoyable whole.

- The enjoyed seminar will then be talked about, generating new business as well as getting repeat bookings from satisfied PSGs.

- As a means of (sooner or later) living spaciously and earning money enjoyably the seminar route has much to be said for it, so let's assume you are ongoing.

- Here are some things to bear in mind whether

207

or not you are going to provide lodging for your PSGs.

- **The house** can be as plain as the back of a bus but should have some grounds and a rurally satisfying view with, ideally, some water to look at and go on.

- That said, the better the house, its decor and its facilities, the more you can charge people to be there.

- For lodging, if you are very fortunate, your house will split itself so as to leave you and your PSGs genteelly separated.

- More likely, as space and money will be at a premium to begin with, you may have to take a spartan view of the space that you can afford to occupy so as to leave enough room for your PSGs.

- Should you have to share with the PSGs most of the facilities, i.e. bathrooms, w.c's, lounge, etc., your family of say four only actually needs for itself two bedrooms of about 100 sq. ft each.

- (Comfort yourself with the thought that one day soon when you are earning enough money . . .)

- Whilst other staff, if any, can be put into slightly smaller space, PSGs should have bedrooms of **at least** 10' × 10' single, 14' × 12' double.

- On to these calculations go the space for your lecture room; about 300 sq ft would be the minimum requirement for say six PSGs, lecturer, all equipment, etc. If you haven't got such a room then build it separately.

- It can be a shed, but remember the heating costs.

- **The decor.** Your house can be decorated and furnished simply or grandly but above all it must be comfortable to the body and the eye, i.e. no uncomfortable seats or beds, no extremes of jarring paint or wallpaper jobs, no fluorescent tubes or dayglo curtains, etc.

- **Lighting** is perhaps the area where more people fall down than any other; it must be **plentiful, warm,** but **not glaring.**

- **Decoratively** it is better to err on the side of shabbiness rather than strain for effect. Go for what you are really at ease with and your PSGs will be happy to follow suit.

- If you have genuine doubts then afford a few hundred pounds and call in a well-referenced professional decorator to get out several sketch schemes for you, your budget and your audience.

- The aim is what you would expect if you were a PSG: to be put at ease as soon as you step through the door (or hobble or wheel yourself; remember the disabled).

- **The plumbing:** No music hall joke this. You have to get it right and it's a costly business so afford an **independent consultant** who will ensure that this very high-demand item actually works.

- Whilst not everyone wants a bath or even a shower **every** day, other bodily needs are obviously imperative.

- A washhand **basin** (and shaver point) in **every** bedroom and lashings of piping **hot water** at all times are minimum requirements.

- Also at least **one w.c.** for every **four** people.

- If there's real and **unavoidable** pressure on room for baths and showers then you have no alternative but to get out a roster so that everyone knows when the facility is available to them.

- Caveat! If you are going for the **Japanese** market, remember they like to shower first, **then** use the bath and, boy, do they like a lot of water! Best to install a special Japanese bathroom away from other important rooms so that if a flood does occur it doesn't bring everything to a soggy halt.

- **Bedrooms:** Well-slept customers are happy customers.

- At least they'll start the day that way, whatever else you may do to them.

- **Beds** should ideally be 4ft wide, two such to a double room, space permitting. If not, 5ft wide doubles. Do not skimp on comfort.

- Use good quality, light-weight **blankets** and plenty of them rather than duvets which some people find not to their taste.

- **Shelves and storage:** It's almost impossible to supply too much of either.

- And **real** coat hangers, not wire or skimpy plastic.

- On one of the shelves there should be a **Teasmade** with a small selection of decent brands of **real** tea and coffee.

- Somehow you must ensure that PSGs can easily get **fresh milk.**

- **Privacy:** The smaller the house the less you'll be able to give your PSGs space like reading rooms, libraries and so on.

- Therefore ensure that each bedroom has at least one very comfortable chair, some topical reading, a decent sized coffee table and a TV set (with an **upper limit sound control** so that insomniacs don't keep everyone else awake) then, if your PSGs want to be alone they can be so in comfort.

- In old houses **bedroom walls** are usually discreetly thick enough to cut off the sound of neighbourly activity. If you have to put up partitions ensure that these and all doors are similarly effective, or high jinks in one room will ensure irritation and embarrassment in the next.

- Poor **heating** is a downer. Don't run the remotest risk of someone putting on your notice board a note we once saw: 'In case of fire keep it to yourself or everyone will want one'. Yes, heating is expensive but give it and charge for it.

- **Food:** If you are confident about your cooking **and** your family agrees with you, do it yourself. Your PSGs will love it. Also, ensure your PSGs know whether food is included in the course fees or an optional extra; if so, where locally they might go for some meals and by what time you expect them to tell you if they are staying in for dinner.

- If in doubt whistle up some well-referenced local cook. Either way keep it home-made and country (local specialities always enjoyed).

- **Drink:** Apart from an on-the-house welcoming drink **do not** include free booze in your tariff.

- You are asking for trouble if either it's all there for the taking or you're seen to be too stingy.

- Instead, have a small bar and short, decent wine list and sell the stuff.

- This by itself will act as a partial brake upon any PSG inclined to over-indulge.

- Of course you do not want to be unduly judgmental but if despite this you find yourself saddled with a troublesome **drunk** take action; put them firmly and immediately to bed and the next day tell them to cut it out or leave. Over-eager tipplers are guaranteed to put a blight on any gathering.

- 'Hey,' do we hear you say, 'I thought I was going into the seminar business, not dealing with drunks!' Wrong.

- Remember up front we said you are going into the **people business** and some people are bad drunks. Right?

- Your PSGs have come to learn but they'll also want to get out and about. Consider having available a supply of **all-weather** clothing, wellies, umbrellas, even woolly socks, Barbour jackets and scarves in case the weather catches everyone short.

- Essentially, **plan leisure breaks** and have knowledgeable information re what's on or what's worth seeing locally, or organise walks, bird-watching or fishing.

- Some **bicycles,** even a pony and trap, would provide a feel of country transport.

- **Time and frequency:** How much time you spend actually teaching your PSGs and how much free time they have will depend as much on the subject matter of the seminar as on your own inclinations and common sense.

- For example, the worst seminar we ever attended

was a two-day affair. The subject, whilst of intense interest, also demanded intense concentration and at the end of two nine-hour-long days with only brief breaks for awful coffee and a gulp of lunch we lurched away absolutely shattered. Verdict: Never again!

- Undue rigour is not going to bring much repeat business or encourage PSGs to 'spread the word'.

- So the point to remember is that the greater the concentration required, the greater the need to break up the sessions into bite-sized chunks and the greater the need for relaxing diversions during the breaks.

- That said, you must maintain sensible momentum or interest, concentration and the whole enjoyment of a group activity will begin to wane, i.e.

- Balance is all.

- As to frequency, it's obviously your choice as to how many seminars you do per week.

- The bigger money-making route might seem to indicate packing your calendar.

- Even then, and certainly in the early stages, it's necessary to leave at least two days a week clear for R&R, and reviewing the business as a whole with, say, two × 2½ day-seminars per week.

- For the more leisurely minded, one × 2- or 3-day seminar event per week may be ideal.

- In the event you have to have larger numbers of PSGs (than you can actually house) to get the desired profit hire local bedrooms to accommodate the extra numbers.

- If so, try still to ensure that everyone eats together at lunch and dinner to get the chat and atmosphere going.

- An important point on the **seminar talks** themselves: Use theatre, a little drama, anecdotes to keep your PSGs enthralled, e.g., a dramatic tool is the **blindfold.**

- Where you have no need to illustrate your lecture with slides or videos but need to make points of central importance to your theme, distribute blindfolds to your students and cheerfully but firmly persuade them to put them on.

- Why? If you have studied audiences, even in a learning situation that really interests them, you will have noticed how easy it is for the attention to wander.

- They look at one another, (particularly if there's a very pretty girl around; for heaven's sake see that she's put at the back of the room), study their finger nails, pick their teeth and fidget generally.

- By cutting off all visual distractions they have to listen attentively.

- The blindfold is an unusual teaching tool but it works and will also provide the invaluable bonus of getting you and your seminar talked about.

- **Note:** Don't use blindfolds for stretches longer than 10 or 15 minutes; after that they can be counter-productive.

- Bearing in mind what we have said above about the need to concentrate attention, also be prepared as appropriate to plunge your room into darkness, the only illumination coming from the (preferably large) video screen and small individual lights over your PSGs' desks.

- Another important consideration for you and your PSGs is for both of you to know how well you've all done during the time they've spent at your seminar.

- Therefore, if you have enough confidence in your abilities as a guru (and if you haven't then don't yourself run seminars) set them **exams** to test what they knew before and what they've learned after your seminar.

- There are two reasons why most if not all PSGs will take the test: (a) adults usually love quizzes, and (b) you can issue appropriately framed **certificates** for the various levels of 'pass' that you determine.

- There are bonuses for both parties: Most people cannot resist hanging up for display and talking about something they've won and, therefore, you get perfectly valid, free word-of-mouth publicity.

- Vitally for you is that you are finding out in the most direct way how **successful** or otherwise your seminar really is, and can make necessary adjustments accordingly.

- This is a growing business but you have to compete hard to ensure that it's **your** seminar people choose.

- Be on the lookout for every discreet, profitable opportunity to **sell** your PSGs relevant things to do with the course.

- Books (ideally, one day, written by you), videos, audio tapes — whatever is germane.

- Having created your seminar set-up don't over-look the possibility of extra income from letting the space out on blank days to others wanting to run **their** seminars on your premises using your facilities.

- If by chance the house of your dreams (or means) is too small to accommodate seminars this still need not deter you because there are always **other spaces** for hire (hotels, village halls, schools, universities, etc.) where you can run your seminars, booking your PSGs into B&B and using local pubs and restaurants to victual them.

- If at any time after you've run seminars for a while you feel the need to find out what's going on elsewhere then remember that companies are always on the look out for capable people to organise **their** events. Nice pickings too at around £200+ per day.

••• INFORMATION CHECK LIST

- According to the seminars you're proposing to run there may be student subsidies available. To start with discuss this with your LOCAL ENTER-PRISE AGENCY, and

- At the same time your LEA may be able to connect you with potential partners if you need skilled back-up for the enterprise.

- For that local knowledge that your PSGs will want from you see our advice in **NOSTALGIA**.

- Seminars are about knowledge and, increasingly, about showmanship. See our comments in **CULTS, LAUGHTER** and again **NOSTALGIA**.

- In this connection think also about a course in public speaking. Check Yellow Pages or perhaps your nearest ADULT FURTHER EDUCATION source.

- Contact the ASSOCIATION OF CONFERENCE EXECUTIVES (0480 - 457595) for details of their unique 5-day residential course for conference organisers and consider taking this. It will give you the professional objectivity necessary to set up your own seminar. Approx £600 inclusive.

- You may want to attend some conferences and seminars for flavour and information. You will find the average cost per day per person to be around £75 plus VAT, without accommodation. Get hold of a copy of the CONFERENCE BLUE BOOK, pub SPECTRUM COMMUNICATIONS GROUP (01 - 740 4444) for details of what's on offer. As this costs £35 better check it if you can at your reference library first.

- You may well require guest speakers. Contact local PUBLIC RELATIONS FIRMS to see if they have the right person on their client list. This route should ensure minimum fees and maximum **media coverage.**

- You will also need specialist insurance to safeguard you against the oh-my-god situations that do from time to time crop up. Competitive-premium conference and seminar specialists are brokers EXPO-SURE (0892 - 511500).

- Although you are going to be running a seminar not an hotel, you might care to indulge yourself and see if the (not particularly cheap) hospitality of some of the places mentioned in **NOSTALGIA** gives you further ideas as to how to make your PSGs feel even more at home.

- For pointers to do with your house itself see elsewhere in this guide: **ACQUIRING YOUR COUNTRY PROPERTY** and the **Architectural Salvage** section of **RECYCLING; SPECIAL EFFECTS** and **DESIGN & DECORATION.**

• SNOW AND ICE

- The Norwegians founded competitive skiing back in the last century but it really started to take off with the first Winter Olympics in 1924.

- Since those days the sport has continued to grow in popularity at such a rate that in recent years **artificial** slopes have been in much demand.

- However, if the Australian (yes) experience is any yardstick then **indoor snow-covered** slopes will enjoy enormous success here too, because

- **Neil Williams** has built the first indoor snow-covered ski-centre in the world in Adelaide, South Australia, not perhaps a place noted for its frequent snowfalls.

- Despite this the 275 metre-long, zigzag, 12 metre-high run is covered in the stuff.

- An artificial, 99% water, material called **Permasnow,** which is held at $-12°C$, is so much like the real thing that you can make snowballs from it.

- And it takes a long time to melt, making maintenance cheap and easy.

- The moving-pavement-type escalator took 100,000 paying customers up to the top in its first year.

- When the skiers have finally had enough on the slope there is also an **apres-ski** area complete with bars and restaurant; a money-maker in its own right as many drinkers and diners come to watch other braver spirits go hurtling down this artificial piste.

219

- The concept is so appealing that it goes on **year-round.**

- With this success behind him Williams plans further **Snow & Ice Arenas** in other Australian cities and indeed envisions similar centres world-wide.

- Whilst he will not be the pioneer here as well, he has UK very much in his sights so there could be franchise possibilities.

- (Should anyone seriously doubt that under-cover is where the future lies consider the following:

- **Biosphere 2** is a 2½ acre spherical greenhouse created as an experiment in Arizona. It is the largest enclosed **ecosystem** on the planet and, cloistered inside, its eight humans share their little world with, inter alia, a mini-rainforest, a mini-ocean, plants, animals, birds, insects, et al. Not until sometime in 1991-2 will the humans emerge to the exterior world again, their only outside contact in the meantime being by telephone and TV.

- Whilst the experiment is concerned with looking ahead to the environment necessary for us to conquer space, be in no doubt that much of what is learned will be put to use to create more and more ideal covered environments here, environments that will have a profound effect on our lifestyles; e.g. why go to the trouble of travelling to Wengen for snow or Florida for sunshine if the environment and facilities we crave are right here on our own doorstep?

- Already the covered future is happening, as those who have been to **Center Parc** in Sherwood Forest will confirm. There, ex-sportswear salesman **Piet Denksen** has created a **climate-**

controlled dome and holiday resort [two more in the pipeline] that is, not surprisingly, full up all year round. He recently sold out his covered empire for a rumoured £½ billion.)

- As skiing's popularity has been heightened by TV coverage it must also make sense to consider combining a ski slope area with two other sports popularised by TV: **Ice Skating** and **Curling.**

- What's in a name? Well, **Zoom, Skate & Curl** might work.

- Main income would derive from customers paying on an hourly basis to use the slope, with extra money being paid for **lessons** and **hire** or **sale** of equipment from your own **shop.** Also, with the slope activities as a powerful visual attraction, your **bar** and **restaurant** would, as in Australia, have special selling appeal.

- Clearly location is paramount, needing to be near good access roads and substantial population centres to ensure the steady year-round flood of custom necessary to justify the substantial investment involved.

- However, **your** investment need not be so very high; if you can find the site (set-aside farmland?) and get the necessary preliminary Planning approvals then outside investment would be readily encouraged, still leaving you with a potentially significant shareholding as originator and manager.

••• INFORMATION CHECK LIST

- The ICE & SNOW ARENA, Adelaide, South Australia; tel: 010 - 618 352 7977.

221

- For information about the BIOSPHERE 2 experiment in Arizona talk to the INSTITUTE OF ECOTECHNICS on 01 - 242 7367 or PROF KEITH RUNCORN at NEWCASTLE UNIVERSITY (091 - 232 8511, ext 7287).

- CENTER PARC can be contacted on 0933 - 401401; bookings on 0623 - 411411.

- A real-snow indoor ski-slope is included as part of a winter sports complex planned for ACCRINGTON, Lancs. One of the consultants is a specialist in the winter sports field, MR RICHARD CASS of Liverpool architects CASS ASSOCIATES (051 - 236 9074).

- SKI CLUB OF GT BRITAIN (01 - 245 1033). Membership fee varies according to your location, from £26 to £36 p.a., to include five copies of their magazine SKI SURVEY. They can point you to training/practice courses in your locality.

- The other ski magazine that is well-regarded is SKIING UK, six issues per year, £1.50 each.

- Unlikely as it may sound, TAYLOR MADE FILMS (051 - 708 8202) believe that you can become 'a more effective skier' by watching two videos they have made. Mark you, they have taken the precaution of featuring 'Britain's best-known ski teacher' ALI ROSS. Entitled SKI PERFECT, Parts 1 & 2. Each costs £19.95.

- For details on how to become an instructor contact the BRITISH ASSOCIATION OF SKI INSTRUCTORS (0479 - 810407).

- NATIONAL (ICE) SKATING ASSOCIATION OF GREAT BRITAIN (01 - 253 3824).

- Controlling bodies for CURLING appear to have

individual national associations. Start with the
ENGLISH CURLING ASSOCIATION on 0772
- 634154.

- The bigger the project the more research counts.
  For broad background consider studying:
  LEISURE DEVELOPMENT IN THE UK,
  ISBN 086338 328 9 and SPORTS AND SPORT-
  ING GOODS, ISBN 086338 202 9. Both surveys
  are by EUROMONITOR (01 - 251 8024) but,
  as the first costs £375 and the second £235, see
  if you can study (but not photocopy) them at
  your local larger reference library or, failing that,
  at the SCIENTIFIC LIBRARY division of the
  BRITISH LIBRARY (start phone no 01 - 323
  7454).

- **SPECIAL EFFECTS**

- Whatever the ups and downs of the economy there is always a shortage of good **hands-on specialists.** Such people earn exceptionally good money, for their skills can add substantially to the value of property (even actually **creating** the property itself in one instance, see below).

- Consider the following:

- **Floors:** Encourage potential clients to roll back that carpet or linoleum to reveal the battered glories beneath, glories that you can restore.

- (Unfortunately if all that's underneath the carpet is the old lime-and-ash plaster finish, tell them to replace the carpet and forget about it.)

- However, if what is revealed is brick, marble, slate, stone, timber or tile these can usually all be restored to their more-or-less original condition. Where a thorough cleaning and minor repair is inadequate then matching replacement material must be found, shaped, fitted and finished in the original way. For example,

- 18th century timber floors were never polished, but hand-smoothed before having a final dry rub with **herbs.**

- And then there were painted floors, the earliest form of lino. Broadly, these were created by layering numerous sheets of good canvas, each covered in oil paint, and finishing the top sheet with a printed or hand-painted design.

- An alternative, coming back into vogue today, was to paint a design directly onto the floor boards themselves.

- Old tiles may have lost their colour from wear and dirt. Proprietary tile cleaners and colour revivers can do much to solve this problem and replacement tiles can often be obtained from specialist suppliers.

- **Walls & Ceilings:** Spectacular special effects can be created by **scumbling, wiping, sponging** and so on.

- Another special effect lies in the provisions of replica wall and ceiling **plaster mouldings,** either for repair of existing or as matching runs for alterations and extensions to old buildings.

- **Roofs:** By which we mean **thatching.** This craft has been returning to popularity for some time bringing pressure to bear on the limited number of craftsmen.

- Further interest in thatching has arisen because shrewd property-owners have noticed that planning approval is more readily granted, particularly for home-workers who want to build work-and-office-space away from their main house, if the new building has a thatched roof.

- **Conservatories:** There can be few more special effects than that created by a conservatory, an amenity that must be close to the top of very many a house-owner's dream list.

- People will pay well to realise dreams but unfortunately these are sometimes shattered either by finding out the huge price of the good-looking conservatories or contemplating the fairly awful appearance of those in the cheaper range.

- To break into the market requires good design and construction, using quality materials and, as importantly, well worked out factory production turning out **kits** that, by clever mixing and matching, can be used to create an apparently unique design whilst using relatively mass-produced parts.

- Such a conservatory package could in due course be **franchised.**

- **Self-Build:** A very special effect indeed is created if you can build houses at less than **half** the conventional cost.

- This is being done by as yet only a few enterprising firms but surely must be a business for the future.

- Take the example of **Phillip Bixby.** A few years ago he set up a company to teach people self-build techniques and under his tuition students learn the skills needed to build timber-framed houses.

- Bixby and his students can 'complete' one house during every **three-week course.**

- As well as having a house to sell or use these short courses generate a mighty good cashflow: 20 students × **£400 each.**

- **Alternative Energy Systems:** Finally we offer the thought that a special effect of rocketing conventional energy costs is the certainty that alternative systems will soon come into their own.

- Extraordinary and vexatious though it is, the reason that **windmill, wave** and **solar systems** etc have been so slow coming on stream is that government has dithered.

- That is now having to stop as the truth dawns that we can neither afford the conventional energy set-up and running costs, nor the planet be certain to survive with them.

- When government tax encouragement and development money really start to flow the **new power boom** will begin and may be the greatest in history, going far beyond windmills and the like, into, possibly, **biofuels, hot rock power, solar power satellites, plasma** and **fusion** power and other sources still only on the drawing board.

- Much of this takes us into the megabucks category but a visit to, e.g. the **Alternative Technology Centre** in Wales, will show you that there's quite a lot of reasonable-cost basic technology already in place.

- You may have to have another business and income before you are able to cash in on alternative energy systems and installation but you could prepare yourself for the great day by using as much of it as possible in your new country home.

••• INFORMATION CHECK LIST

- Perhaps the first thing to remind you of is that although we are discussing high levels of skill for this venture, this does not mean that you personally have to have these skills. As we point out in **BESPOKE,** craftsmen are not always well up in business and marketing (crafts in their own right!). Consider, therefore, being the business manager to a group of craftsmen.

- However, if acquiring the skills does interest you start by contacting CITB, the CONSTRUCTION INDUSTRY TRAINING BOARD (0553 - 776677) who will tell you what training is required for the skill(s) that interest you and where this may be obtained in your area.

- More detailed information available from the GUILD OF MASTER CRAFTSMEN (0273 - 478449).

- More still from RURAL DEVELOPMENT COMMISSION (0722 - 336255), not only about skills training but also re potential partners and business premises. (Only operates in England. For other UK areas check phone numbers listed in **BESPOKE**).

- The BUILDING CONSERVATION TRUST (01 - 943 2277) run an exhibition as well as an information service.

- For expert opinion and information on cleaners and revivers and potential supply of replacement tiles speak to H & R JOHNSON TILES (0782 - 575575) and/or W B SIMPSON & SONS (01 - 877 1020).

- An adviser on historic tiles and ceramics is TONY HERBERT (0743 - 236127).

- Invaluable sources for all old materials are ARCHITECTUAL SALVAGE firms (see references under **RECYCLING**).

- The SOCIETY FOR THE PROTECTION OF ANCIENT BUILDINGS (01 - 377 1644) puts out a range of pamphlets for 60p each, including one on the treatment and repair of old floor boards.

- There is a NATIONAL ASSOCIATION OF MASTER MASONS (0525 - 72361).

- Read FLOORS & MAINTENANCE, by

SALTER, pub APPLIED SCIENCE PUBS, £20.

- Read PAINT MAGIC, pub WINDWARD and PAINTABILITY, pub WEIDENFELD & NICOLSON, £8.95; both by JOCASTA INNES.

- The PARDON SCHOOL OF SPECIALIST DECORATION (01 - 245 1049) offers 10 videos by the master, LEONARD PARDON. Each half-hour tape shows how to produce a particular finish and effect, £39.95 per tape.

- Also on walls and ceilings read the illustrated (and amazingly titled) COLOUR ATLAS OF PLASTERING TECHNIQUES, by KENNETH, MILLS etc, pub WOLFE MED, £13.95; also PLASTERING: A CRAFTSMAN'S ENCYCLO-PAEDIA, by PEGG & STAGG, pub COLLINS BSP PROFESSIONAL, £7.95.

- See **INFORMATION CHECK LISTS** for **Architectural Salvage** section of **RECYCLING** and **ACQUIRING YOUR COUNTRY PROPERTY.**

- There is a NATIONAL SOCIETY OF MASTER THATCHERS (0962 - 67389).

- The THATCHING ADVISORY SERVICE (0734 - 734203) does rather more than advise, for it may be able to offer you a thatching training course and franchise. It also has a division THATCHERS (MARKETING) LTD (0734 - 730766) that creates and sells the thatched work and study buildings (called **pavilions**) mentioned above. These range in price from approx £3,000 to £21,000.

- Thatch, incidentally, need no longer be a particular fire hazard. Treatment with a Rockwell product THATCHBATT significantly reduces the risk.

- Read A HANDBOOK OF THATCHING, by NICHOLAS HALL, pub INTERMEDIATE TECHNOLOGY PUBLICATIONS, £4.95.

- Read FOLLIES & PLEASURE PAVILIONS, by G MOTT & S S AALL, pub PAVILION, £15.95.

- Also the AMDEGA BOOK OF CONSERVA-TORIES, by BRADBURN, pub DAVID & CHARLES, £12.95.

- The Self-build housing courses mentioned are run by CONSTRUCTIVE INDIVIDUALS (0757 - 82562).

- Read SELF-BUILDER, by SNELGAR, pub DAVID & CHARLES, £12.95.

- Also THE NEGLECTED ALTERNATIVE — SELF-BUILD HOUSING, pub POLYTECH-NIC OF S BANK Dept of TOWN PLANNING, £3.00.

- BUILDING YOUR OWN HOME, by MURRAY ARMOR, £6.95, ISBN 1-85327-028-8.

- The BRITISH WIND ENERGY ASSOCI-ATION (01 - 499 3515).

- Some reading of interest: FOCUS ON ALTER-NATIVE ENERGY, by McGLORY, pub WAYLAND, £4.95.

- As the house of the future must become part of the ecosystem, being built of materials that are renewable, non-polluting and energy-efficient read THE NATURAL HOUSEBOOK, by D PEARSON, pub CONRAN OCTOPUS, £14.99.

- Also WORLD ENERGY, a survey carried out by EUROMONITOR (01 - 251 8024) covers current ground but also looks at future key energy issues. Price £28, but see if you can get a look at it at your reference library or at the SCIENTI-FIC LIBRARY division of the BRITISH LIBRARY (start phone no. 01 - 323 7454).

• THE TEA CEREMONY

- Further on in this guide we suggest wine appreciation for serious consideration. Tea (Camellia sinensis) is every bit as fascinating, complex and ritualised.

- There are more tea drinkers in the world than wine drinkers. Nearly half the world drinks tea. (Coffee is the second most popular beverage.)

- In fact more coffee was drunk in England than anywhere else in the world until tea went on public sale at **Garway's Coffee House, London, in 1657.** By 1676, however, public coffee houses had to be licensed (because Charles II claimed they were centres of sedition and intrigue).

- Nevertheless, tea was here to stay. The rest is history: Britons now drink an average 3.76 cups of tea per person per day (that's an 8 fl oz cup!) or over 180 million cups a day, more than twice the amount of coffee drunk.

- Despite this huge consumption the market could still be considerable for exploiting tea detail and ceremony.

- What is there about tea, other than you boil freshly drawn cold water, warm the pot, throw in the tea (one teaspoon per person and one for the pot), pour on the boiling water, let it infuse for five or six minutes, stir and pour. Simple.

- Not entirely. **What** tea are you drinking? Is it, e.g. **green** (unfermented), **black** (fermented) or **oolong** (semi-fermented)?

- **Where** does it come from? England imports the beverage from at least **25 countries** and there are more than 30 countries growing it, from

Soviet Georgia to **South Africa.** Britain's imports represent nearly 25% of the major growers' exports, more than the total of Europe and North America imports.

• Is it the best quality from the **top bud** and **first two leaves,** or is it a blend of qualities, from different pickings, including lower leaves and the stem and the 'dust' (tiniest grade)?

• Perhaps it comes from the single-stem **Assam** plant which grows up to 18 metres high and has an economic life of 40 years; perhaps from the multi-stemmed **China** variety which grows to 2.75 metres high and has an economic life of 100 years; maybe its from the latest production methods of **Kenya** where they **clone** the best plants.

• As the Chinese writer Lu Yu said in A.D. 780, 'There are a thousand and ten thousand teas'. The most familiar come from **Ceylon, Assam, India** and **China,** which has been cultivating it since about 2737 B.C. (How come it took over 4,000 years before we got the taste?)

• The Chinese took it to **Japan** from where it has spread around the globe developing its own culture and ceremonies.

• It took Japan half a century to popularise it and there it is now not only the national beverage but a multi-billion yen business with special **Tea Ceremony Universities** taking in residential students for a three-year course to learn the ritual and culture of **Chado (The Way of Tea).**

• So highly revered is the taking of tea that special rooms are built in **Japanese gardens** for the ceremony, with warning signals given to people that the ceremony is taking place and not to interrupt.

- It is a time for being calm, for resting, for becoming rejuvenated.

- Even the **Samurais** had to take off their swords to enter the **chashitsu (tea room).**

- The Japanese see it as an other-world experience, serving twig or powder tea in earthenware bowls, not one utensil matching the other.

- In Australia tradition has the drovers drinking it from a tin at the billabongs.

- In Russia, they serve it in gleaming silver samovars.

- Here, of course, we also have our own rituals, serving tea in anything from a battered mug to the full kit of silver service or bone china with matching cups, saucers, teapots, sugar bowls and milk jugs.

- **Queen Catherine,** wife of Charles II, introduced tea as a social and family habit; a Mrs Harris was the first **'tea lady'** who introduced the tradition by making tea for the directors of the East India Company; later there were **tea breaks,** vigorously fought for when some employers in the late 18th century tried to stop them; and of course the **tea tray, tea gardens, tea dances, nursery tea, high tea,** etc., were all peculiarly British inventions.

- It was the **Duchess of Bedford,** around 1840, who introduced a new twist to tea by serving it with cakes and sandwiches. And when Englishman **Richard Blechynden** found he couldn't serve the conventional hot brew to the Americans in the steamy atmosphere of the St Louis' World Fair in 1904 he poured it over ice cubes and as a result the Americans began to strongly favour **iced tea.**

- They it was too who made a big political issue out of tea in 1770 when a band of irate colonialists, dressed as Indians (and maybe stoked up on the narcotic local brew **Cassina**) threw a valuable shipment of imported tea into Boston Harbour as a protest against the English taxing it too highly, thus precipitating the **American War of Independence.**

- Two thousand bushshoots of China tea make 1 lb, while the same number of Assam shoots may weigh 2 lbs.

- Tea contains only four calories and no carbohydrates or fat (without added ingredients) but it is the **caffeine-content** that gives tea-drinkers their 'high'.

- That said, tea is one of the most healthy, natural drinks you can get. It contains several of the B-complex vitamins, mineral elements such as zinc, manganese, potassium and nicotinic acid, and even small amounts of fluoride, but has no artificial flavourings, colourings or preservatives. And most of the tea imported into the UK is totally organic.

- Remember, keep your tea in an airtight caddy as it is easily contaminated by other flavours and smells.

- Arguments range over whether milk should be added to the cup before the tea or after, whether the cream goes in first or last. Should you in fact add anything?

- The tea tasters do add milk but no sweeteners when they are tasting because most Britons take milk and therefore the tea has to be judged that way to get the flavours right.

- The **Turks,** forbidden alcohol under their Moslem faith, perhaps drink more tea per head than any other nation. It's quite something to experience the joy and quietude of smoking a water pipe, having your shoes cleaned and topping up your tiny glass cup with tea from the enormous samovars in the lovely tea gardens of Istanbul or Cesme.

- The rituals of the drinking are but the end of an interesting cycle that starts with the growing and progresses through the tea auctions to the tea tasters and their routines — they have over 120 words in their specialised vocabulary, ranging from 'stringy' (= very good, orthodox tea) to 'dirt' (= sweepings off the floor) — not unlike those of wine tasting, to the retailing and on to the making ceremonies.

- Tea is normally sold loosely but it can come in tea bags or as twigs, which can be reused over and over again, or as a powder; even in brick form.

- If this isn't enough scope then look to other 'teas' which are not made with the tea plant but are really infusions of herbs and spices.

- What money-making here, you ask?

- We see the scope as three-fold: as a **leisure** course, taking your PSGs into the mysteries of tea in its many fragrant forms and making it in a theatrical performance.

- From there developing courses in the Japanese

tea ceremony itself (**Sen Rikyu** codified the ceremony in the 16th century and emphasised the
harmonious, restful, cleansing and tranquillising
effects that the properly conducted ceremony
had upon the participants).

- And finally the sales to PSGs, the public and by
  MAIL ORDER of exotic teas and **tea utensils.**

••• INFORMATION CHECK LIST

- Read ALL ABOUT TEA, 2 vols, by W H
  UKERS, dealing with the historical, technical,
  scientific, commercial, social and artistic aspects
  of tea production.

- Also, THE CULTURE AND MARKETING
  OF TEA, 3rd edtn, 1964. Track down these
  books through your library.

- Contact THE TEA COUNCIL (01 - 248 1024)
  for their FILE ON TEA, cost two first class
  stamps; or their HEALTHY DRINKS REPORT,
  £15.

- The TEA COUNCIL also offers AFTERNOON
  TEA KIT, £3.25, and the TEA PACK (prices
  £4 or £6) for the catering trade.

- A quite beautiful book is A JAPANESE TOUCH
  FOR YOUR HOME, by KOJU YOGI, pub
  KODANSHA, £17.95. This gives simple instructions and illustrations of the TEA ROOM for
  the TEA CEREMONY; the room can be as
  small as two tatami mats, 6′ × 6′, or as large as
  4½ mats, 9′ × 9′. The book is available from
  HARPER & ROW (0752 - 705251).

- Other Japanese reference books in English

include THE TEA CEREMONY, £5.95; ZEN IN THE ART OF THE TEA CEREMONY, £6.95, and CHADO — THE JAPANESE WAY OF TEA, £14.95; all available from the JAPANESE CENTRE (01 - 439 8057).

- Read CONSTANCE SPRY COOKERY BOOK, pub J M DENT, ISBN 0 46004382, on English tea-times and recipes.

- THE HERB BOOK, by JOHN LUST, pub BANTAM, £4.95, on herbal teas.

- Look up your local YELLOW PAGES under TEA BROKERS if you want to find out more about becoming a tea taster (requirement: good palate as you will be expected to taste between 500 and 1,000 teas per day, every working day; five-year apprenticeship, but you will get to travel around the world visiting growers); and TEA BLENDERS (usually the name is on the pack of your favourite tea) if you wish to visit one of the tastings. Auctions are not particularly interesting as there is **no** tea present; it will have been tasted a week or so beforehand and will be sold off-the-catalogue.

- If you want to experience a real Japanese Tea Ceremony then phone MRS TAKAHASHI on 0628 823876, who conducts ceremonies in London.

- Or, if you want to study it seriously MICHAEL BIRCH (01 - 853 2595) is (we think) the only teacher in the UK doing this. He travels throughout the UK and Europe spreading the word and has faithful students who have been attending his courses for 13 years. His charge is £10 per lesson.

- The UK's first TEA HOUSE (a three mat-room)

is being built by the URE SENKE FOUNDA-
TION at the British Museum, London.

- WHITTARDS (01 - 924 1888) offer a wide range
  of teas by mail order throughout the UK, including Japanese twig and green teas, and the
  naturally-caffeine-free ROISBOSCH 11
  O'CLOCK TEA, in tea bag form, from South
  Africa.

- Read (and sell?) THE ECCENTRIC TEAPOT,
  by GARTH CLARK, pub ARUM PRESS,
  £13.95.

- Finally, feeling tired, got puffy eyes from reading
  this guide? Then put some warm tea bags over
  your eyes, lie down for 15 minutes' rest, then
  make a cuppa (**Lapsang Souchong** or **Earl Grey**?)
  and carry on reading . . .

• TELEPHONE DYSPHORIA

- Since **Bell** invented the thing in 1876 the telephone has been developed into a masterpiece of sophistication.

- A masterpiece created for purposes that the majority unknowingly abuse:

- During research for this guide we have had to speak to hundreds of people by telephone. The experience confirmed a niggling suspicion: Few people understand the need for **CTP — Correct Telephone Personality.**

- The commercial consequences of this are devastating because there are countless managers running painstakingly efficient organisations otherwise but who still let any old body who happens to be near it answer the phone. (And possibly then only after it's been ringing for several minutes. . . .)

- Less than 20% of the people we tested came across in an acceptable way; four out of five respondents did themselves (and in many cases their **employers**) a disservice.

- In short the telephone still remains an area of major management cop-out.

- Lest you jump to the wrong conclusion we should make it clear that, yes, we had taken the trouble to study the basics of our own CTP beforehand.

- As a result what we did was to:
  - Smile when we spoke
  - Speak distinctly, with the microphone about 1″ from our mouth
  - Speak in an optimistic tone of voice
  - Speak at a moderate speed (180 words a

minute is ideal)
- Introduce ourselves clearly
- Politely find out precisely who we were talking with
- Prepare our questions ahead of our call and then
- Pleasantly and succinctly state our requirement
- Have pencil and paper ready to hand to record the information
- Save their time and ours by keeping the call as brief as possible
- Listen through the left ear
- Use body language when necessary
- Concentrate

- Regarding all these basics we should just clarify that:
  - Only a small percentage of communication is received through the **words** used
  - When you smile this communicates to your listener; important because a larger percentage of communication between people is understood because of the **tones** used
  - Left ear intake goes to the brain's right, intuitive, hemisphere, enhancing **empathy**
  - Where you are unavoidably stuck with either a reluctant or not-very-bright respondent it can help if you **stand up** and gesticulate. A more **authoritative** message results.

- Of the 80% of poor respondents, as many as half of those failed on **12** of the 13 points. (We could only guess at which ear was being used!)

- Before we try to understand the underlying problem we should say what we're measuring here: whether social or business the telephone call has but two objectives: to **exchange information** and **to do this pleasantly.** Ideally we should put down the phone feeling better; at the very least we should end the call with our equi-

242

librium still in place.

- Back to the problem. It is **Let-it-all-hang-out Spillage:** This is the presumption that whatever the sufferer is feeling at the time you call him can be allowed to pollute the resulting conversation. Totally and completely wrong, of course.

- Sadly, many people are **bored** with what they're doing. This boredom (indeed **any** feeling, negative or positive) comes quite clearly down the line. The voice arrives unclothed, revealing all too often, for example, resentment at the 'intrusion' or disinterest in the matter at hand.

- A slack-jawed mumble or a steely bark (not to mention all the other aberrations in between) are all very, very bad for business.

- After all, who wants to start by making an innocent phone call and end up making war?!

- Our contention is that any training will only win if it is based upon respect for communication by telephone as an extremely valuable part of our lives. At the moment it is treated with contempt by far too many people who wouldn't understand the need for a CTP if you sky-wrote it for them. Management **must** take a decisive hold on the problem.

- Does all of this mean that we have to have a telephone personality which is **consciously** bolted on to our other self?

- Until we begin to compare with the Americans, who are masters of the art of using the phone, the answer should be **'yes'**.

- There are no doubt telephone training courses on offer; judging from the above they are not very effective.

- What we discovered that compounded the problems was that many telephone receptionists were badly-briefed temps ('Dunno — I'm only here for the day'), who, as often as not, had to be 'rescued' by some other staff member — if there happened to be a rescuer to hand. If not, forget it.

- We can see a business aimed not only at properly **teaching** the required telephone personality but also **supplying** the graduates to firms.

- Whilst such a course would be business-oriented, if enough **humour** was injected a more social course would also certainly interest, educate and entertain the public at large as well.

- Let's face it, for those who just don't begin to adequately communicate on the telephone, such a deficiency impairs their dealings with, indeed even cuts them off from, the wider world out there.

- Your course could bring some **euphoria** rather than the pain implied in our heading.

- In addition to possibly selling to your PSGs some of the items mentioned below, consider also that only 2 or 3% of households have **telephone-answering machines.** A profitable sideline would be to have the best on offer and sell them to your PSGs. (Be prepared to throw in a mini-course on **how** to use them — and how to persuade callers to actually leave messages!)

- Check out the range in your local electronic equipment stockist then buy your choice(s) wholesale. There's between 18 and 35% markup.

••• INFORMATION CHECK LIST

- Read BE YOUR OWN BOSS, by DAVID LEWIS, pub and distributed by BRITISH TELECOM. Ring 0800 800 865. Lewis is a psychologist and brings his professional technique to bear on how to solve telephone hang-ups.

- Also YOUR TELEPHONE PERSONALITY, an American series of booklets that are issued each fortnight. Cost £1.35 each but this reduces with numbers. Contact the distributors, IBIS INFORMATION SERVICES on 0727 25209.

- GUIDE TO EFFECTIVE TELEPHONE TECHNIQUES, by PEMBERTON, pub INDUSTRIAL SOCIETY, £2.95.

- As we have said, the Americans are the master telephone technicians. Contact NIGHTINGALE-CONANT on 0101 - 708 647 0300, or write to them at 7300 NORTH LEHIGH AVENUE, CHICAGO, ILL., USA, zip 60648, re their catalogue no. 918TD. This is a series of 13 cassettes collectively called PHONE POWER. The cassettes cover every aspect of effective commercial telephone use. Also available, the video PHONE POWER, catalogue No. 580.

• WEATHER MAN

- As we note elsewhere, doing anything where you are dependent for your money on the weather is not a good idea. However, here's one way that you **can** cash in on it, regardless of its temper.

- Perhaps it's all because of our environmental concerns but it's hitting the Met Office hard — there is a shortage of weather men (or Scientific Officer/Forecasters as they are more correctly known).

- Whilst the salary scales at the MO are, shall we say, somewhat modest (around £20K) the more glamorous media stars will probably be earning twice that or more.

- Since the 1830s when the telegraph system helped quickly spread information about prevailing conditions, forecasting the weather has developed from hit-and-hope into a more exact science, although despite all the technology there is still a degree of pure intuition involved.

- Nevertheless, if you have an interest in physics, maths and wisdom in computers, you might consider setting up your own commercial **weather service.**

- Most people assume that the only source of reports is the Met Office. Not so: there are a small but growing number of **private firms** in the field.

- Typical customers are **radio stations** and **organisers of outside events;** indeed anyone whose regular or occasional cashflow is dependent on the weather.

- The Met Office is by law compelled to release certain information free of charge and this is used by small firms as their base starting-point from which to prepare more detailed local reports for their customers.

- Sensibly, weather forecasting might be a **second-string** business with main income arising from another activity.

- However, if this second-string could find a market niche and simmer along profitably you could just be laying the foundation for significant future growth if the environmental concerns we mentioned above should suddenly magnify even further.

••• INFORMATION CHECK LIST

- METEOROLOGICAL OFFICE (0344 - 420242) for details of how to become one of their WEATHER MEN. (There are basically three bands: Assistant Scientific Officer, four 'O' levels required, plus competence in physics, maths and computers, salary up to £10,000; Scientific Officer Band 2, university pass degree in meteorology, physics or maths, salary up to £15,000; Scientific Officer Band 1, 1st or 2nd Honours degree in meteorology, physics or maths, salary around £20,000.)

- READING UNIVERSITY (0734 - 875123) do a three-year BSc course in meteorology; a further one-year post-graduation course can land you a MSc.

- Another three years on your thesis and you could become a PhD **and** FELLOW of the ROYAL METEOROLOGICAL SOCIETY

(0344 - 422957). More modestly you can be an ordinary member for £24 per year which also gets you WEATHER magazine, monthly. (Cost for non-members £1.50).

- Another met mag is THE JOURNAL OF METEOROLOGY (02216 - 2482), 10 issues per year, £1.50 each.

- Of course, many amazing weather forecasters have never had any scientific training at all. Perhaps that's because they've read THE COMPLEAT METEOROLOGIST, an illustrated book by MEAD, pub NEMEC, £6.00.

• WINE & MALT WHISKY

- Wine has marched hand in hand with the history of civilisation, so surely there can be no more civilised a subject for study, discussion and, of course, tasting.

- It is probable that wine first made its appearance in Mesopotamia some 5000 years ago.

- In due course the vine was planted in Egypt and Greece but it was **Rome** that accorded it and its noble produce the greatest appreciation and, through the Legions, spread it westward and northward into practically the whole of Europe.

- Unlike much other wine 2000 years ago (which was often watered, spiced and seasoned) Roman wine was similar to that which their descendants drink today.

- By the time of its decline in the 5th century, Rome had laid the foundations for almost all of the greatest vineyards; only **Alsace** and **Champagne** do not have Roman origins.

- The **Church** carried on the good work and for centuries owned some of the finest vineyards of Europe, for wine was essential to ritual; also as medicine, restorative (and disinfectant!).

- With the rediscovery of **cork** came the realisation that wine kept in a tightly-corked bottle lasted much longer and tasted better than if kept in a barrel.

- The rise of the great estates and the evolution of modern wine dates from that time, the 18th century. Truly the Age of Enlightenment. . . .

- It is thought that we owe to the **Chinese** the

development of distilling **spirits.**

- Around 800 BC they were distilling a beverage from rice beer.

- Production in Western Europe gained impetus after our contact with the Arabs (the word **alcohol** is of Arab derivation).

- **Single malt whisky,** a corruption of the gaelic **usquebaugh** (= water of life), is distinguished from grain whisky in two ways:

- It is made entirely from a mash of malted barley and it is aged in oak casks for a minimum of **eight years.**

- On the other hand, **grain whisky** (with which the single malts are mixed to provide the usual run of popular blended whiskies) is made from a mash of pre-cooked maize together with a proportion of barley and is drunk sometimes with as little age as **three years.**

- Malts of 30 years ageing can be found on a few discriminating off-licensees' shelves.

- However, perhaps malt whisky's finest feature it does share with its humbler, grainy cousin and that is the variety in flavour of the delicious **Scottish water** used in its production.

- This variousness of water source (not forgetting the human loving care and idiosyncrasy lavished on producing each individual malt) ensures that there is a truly astonishing range of flavours for the palate to enjoy.

- (And consider some of the names: Immortal Memory, Grogsblossom, How Tow Die, Tax Collector and Pig's Nose mingle robustly with the likes of the staider Laphroaig and The Glenlivet).

- Despite rationalisation in the industry there is still a huge and pleasantly bewildering range of different malts on offer, each distinctive from the other.

- Consider the even greater range of wines around the world and you have material enough for courses stretching a long way into the future.

- Added income to be gained too from the sales of bottles, cases, books, and ancillaries like cork screws and cellar systems, for your PSGs' home pleasure. You could perhaps also consider importing some of your own medium and higher-priced wine, leading you into **MAIL ORDER** (qv).

- As you will know by reference to **HIT LIST** (qv) we do not recommend any venture where your cash can be put at serious hazard by the weather.

- Why then are we now going to suggest that you perhaps consider running your own **vineyard?** Because grapes can be grown **hydroponically** and **under-cover** (see **GROWING THINGS**).

- For example, using volcanic substrates, grapes are grown hydroponically on **Lanzarote** in the Canary Isles.

- Whilst purists will probably be horrified, the fact is that not only do you need no soil (indeed soil is literally at the root of many troublesome diseases) but you can also control the **flavour** of your produce much more closely by the use of hydroponics.

253

- Because under-cover hydroponic growing is an ecosystem of its own it does more than protect crops from the weather; unlike conventional UK vineyards which go no further north than Leeds it provides **geographical freedom** of site location.

- It is a further fact that the clever hydroponicist can get a denser, higher crop than his outdoors counterpart. Bearing this in mind the **outdoor** figures look something like this:

  - 2 × 75cl bottle of wine can be harvested from one vine
  - you can reckon on 1500 vines per acre
  - 3000 bottles per acre multiplied by an average £4 per bottle **retail** totals £12,000 gross per acre

- No wonder wine is considered to be such a prized crop!

- In a good weather year the UK produces over **5,000,000** bottles but the obvious downside is that the crops are frequently sorely afflicted by unfriendly outdoor conditions, a hazard avoided by the method outlined here.

- In addition to the income sketched out above you will make extra cash if your site can attract tourists to whom you will certainly be able to sell both wine by the glass and cases to take home.

- The caveat is that, as something of a pioneer, you will have to spend time and money on experiment so get plenty of expert advice up front and start **small.**

- Wine does not **have** to be made from grapes of course; there's a growing trend to experiment in other 'country' flavours: elderberry, apricot, damson, etc.

- Meantime your wine and whisky appreciation courses (and the sales therefrom, and don't overlook organising wine sales to local businesses and private consumers, or being even more energetic and taking parties on tasting tours abroad) will be needed to finance you through your vineyard start-up period.

- If it had crossed your mind to create your own malt whisky then of course Scotland is the only place to do it. There is no substitute for the Scottish waters — as you'll know well enough if you've tasted whisky made anywhere else!

- A last but not terribly serious thought: If you are going to, so to speak, 'combine' wine and whisky then you can give your PSGs a taste of an unique drink recently on the market; it's a combination of British wine and Irish whiskey! (Not an Irish joke; it's called **Glen Dew** and is on sale in major supermarkets.)

••• INFORMATION CHECK LIST

- SOTHEBY'S WORLD WINE ENCYCLO-PAEDIA, by TOM STEVENSON, an illustrated book, pub DORLING KINDERSLEY, £30.

- THE STORY OF WINE, by HUGH JOHNSON, pub MITCHELL BEAZLEY, £25.

- A TASTE OF ENGLISH WINE, by HUGH BARTY-KING, pub PELHAM, £15.95.

- THE DIRECTORY OF WINE SOCIETIES

255

AND COURSES, by P BARBOUR, pub WINE BUYERS GUIDES, £6.95.

- DECANTER, monthly magazine, £2.

- THE 1990 WHICH? WINE GUIDE, pub CONSUMERS ASSOC & HODDER & STOUGHTON, £9.95.

- ENGLISH VINEYARD ASSOCIATION (01 - 857 0452) for information and for further suggested reading. They publish a quarterly magazine GRAPE PRESS.

- WINE & SPIRIT EDUCATION TRUST (01 - 236 3551) for training information.

- WORLD GUIDE TO WHISKY, by MICHAEL JACKSON, pub DORLING KINDERSLEY, £14.95.

- ALMANAC OF SCOTCH WHISKIES, £5.95, pub LOCHAR PUBLISHING, by WALLACE MILROY who, in addition to writing this authoritative book, with brother John runs the SOHO WINE MARKET (01 - 437 9311). You not only get the book from them but they have perhaps the biggest range of malt whiskies on offer in the UK. Get their list for mail order buying.

- If Hebridean malts interest you then also from the Soho Wine Market get SCOTCH & WATER, by NEIL WILSON, pub LOCHAR PUBLISHING, £12.95 and also

- For the historically-minded a Victorian account of THE WHISKY DISTILLERIES OF THE UNITED KINGDOM, by ALFRED BARNARD, pub LOCHAR PUBLISHING, £20.

- ALCHOLIC DRINKS IN THE UK is a survey worth reading giving not only an overview of the market but a look into the future. Contact EUROMONITOR (01 - 251 8024) or, as the survey costs £375, try your local larger reference libary or the SCIENTIFIC LIBRARY division of the BRITISH LIBRARY (start phone no 01 - 323 7454).

- Wine taster breaks are not difficult to find, either from studying the magazines mentioned, the general glossies or from THF (0345 - 500400) or HILTON (0923 - 38877).

- Many of the major distilleries conduct whisky tours and tastings. Contact them first for opening times; or try the SCOTCH WHISKY ASSO-CIATION (01 - 629 4384) who, apart from pointing you in the right direction, have a permanent display on the workings of a distillery with models and audio visuals in London.

- Also for whisky tastings check with JOHN or WALLACE MILROY (see above).

- UISGEBEATHA GU BRATH (= water of life forever)!

• WRITING

- **Abraham Lincoln** was pretty good at the smoothly-rolled-out phrase himself: 'You can fool some of the people, etc.' and, of a book, 'People who like this sort of thing will find this the sort of thing they like' et al. He also said that 'Writing was the greatest invention of man'.

- Few of us have his gifts of expression but a master in another branch, **Robert McKee,** an American screen-writer, maintains stoutly that technique **can** be taught in **any** art form, including writing. So

- A large subject but here for you to consider because of the palpable current surge of interest in self-development and expression.

- Because of its very range and complexity you may choose to **specialise** (see below) or call on a variety of practitioners to cover the subjects: novelists, short story writers and playwrights for theatre, TV, film and radio.

- Then there is factual writing: history, biography, technical, documentary, etc., and, to give the other bloke's point of view, your PSGs will also want to hear the publisher's angle.

- Then there is journalism . . .

- Whilst a lot of people profess contempt for the media, journalists themselves actually enjoy an interestingly racey, gamey image.

- Because the profession is so little understood — there's a good deal more to it than the 5 Ws: WHEN, WHAT, WHERE, WHO, WHY — a lot of people would pay to know more about the skills involved.

- There will perhaps be some specialised market niches of your own that you have in mind. But meantime consider:

- **TV Writing:** With the huge increase of **TV satellite channels** and their cost to the consumer, it is clear, surely, that viewers will soon want not so much more channel choice but a bit of quality when they do come to rest. There is a looming shortage of TV writing talent. Could you devise a course to start meeting this imminent need?

- **De-jargonising:** Ultra-specialists tend to write in other-planetary non-language, e.g. the creators of computer manuals. The computer may be elegantly simple as its supporters sometimes claim but, if so, this simplicity is shrouded by the obfuscations of the accompanying 'explanatory' books. A widespread problem.

- **Translating** the translation: Translators may be brilliant linguists but are seldom as skilled when it comes to making understandable the translation into the new language. Another widespread problem.

- Talking of skill, consider the true story of one **Rupert Downing,** a talented old Fleet Street hand given to the frequent boast that he could tell **any** story in a single sentence.

- Exasperated by this, one evening some colleagues challenged him to use the Bible as reference and prove his point. 'Certainly,' he replied, 'give me five minutes.'

- Going to a corner of the bar he ordered another large whisky and soda, sipped it thoughtfully then started to write in his notebook.

- Well within time he returned, tore out the page and threw it on the bar in front of the others.

- The somewhat tipsy scrawl read: 'In the beginning God said "Let there be Light" and by Christ there was.'

- If you can teach your PSGs such matchless brevity the hopeful writers of this world will beat a path to your door.

••• INFORMATION CHECK LIST

- Contact the SOCIETY OF AUTHORS (01 - 373 6642). They publish THE AUTHOR, quarterly, £3, and will be able to point you towards agents of members who give talks.

- Equally the INSTITUTE OF JOURNALISTS (01 - 252 1187).

- For information about ROBERT McKEE and his courses contact INTERNATIONAL FORUM (0732 - 810925).

- If this is your area contact THE CRIME WRITERS ASSOCIATION (01 - 493 9001).

- Or the ROMANTIC NOVELISTS ASSOC (051 - 5464014).

- WRITERS AND ARTISTS YEARBOOK, pub A & C BLACK, £6.95.

- WRITERS HANDBOOK, by BARRY TURNER, pub MACMILLAN, £6.95.

- WRITERS MONTHLY magazine (01 - 888 1242), £33.50 per annum.

- Perhaps one of the most reliable correspondence courses we know of is so because it's run by a firm of publishers you've seen mentioned several times throughout this guide: DAVID & CHARLES' WRITERS COLLEGE (0626 - 63226). Their course costs £149 **and** they **guarantee** a return of the money if your earnings from writing have not at least covered their course fees by the end of the tuition.

- Read HOW TO WRITE FOR PUBLICATION, by McCALLUM, pub NORTHCOTE HOUSE PUBLISHERS, £5.95, and BECOMING A WRITER, edited by CHAPPLE, pub NELSON, £3.95.

- Consider the six audio cassette course YES! YOU CAN WRITE! It's numbered 169AC in the NIGHTINGALE-CONANT catalogue. You can contact them on 0101 - 708 - 647 0300, or write to them at 7300 NORTH LEHIGH AVENUE, CHICAGO, ILL, USA, zip 60648.

- The BRITISH COMPUTER SOCIETY (01 - 637 0471) is the friendly face of that much-maligned machine. Talk to them if you're interested in a dialogue about improving computer manuals.

- Check with THE ASSOCIATION OF TRANS-LATION COMPANIES (01 - 821 6560) referred to in **LANGUAGES INFORMATION CHECK LIST** (qv).

- Equally the INSTITUTE OF TRANSLATION & INTERPRETING (01 - 794 9931).

- If you're interested in getting into a course the hard way contact CITY UNIVERSITY LONDON (01 - 253 4399 ext 3266) regarding their intensive SUB-EDITING and/or FREE-

LANCE JOURNALISM courses (£275 and £150).

- Any study of writing is incomplete without some informed idea as to how the publishing end works. BOOK HOUSE TRAINING CENTRE (01 - 874 2718) offers some 50 different courses covering publishing: e.g. editorial, law, production, marketing and management. The specialist copy-editing course relative to SCIENTIFIC, TECHNICAL & MEDICAL (STM) work is of particular relevance.

HIT LIST

• HIT LIST

- During the course of compiling this guide we have looked at hundreds of different ventures. Many were discarded early, lacking the zing that really motivates people (bed and breakfast houses, corner shops, sub-post offices, etc).

- Others we looked at closely before giving the thumbs down.

- Whilst respecting the fact that there are people who make some money from these occupations, we thought nevertheless that you would be interested to have some **samples** and our reasons for putting them on this list:

• AIR PURSUITS

- Training people to fly small planes, micro-lights, gliders, balloons; teaching parachuting/scending etc. It all sounds great fun but our information is quite clear: Not only is the competition hot but critically the British weather ensures that you will always struggle to make money.

• ANIMAL EXOTICS

- Rearing and selling camelids (llamas, alpacas), angora goats, etc. This potential venture had all sorts of people smiling and aahing. Alas, the commercial realities soon intruded.

- As animals are a great tie it is essential to be able to see up-front what the profits will be in return for the very heavy investment of your time and the not insignificant capital concerned.

- Particularly with camelids and angora goats the market has been turbulent causing those involved some painful financial shocks. There have also been health and import difficulties.

- The alternative to selling the animals is to go for the wool harvest but experts have concluded that at current market prices that's not economically viable either.

- Make your money elsewhere then try and run your favourites commercially if you can. Better still, see animals as an expensive hobby.

• ANTIQUES

- Taking the definition literally (to qualify an item must be at least 100 years old) would involve tying up hefty capital because, due to years of exports, there simply isn't any longer enough good stuff around to freely buy and sell. What little remains is now extremely costly.

- Even when you sell and make a large profit therefore you're faced with the expensive difficulty of finding genuine replacement stock.

- The result is what you see around you: so-called antique shops with few if any genuine pieces and plenty of poor quality, but high-priced, tack.

- Better make new 'old' furniture (see **BESPOKE**) or bite the bullet and run a real junk emporium (see **RECYCLING**) or teach others how to enjoy (see **ANTIQUES APPRECIATION & RESTORATION**).

• COUNTRY HOUSE HOTELS

- Another charming idea (and yet another where you need to go and lie down somewhere until the feeling goes away).

- Whilst a substantial investment should never by

268

itself frighten you off (several ventures call for it), before you go in you've got to see the required profit beckoning at the end of the tunnel.

- You've also, if you're wise, got to be satisfied that you'll **enjoy** what you're going to do.

- If you'd revel in spending hundreds of thousands of pounds setting up your luxury palace; think you'd also enjoy 25-hour days, eight-day weeks, brutal staff problems and pilferage that can become grand larceny, then no doubt you will go and open a country hotel.

- However before you do just reflect on two other awkward little matters:

- Getting to break-even is a slow affair; this is a business that mainly works on word-of-mouth. Also the big hotel chains are starting to fancy the idea of getting into country house hotels themselves.

- Actually we don't think they'll make money from them either but they can afford the loss. Could you?

- If you can command the sort of cash needed to start up one of these places why not go for something with much fresher and wider appeal? e.g. **SNOW & ICE** (qv).

• COUNTRY PUBS

- Many of the comments made for country house hotels apply to country pubs; big ingoings, staff difficulties (which are quite unavoidable due to the unsocial hours), pilferage, etc.

- However hard they try, brewers still struggle to break away from 'institutionalitis'. This can make them, at best, very frustrating to deal with. In addition, deliveries are frequently a problem and where's your profit if you're short of beer?

- Also, country pub customers are very exposed to breathalyser crack-downs by energetic local police who have rather more time to make their presence felt than their city counterparts.

- Unless you're content to run a lager house, with all that that implies, it is only feasible to build a healthily strong and steady trade by serving a range of real ales.

- However, this is a Catch 22; as real ale goes 'off' within a few days, you have to have plenty of customers around to drink it whilst it's fresh. As to begin with you probably won't have many customers, you'll find yourself either throwing the expensive stuff away or serving sour beer. As nothing empties a pub quicker or more permanently than that. . . .

- If the feeling is strong within you to make people feel good then there are plenty of other ideas in the guide and, if serving a beverage must feature, consider **TEA CEREMONY** (qv).

• COUNTRY RESTAURANTS

- Country folk like eating out — at weekends and, **in numbers,** only then.

- This is no basis for a business where your overheads go on seven days a week.

- As country people are conservative you could also have a long lead time before you become popular.

- All this can mean that you're running a polarised

business; extremely busy on a few occasions, slack on others. It's very difficult to train staff under circumstances where they're either rushed off their feet or bored rigid staring at each other and the empty tables.

- As most people dislike extremes staffing becomes a major hurdle. A problem as intractable as this can close businesses down and has done many times.

- Our old friend pilferage features again.

- Why not consider **WINE & MALT WHISKY** (qv) courses? Much safer and much more enjoyable. **MICROWAVE MAGIC** (qv) or **KITCHEN FACTORY** (qv) are other, foody, alternatives.

• FARMING

- Conventional farming is going through a volatile period, lacking security but still with plenty of bureaucratic interference.

- And, yet again, there's the weather. . . .

- The general view seems to be that you have to run at least 150-200 acres to have a chance of making a living; even then this is a venture at the margin, with far too heavy a capital investment for erratic and very hard-earned returns.

- However for unconventional ways to go see **GROWING THINGS.**

• RESIDENTIAL CARE/NURSING HOMES

- Many of the comments we make about country house hotels apply to this venture.

- In addition there are others:

- No doubt due to some corner-cutters in the industry, the authorities concerned with residential homes are becoming positively draconian in their demands regarding the facilities and safeguards needed before they will permit operation.

- You may think that, before you invest, you can solve these problems by spending (quite a lot of) time and money finding out what the requirements are and how much it is likely to cost to meet them. Not necessarily so.

- We've heard of hapless owners spending significant sums on meeting requirements only to find that, because of revised thinking and/or a change of Authority staff, the goal posts get moved and yet more expense arises.

- This is a business only for the well-heeled **professional,** who can calculate and get the return on his investment of money, expertise and, let's face it, heartache.

• WATERSPORTS

- What was exhilarating when you were water-skiing, wind surfing, jet-skiing etc and generally enjoying yourself in the sun and as a hobby may not look so great when the British weather intervenes.

- To the real enthusiast of course this doesn't matter but, from what we've heard talking to teachers and watersports operators, it's quite amazing how many "enthusiasts'" enthusiasm drains away when the skies open up.

- The days and weeks lost to weather mean a fall

in income you can never make up.

- As we understand it the biggest watersport of all is angling; also that the fishing aficionado is undeterred by the weather. However, we haven't figured out how you could make much money out of this sport. If we're wrong, no doubt you'll tell us.

- **To summarise:** Avoid like the plague any venture where success or failure ultimately rests on factors largely or indeed totally outside of your direct control.

- Inevitably the **weather** is one of these factors.

- **Staff** working unsocial hours can be another, however good your training.

- It's a fact of life that high-calibre people do not care to work unconventional hours for other people. If you do not have capable, reliable staff working for you who must do the work? **You,** of course. If an excessive burden continually falls on your shoulders you will soon start to suffer mental and physical exhaustion and no one ever ran a successful business in that condition.

- **Institutions and Authoritative bodies** can have (and misuse) quite awesome power in some types of business. Make sure it's not your's.

- ## COMPUTERS

- Unless you are already **fully** computer-wise it does **not** follow that your new business must be computerised; indeed, there are some powerful reasons why you should only consider this step **after** your venture's up and running satisfactorily:

- Whilst no one should suggest that the computer industry is dishonest, it is regrettably a fact of life that, perhaps because of its rather mysterious nature, it has attracted some pretty unreliable people into its midst.

- Should you have the misfortune to strike one of these dodgy fellows you will certainly wind up paying more for your system than you'd bargained for.

- By this we mean not only will you be charged for endless **extras** (in which case you'll get off lightly!) but you may also have been landed with the **wrong** system altogether.

- Mysteriously, too, you may find that just when you need your **supplier** most (like when your system's gone down on you) he's simply not 'available'; even if he is around he would be a rare bird indeed if he actually took positive action to get the maintenance engineer to you remotely within the time stated in the on-site contract (for which you've usually paid heavily!).

- However, poor though the back-up usually is, with new equipment you do have a bottom to kick and it's called a warranty — you can legally get **someone** to help you, albeit belatedly. Do **not** therefore be tempted to buy second-hand gear. If something goes wrong with that you've usually lost the lot.

- In a start-up situation there are really only three ways to go with computers: either do without (recommended); or go cheap (Amstrad) or, if and when you can afford, go IBM (expensive). Why IBM? Well, they say no-one ever got fired buying IBM; it's the Rolls-Royce of the industry, has a name to protect and will probably give

274

you something like the result you're looking for. But forget the budget **or** try renting.

- So there can be very real problems on the supply and maintenance side; but that is not the end of it because you may well have difficulty in mastering the complex techniques necessary to make the system run satisfactorily to your business's needs.

- This can be a critical difficulty, because the first call on your personal time must be to get your business running.

- e.g. If the computerised records fall behind you are building up to a major and expensive-to-solve problem.

- It is not overstating the case to say that computer cock-ups have bankrupted even **mature** businesses. To run such a risk in a start-up situation is to court potential disaster.

- Need we add that anybody you talk to who is **in** the computer industry will vehemently deny everything we have written; but then they would, wouldn't they?

- However, we write from experience learned the hard way.

- ## INSURANCE & INSURANCE COMPANIES

- You must have full insurance cover but strangely you may find it rather difficult to obtain.

- This will have nothing to do with you, everything to do with the fact that many insurance companies themselves have got hopelessly behind with their paperwork (**computer breakdown** being frequently the culprit. . .).

- The sinister aspect of this is that, whilst you may **think** you're on cover, you may **not** be.

- Again, you may calculate that if you go through a reputable **broker** you will be protected. Again, sadly, this ain't necessarily so because your broker is powerless to control what the insurance company's doing.

- This is too important a matter to leave to chance. Your best bet therefore is to actually **visit** (do not telephone) insurance company office(s) in your area, compare quotes and do your deals **direct** with the office(s) of your choice.

- When you pay your money you get a receipt and **cover note** so there can be no doubt that, however long the policy actually takes to reach you, you **are** insured.

- We write the above from more experience learned the hard way, we're afraid.

• LAWYERS

- We refer elsewhere to the need for considerable care in selecting professionals. You will sooner or later find that you must also use a lawyer for, alas, there are certain situations where this is virtually unavoidable.

- More than with any other professional, you must use discrimination in making your choice of legal representative.

- For many centuries lawyers have had a poor press: Shakespeare put the lines 'The first thing we do, let's kill all the lawyers' into the mouth of a player in Henry VI, and later on John Gay, in The Beggar's Opera, suggested 'A fox may steal your hens, sir . . . If lawyer's hand is fee'd, sir, he steals your whole estate.'

- More recently, Will Rogers said 'I don't think you can make a lawyer honest by an act of legislature. You've got to work on his conscience. And his lack of conscience is what makes him a lawyer.' Not, you note, a 'good' lawyer, just 'a lawyer'!

- P G Wodehouse was even blunter. 'That's what comes of being a solicitor, it saps the vital juices. Johnny doesn't even embezzle his clients' money, which I should have thought was about the only fun a solicitor can get out of life.'

- Even today, lawyers seem relatively disinterested in improving their image and the consequence is that they are perceived as aloof and arrogant, expensive and poor value. Going into litigation is generally regarded as the act of a spendthrift maniac, determined on no other course than lining the pockets of grasping solicitors and briefs and probably bankrupting himself in the process. The Law does not appear to have a compassionate face.

- Unfortunately, this impression is well-based and the reason is not difficult to see: the lawyer's training fits him mainly for the role of an academic, someone removed from the world as it really is, from human beings as they really are.

- However, although many lawyers have a very poor understanding of business, do not for a moment be misled into thinking that your average lawyer is merely a naive and bumbling incompetent; his training may be unworldly but it does enshrine "Me first", i.e. your lawyer will

be very alert to protecting his own backside —
and his own bank balance, as you'll discover
with an unpleasant shock when you start to
receive his fee notes.

- Here are some ground rules for dealing with
  these people:

- Do not go near a lawyer unless he is personally
  recommended to you by someone who has found
  him satisfactory **over time,** in handling **business
  matters.** Such a lawyer is a rare bird so you may
  have much ferreting ahead of you.

- Accept that a lawyer's main concern is his **fees.**
  Before you issue instructions get in writing a
  clear financial estimate from him for any work
  you want doing and define that work with
  precision.

- Although many of them would like you to believe
  otherwise, lawyers are not gods. Any two lawyers
  are quite likely to differ in their interpretation
  of the law. Therefore use your own common
  sense and have the courage to question advice
  which strikes you as nonsense. (As very few
  clients ever do this it is not surprising that many
  lawyers have delusions of grandeur!)

- Equally, do not assume that your lawyer has
  automatically done his homework thoroughly,
  e.g. because lease documents are long, boring
  and **in most cases** in a fairly standard format
  the fine print does not always get the close
  attention it merits. The outcome could be a
  lease that lands you with some unnecessarily
  onerous responsibilities. Therefore **always** read
  through such documents yourself to check that
  both you and your lawyer have spotted anything
  objectionable.

- Assess all situations for litigation potential. If such potential is high, run a mile. If, despite these precautions, you find yourself facing court action, explore every possibility of settling **out of court,** for once you're into court you're on the Cresta Run — without a particularly secure sled!

- Should you find that you're stuck with a lawyer who is both expensive and incompetent (and the two almost invariably go together) be aware beforehand that he has a lien on any of your papers and documents in his possession and will not part with these until **all** his fees are paid. However unfair it appears you have to pay him first and sue him afterwards!

- In short, in dealing with lawyers bear well in mind one of their very own dictums: **caveat emptor** = 'Let the buyer beware. . . .'

WHAT TO DO NOW

• WHAT TO DO NOW

- There follows a sequence of questions to address if you are serious about pursuing a venture:

- How do I get an initial, rough idea of the venture's **viability**? See the **SR FORMULA**.

- Will I **win**? See **PERSONAL STOCK TAKE**.

- What do I **want**? See **YOUR VENTURE PHILO-SOPHY**.

- What **must** I **watch** closely? See **THE CRITICAL SUCCESS FACTOR(S)**.

- What's my **medium-term concept** for running my business? See **MARKETING STRATEGY**.

- What if I may need **money**? See **FUNDING YOUR VENTURE**.

- What's the next **move**? See **SELLING YOUR PRESENT HOME**.

- And the next? See **ACQUIRING YOUR COUNTRY PROPERTY**.

- How do I get **into play**? See **MARKETING PLAN**.

- Before reading through the sequence we offer this tip: If you are determined to go ahead then, in the initial stages, **do not** discuss your intentions with anyone **other** than the person or family member who will be directly involved in running your future business with you. The best of ideas will crumble under the weight of too much random talk, particularly to the unqualified cynics who will sap your enthusiasm. Don't talk it — do it!

• THE SR FORMULA

• Now you need to get some idea of whether or not you can make an acceptable profit.

• The SR FORMULA is a quick method of telling yourself whether you're on the right financial track or wasting your time. So:

• Do preliminary investigations sufficient to give you a broad idea of the **gross weekly income** of each venture that interests you. Then

• Calculate the approximate total **capital** costs of acquiring the property, moving in and getting started.

• Divide this figure by **50** (see below).

• Your venture could be a runner if your **guesstimate** of its gross weekly income is within 10-15% either way of the figure arrived at by dividing total capital cost by 50.

• If your weekly income guesstimate is **significantly lower** than the SR Formula figure then you should recheck, particularly asking if you have not tried to put yourself and your venture into too grand and expensive a property.

• A cheaper property that you can extend later out of profits could correct the distortion in your figures.

• If you still have a problem but you're **convinced** about the venture then base your calculations on **renting** your property, not buying (see **ACQUIRING YOUR COUNTRY PROPERTY**).

• Why divide by 50? It's an arbitrary figure for a number of reasons, one of which is because different people have different ideas as to how quickly they want to see their capital returned out of profits. However, on the basis that dividing by 50 returns capital **gross** in one year **and** that you achieve average **nett** profits you will return your capital within four to five years which, again, is a reasonable average.

● YOUR PERSONAL STOCKTAKE

● Your venture **is you.** Therefore

● If:
● You've thought it through from **every** angle
● You're prepared to change your **life-plan**
● You're prepared to learn **new skills,** if necessary
● You're ready to bring to your venture the very **best** of you
● You're able to make success in your venture a **treasured objective**
● Then you **will win.**

● To help you toward that target here are a few pointed questions you might ask yourself:

● This venture will involve me in discharging the following responsibilities. (List these, as best you can, paying particular attention to responsibility for repaying **borrowings**);

● Will I **enjoy** and **measure up** to these responsibilities?

● Supposing I hit snags? Am I tough and resourceful enough to keep going till I beat them?

● (Snags can crop up in surprising places: you'll be disturbed at how defensive, unhelpful even obstructive people can become when you put them under pressure to do their job. A not unimportant example concerns **suppliers:** Whilst the top man will usually want to sort out the problem, you may have to be **very** blunt and firm with a lot of his juniors before they allow you to get to him!)

● If I have finance problems will I have the guts to go and talk them through with my funders? (You'd be surprised how daunting this can be!)

- When I succeed I'll want a handsome reward. **My** reward concept is:

- A reasonable living, giving me more time with my **family**? (How much **is** my 'reasonable'?)

- Or

- Becoming **wealthy**? What is my **wealthy**?

- £40/50,000 a year?

- More? £100,000 per year?

- More? The sky's the limit?

- If **'more, more',** how will this affect me?

- Could I **really** cope?

- And my **family**?

- In short, try hard to define **now** the size of the income and therefore the business you want to achieve.

- These sample questions will probably raise others. The best time to ask and answer them is, as far as possible, before you go ahead.

- The possibility arises that you may not yet have found the right venture. In which case ask yourself this rather extreme question:

- 'I'm convinced of the need to switch my life-plan to a country context. Should I do so **now** — even though I still haven't got a desirable venture with which to earn money?'

- This sounds like a gambler's question but there is a weird entrepreneurial logic in the answer:

288

- If you're convinced but you let the moment pass you may never again have the determination, the moral force, to make the break.

- Shakespeare was no mean entrepreneur and he, if you recall, put it like this:

  'There is a tide in the affairs of men,
  Which, taken at the flood, leads on to fortune;
  Omitted, all the voyage of their life
  Is bound in shallows and in miseries.
  On such a full sea are we now afloat;
  And we must take the current when it serves,
  Or lose our ventures.'

- Remember also that:

- Once you **have** committed yourself you will focus and concentrate harder. It is from that mental high ground that you will more easily discover the venture for you.

- But to return to the assumption that you believe you have found your venture. The next discipline is to:

- Put it from your mind for at least two weeks! If when you look at it at the end of that time it still makes sense then you and your venture have passed the **'blowing hot and cold'** test.

- If however, the answer's not a black 'no' or a white 'yes' but a grey '?' then the answer is that you need more information.

- Go out and get it (still endeavouring to solve the problem without talking about your venture to others not intimately connected with it).

- There has to come a time when you **quit or commit** to your venture:

289

- If you are with someone else, you may not agree: the other person simply doesn't think it will work, or maybe, at a deeply personal level, they fear that working together round the clock could damage your social and emotional health.

- Who decides?

- Ideally, both of you, for any venture's prejudiced if there's initial disagreement.

- In our experience it is the person who has **all** the facts and who has thought them and their consequences through most cogently who is entitled to prevail. (**NB:** This person may not be the usual family decision-maker!)

- If there is still concern about going ahead then consider attending a **transition seminar** geared to helping you cross the perhaps frightening chasm that separates the entrepreneur from less adventurous mortals.

- You next have to grapple with another intensely personal challenge, **YOUR VENTURE PHILO-SOPHY.**

••• INFORMATION CHECK LIST

- Contact PSYCHOLOGICAL PRESSURE POINTS LTD (01 - 530 2920). Their JACK MITCHELL runs transition seminars.

- GOOD HOUSEKEEPING (01 - 439 7144) have joined forces with the OPEN UNIVERSITY to produce the LIVING CHOICES pack, £15. Appreciating that irrevocable decisions and change are very difficult, their book-cassettes-study guide-kit is geared to help you master the forward planning and clear thinking necessary to reach the right decision.

- Consider taking THE PHOENIX SEMINAR, see under **PERSONAL DEVELOPMENT;** change **can** be programmed.

• YOUR VENTURE PHILOSOPHY

- This consists of the core objectives you **intend** to achieve through your venture.

- Decide on these and the methods of achievement.

- Naturally they must be consistent with the results of your **PERSONAL STOCKTAKE** — so don't soar off on grandiose wings!

- These objectives will only be achieved by a hard-nosed assessment of the relationships that your intended venture will have to have with its **environment** (which includes **you personally,** your **customers, suppliers, competitors,** the **authorities,** etc) to hit your targets.

- Typically, an effective VP will go to 20 or more points, from describing the initial business, on to what it is intended are future goals, via customer dedication, pricing, ownership of the venture, decision process, profit targets, success yardstick (i.e. profit targets achieved within time and money budgets); growth (how?), what you propose doing about money (both coming and going), how all concerned will operate, the conditions under which they will operate, etc.

- Be **trenchant.** Say what you really **want.**

- This in turn involves an analysis of the components in your product/service which will lead you to finding your **CRITICAL SUCCESS FACTOR(S).**

• THE CRITICAL SUCCESS FACTOR(S)

- Activities that can contribute to big **losses** or big **profits** point to **CRITICAL SUCCESS FACTOR(S)**

- However, on the face of it, identification of CSFs may not be easy and sometimes **survival** can be confused with **success,** i.e.

- Survival is not winning, **but**

- If you don't look after survival you can be left on the rocks, **but**

- If you don't concentrate hard on your CSFs you will not win.

- CSFs lie somewhere in what is called **a value chain;** the chain of activities that **add value** to the product or service. These are broadly: **Research, Design, Development, Production, Marketing, Sales, Distribution.**

- Before the jargon takes over let's look at a couple of examples:

- Mobil Oil's CSF is their ability to find the gushingest, oiliest **holes** in the ground and **own** them; **not** refining the stuff, which may determine survival. The CSF therefore lies in **Research.**

- For Heineken lager their success depends upon reaching the parts other **advertisers** have not reached, hence their CSF lies in **Marketing,** not in the quality of the product, which may determine survival.

- By reducing the activities of your proposed venture to its few absolutely **essential** operations you will reveal its fundamentals.

● These fundamentals must be **strengths;** these strengths are your CSFs and you must concentrate on their promotion and development.

● This is helped by having a **MARKETING STRATEGY.**

●●● INFORMATION CHECK LIST

● THE MANAGER'S HANDBOOK, by ARTHUR YOUNG INTERNATIONAL, pub SPHERE REFERENCE, £9.95.

- ## **MARKETING STRATEGY**

- Surrounding which there is much mystique and no little confusion, largely because it is often muddled with the **MARKETING PLAN** (qv).

- However this definition of marketing strategy may help:

- 'The process by which an organisation satisfies the needs of its **customers,** at a **profit** which satisfies **its** needs.' For very good example:

- In the last century one small business was founded on ideas that did much to clarify marketing strategy:

- The founder's lodestar was **'Five Times R'.**

- Promote to the **right people**
  in the **right way**
  the **right product**
  at the **right price**
  in the **right place**

- The founder's name was **Michael Marks.**

- His business today is known as **Marks & Spencer.**

- Here are some other points that will be helpful:

- **The customer is King.**

- Understanding him is at the core of any marketing strategy. So it follows that

- Anything you do to **distance** yourself from him will cut off your organisation's life-support system. For

- He not only pays you money **today;** by asking

him, directly or indirectly, what:

- He thinks of your **product/service**

- And its **value-for-money**

- He feels about **improvements** or **additions**

- **Unfulfilled needs** he has that you might meet

- **And** responding **positively** you are also ensuring that he will be paying you money **tomorrow.**

- 'The market' is everyone. 'Everyone' is not **your** market. To find out who **is** you have to:

- Break down the market into understandable **chunks** or segments.

- Be reasonably sure that the perceived market(s) have the **money** to afford, and the **need** to buy, your product/service.

- As buyers in different segments are unlikely to be satisfied by the same features you may have to promote **different** features of the same product/service.

- Be ruthless in assessing the **competition.**

- Always **over-estimate** their threat.

- That way you try harder to be better and will probably succeed.

- Find out approximately:

- How big in cash terms is **my** market segment(s)?
- What percentage can **I** reasonably expect to get?
- How long will it take **me** to get it?
- What makes **me** think so?

- Getting market information involves leg work. According to product/service involved sources could include: electoral registers, trade directories, development agency directories, Chambers of Commerce, trade associations and publications dealing with your area of interest.

- Consider **carefully** before using a market research company and ensure that it comes to you **well-referenced.**

- It's, unfortunately, received wisdom that every forecast based on market research will be **wrong** in some way or another but, nevertheless, that research-based judgement at least will help you to be able to **make** strategic decisions.

••• INFORMATION CHECK LIST

- Bone up on the subject by reading, for instance, UNDERSTANDING MARKETING, by ALAN WEST, pub PAUL CHAPMAN, £7.95 and MAKING MARKETING WORK, by GERALD EARLS and PATRICK FORSYTH, a BUSINESS ENTERPRISE GUIDE, pub KOGAN PAGE, £7.99.

- Contact THE INSTITUTE OF MARKETING (062 - 8524922) for further information and copies of their formidable lists of further reading.

- After the strategic analysis is completed you'll need a **MARKETING PLAN** to make it all happen. However, this comes after you've dealt with **FUNDING YOUR VENTURE.**

• FUNDING YOUR VENTURE

- We assume you have to find cash to launch your venture. If not, congratulations, but read on anyway; you may learn something because

- Each financial package is a highly **individual** cake; the successful ones contain some of the following ingredients:

- Clever funders look for committed, confident **people** to invest in, **not** ventures. So

- In **no circumstances** go and see a funder till you have done your **homework.**

- There's a lot of homework to do and it's a test of your commitment.

- The other test homework makes you pass is the **knowledge** test. You can't present a whole, clear picture until you **know.**

- Get a copy of each high street bank's **Business Plan** and **Cashflow Chart.** Inter alia, the Business Plan requires you to describe your service/product, define your market, show how you will beat the competition and ultimately achieve a projected profit figure.

- The Cashflow Chart requires that you set out your idea of the probable inflow and outflow of cash in a given period. The completed Chart will indicate probable **borrowing needs** and **repayment** potential.

- Choose and use the Business Plan and Cashflow Chart forms that make most sense to you, whether or not you actually intend to use the bank(s) concerned. It's the formats you want.

- Complete the forms with **great care.** They are demanding of detail but, if they are rushed and inadequate, you will be dooming your venture to the **waste bin** before it ever sees the light of day.

- Critically, **decide** whether you are going to **buy** or **rent** your property. If you rent you may not **need** any outside funding. (See **ACQUIRING YOUR COUNTRY PROPERTY**).

- Complete the forms **alone.** You must be the first person to see and rectify any **weaknesses** thrown up by the completed forms. Why? Because

- There is nothing so damaging to confidence as for someone else to immediately spot a basic flaw that you've overlooked.

- To complete the forms involves a lot of guessing.

- Make these guesses as informed as possible. Get information, e.g.

- Comparable **companies' accounts** are invaluable sources (every Limited Liability Company has to publish them).

- To understand what you're looking at you'll need some basic accountancy knowledge. See **IN-FORMATION CHECK LIST.**

- We can't construct your Business Plan for you but what you and other interested parties should be looking for is a plan that sensibly demonstrates the **maximum possible reward measured against the minimum degree of risk.**

- Your reading will show you how accountants think which is very useful because

302

- Once you've done the homework, completed the forms and found that the idea still looks viable, your next call is on an **accountant** (and **he** should be the **first** outside person you tell about your venture).

- Accountants can be brilliant but don't count on it.

- Pick a couple by asking around. See them both.

- Select the one who is most on your wavelength.

- **Don't** try to economise with your accountancy. Big firms anyway maybe no more expensive in the long run and, because they're equipped to handle start-ups, will probably be more effective when it's vital — at the **beginning.**

- What do you want of your accountant?

- A constructive (but not over-optimistic) view on your venture and

- A global up-date on the current enterprise scene and an introduction to the appropriate counsel at your Local Enterprise Agency who will give you details.

- Between them, your accountant and the LEA will give you informed information on the present structure of grants, allowances, seed capital, funding guarantees, subsidised consultancy advice, etc. (However don't **rely** on getting a consultancy **guru; they're** invariably too busy to give you the time you need.)

- They should also advise on the best core funding and who to approach for it.

- Your accountant must give you detailed help in

getting your paperwork and proposals polished and absolutely 'right'. (This is, of course, impossible because you're guessing but a clever presentation is the best 'proof' of profits that you can offer.)

- You should insist on your accountant's presence when you meet potential funders.

- (Up-front try and persuade him to operate on a contingency basis: an agreed fee if he actually helps you get the funds, a nominal agreed fee otherwise.)

- Your accountant will be particularly interested to hear that you will be running a business from your home because there are tax aspects.

- Other points he will advise on: whether you should start from scratch or, if available, buy an existing business; what legal form is best for you to trade under (sole trader, limited company, partnership, etc.); tax, VAT, National Insurance, Pensions, Bookkeeping — will you do it or he? — employee obligations and so on.

- As your information-gathering builds so will your self-confidence; soon you will be ready to begin meeting potential funders. However,

- Beforehand, one of the last pieces of homework is to learn more about the banking mind. For reading see **INFORMATION CHECK LIST**. Points:

- Funding is a very political, very **competitive**, game, especially concerning small businesses.

- Bankers believe that they aren't money-lenders any more; they're

- **Problem-solvers.** (If you're fortunate enough to find one of **these** paragons, you've struck gold.)

- They won't make a 'bad' loan however good the security but

- They won't refuse a 'good' loan because there's no security.

- They're amazed at borrowers' lack of knowledge about the range, flexibility and sophistication of the lending packs on offer:

- Overdrafts, HP and mortgages are only the tip of the iceberg.

- Inter alia, there are term loans, participating loans, bill discounting, leasing, factoring, grant, royalty and equity deals, debentures, sale-and-leaseback, interest and capital repayment 'holidays', 'balloons', and so on.

- In short, the right funder can tailor-make **any** money pack you want.

- And **he** should want to: after all, small businesses account for more than **half** the big banks' corporate business. However

- You must know what to ask for.

- Funders can be good friends. Friends sometimes tell you about things you'd sooner not hear. Like

- Failure:

- One in three new ventures go belly-up in the early years.

- Why? Some reasons:

- Incompetence; low profits; bad debts; no cash to meet the bills and consequent credit dry-up; poor or no accounting information to management; failure to foresee or respond to change and inability to cope with adversity.

- All of this reflects on the venturer's **management ability** so that's what funders are obsessed with.

- You are intending to become an entrepreneur so you must, of course, know how to manage your company. See **INFORMATION CHECK LIST** for further reading. This type of reading and your other homework will all go to generate self-confidence and help you to communicate it in the right way.

- Consider what the funder will want to know about **you:** Amongst other things,

- **Background; experience; any qualifications; capacity for personal development; adaptability; family circumstances; health; ability to generate new business, maintain and increase volume, motivate staff; competence in marketing, financial control, organisation and administration; ability to train and delegate.**

- The funder's looking for a lot and in particular he's looking for one other thing he doesn't find as often as he would wish:

- A venturer who's prudent and courageous enough to face up to, and make provision for, the **downside** in his Business Plan and Cashflow Chart.

- The entrepreneur who doesn't do this is a wally.

- Would you invest money in a wally?

306

- You'll have learned from your reading that you want nice **matched packages** that also keep the strain off the venture in its delicate early stages. These include a

- Capital and interest **holiday** up-front; no payback for, say, the first year. Fight for it, it could be crucial, i.e.

- If you need to borrow yet more expensive money from Peter Loanshark to pay Paul Funder you've almost certainly got a terminal problem.

- And talking of expensive money, it's not necessarily clever to borrow very high-interest money for start-ups, so how about really getting the funder on your side by persuading him to **buy shares** in your venture — thus making him a partner?

- What's that: **AAARGH!!!** Yes, we thought that's what you screamed, but consider:

- The funder's unlikely to want majority share control (he usually won't need it. The reason is that in most cases he will also have to make a moderate-interest loan; this will carry safeguard provisions ensuring that the funder is largely protected against downside.).

- Anyway up-front you can negotiate an agreed share buy-back at a certain date under certain circumstances.

- Meantime he may want a **seat** on your board and he certainly will want

- **Monthly budgets** and **management accounts.**

- But then, don't you? You **can't** monitor the health and progress of a business without them.

Also

- If you hit snags he'll listen, advise and support, not cream off monies that really should stay in the business.

- It might **underwrite** the success of your venture in a way that no other method could. And

- If ever you want money again (successful people **always** do) ask yourself which funder's going to fall over himself to ensure you get the money from **him**?

- However, before you eventually find yourself sitting down with the funder of your choice you have to look at the field:

- There are some funding resources more in tune than others with certain types of venture;

- Identify them but do **not** go to them first.

- Try less likely funders first.

- As you will have done your homework immaculately don't be totally surprised if they offer you what you're seeking.

- If not, you will have gained invaluable information on any weaknesses in your proposal and can strengthen accordingly and so complete your preparation for the assault on the summit of **probable** funders.

- Ideally, get two funders genuinely interested and, all other things being equal, go for the one who gives you the best terms. (All other things are **not** equal if the best terms come from someone who makes you uneasy and with whom you feel you may not get on. Be prepared to listen to your intuition on this.)

- You are entitled to, and should insist on, a reasonably speedy answer.

- Delay can come if your potential funder has to ask too many other people higher-up. If so, you are talking to someone who is too low down.

- Either reach the right person or, if this proves difficult, go elsewhere because

- You must always have ready access to the **actual** decision-maker.

- Finally, whilst all of this is going on, you may think you'll need an office. Fair enough and there are usually plenty of nicely furnished ones around, with a pleasant atmosphere, ideal for holding meetings in. Their only cost is the price of a meal or a few drinks and they're called hotels.

••• INFORMATION CHECK LIST

- Read HOW TO UNDERSTAND AND USE COMPANY ACCOUNTS, by ROY WARREN, pub CENTURY HUTCHINSON, £13.95.

- Written by bankers for bankers to better enable them to fund is LENDING PACKAGES FOR SMALL & MEDIUM-SIZED COMPANIES, by ROBBIE, COULBECK and MOULDS, pub CROOM HELM, £8.95.

- Because we've slogged through the text books ourselves it's easy for writers to hector readers to do the same. However, although they have to be read, text books can be heavy going. For an introduction to finance that eases you in more entertainingly try THE BOTTOM LINE, by ALAN WARNER, pub GOWER, £18.50.

- Back to text books again. We've mentioned one manager's handbook; another that takes a different and valuable approach is HANDBOOK OF MANAGEMENT SKILLS, edited by DOROTHY M STEWART, pub GOWER. This pools the knowledge of 25 individuals acknowledged as experts in the field of business. At a hefty £32, however, you may first prefer to give it the once-over at your local large reference library.

- Of course, books on how to be a manager are all very well but, for you who may never have managed before, it's all **theory.** Nevertheless, slogging through them ahead of **hands-on** has two obvious advantages: you'll be able to talk more knowledgeably to your potential funders and the skills **will** be of great use when you get going. So read.

- And perhaps view: BBC ENTERPRISES (01 - 576 0361) offer a range of skills videos. Ask for their current list of **trainers.**

• SELLING YOUR PRESENT HOME

• On the assumption that plans for your venture and its funding are by now firmed up you can address the next challenge, selling your existing house.

• This can be a **traumatic** or **bearable** experience. Which it turns out to be is actually up to you, believe it or not.

• We will guarantee that it will not be traumatic if you first of all get you and yours in to the **right frame of mind** (see below).

• In a residential property **seller's** market you should question whether or not you need an agent (apart from calling in a few to get a line on current prices). Your own board (and just to be a little more eye-catching say **'For Purchase'** instead of the dreary For Sale) and a few well-worded adverts may save you the agent's hefty fees.

• In a **buyer's** market the same advice **can** hold true, only now you have to try a lot harder and take a pessimistic (some call it realistic) view on selling price.

• Remember swings and roundabouts; thus, in a buyer's market, although you're **selling** cheaper, you're also **buying cheaper.**

• If you're going to **rent** not buy your country property you give yourself an even better chance of selling your existing one, being able to take a lower offer; and in a buyer's market even getting these can be tough.

• In short, being greedy at one end and hoping to screw down the buy-in price at the other doesn't

311

work because you will **not** sell, i.e.

- Stalemate — and there's your venture sitting out there waiting, with no place to go.

- So, get several agents' advice on price then aggregate the figure, get the mean and **reduce** the resulting selling price by at least **7½%**, or better and more realistically still, **10%**.

- Before **finalising** your selling price step back and look hard at your property, as a potential purchaser would, and try to see if you are offering **value-for-money:** you may decide that a few hundred pounds could be well-spent on a tidy-up but in no circumstances go berserk and spend thousands — you may never get it back!

- (Sadly, some 'improvements' turn out to have been a waste of money: outdoor swimming pools and crushed strawberry triangular baths for instance can be disadvantages in some buyers' eyes.)

- Do some market research: Who is the most likely buyer for my house? What are its **unique selling factors?** and so on, then

- Consider the expense of a professional to produce **photographs** that handsomely show all the really important aspects of the property.

- Draw up **honest particulars** (one's that don't match the facts will fool no one but you).

- Indicate clearly on the particulars if carpets, curtains, plumbed-in washing machines, cooker, etc., are included in the price.

- Get the details neatly typed up (and **copied** × **12**) and attach pictures and

- Make up into business-like dossiers ready for mailing to enquirers, then

- Remembering that ladies play a decisive role in house-buying, choose your media.

- Set a generous budget for your ads and illustrate them with one of your **pictures** if it says something, special ('one picture's worth a thousand words', remember?).

- Don't waste lineage with burble and hype; emphasise the positive and, crucially, the **fairness** of the price. Also feature your **phone** number and availability precisely. Consider also a full message on your **answerphone.**

- When showing:
- Be welcoming but **business-like**
- Ensure the house is immaculately **clean** but balance this, because every house benefits from looking **lived-in.**
- Emphasise **space, light** and **features.**
- **Don't over-crowd;** husband, wife, the kids, dog **and** your prospects crowding into every room make for an uncomfortable muddle and will leave a messy, negative impression.

- You may have to leave prospects by themselves for a short time so they can talk amongst themselves **so** see that all **valuables** are under **lock and key.**

- Even though it may be convenient for you, don't insist on selling your house with all the **furniture.** Most buyers have their own kit. However, do draw up a list of items that you want to sell, price them fairly and offer a copy as appropriate.

- **Genuine** cash buyers are very rare birds; if you find one take his offer rather than hold out for 'more' money from a chain-trapped prospect.

- But beware the 'dealer' who will offer you probably only ⅔rds of the proper value.

- When it comes to final negotiations agree only **'subject to contract'.** This lets you free if your prospect wants to delay things and another buyer appears.

- Once a signed contract is **exchanged** and a **deposit** laid you're still not quite home and dry, but at least you will benefit from keeping the deposit and having legal rights to sue for shortfall if the purchaser decides to drop out.

- Earlier we mentioned the right frame of mind.

- This in essence depends on living in the **real** world of: fluctuating market prices and keeping abreast of these by being certain that the price for your house is really **competitive;** people who have difficulty in always doing their job efficiently (e.g. estate agents — if you decide to use them, and **conveyancers** or **lawyers** who you have to use whether you like it or not); those who have trouble making up their minds (**prospective purchasers**).

- Learn to live in this world and you will sell your house and the process will be bearable.

- It's only in the world of **fantasy** that trauma breeds.

●●● INFORMATION CHECK LIST

- Whether or not you decide to use an estate agent you should be aware of the very strong concerns expressed by the LAW SOCIETY (01 - 242 1222) regarding your need to protect yourself against the unscrupulous. The Society has published a leaflet DEALING WITH YOUR ESTATE AGENT: HOW TO PROTECT YOURSELF. Free on request.

- As an alternative to a photograph consider using and publishing a **line drawing** of the property. This will give a greater sense of character and desirability. An artist who does this work is JANE ANDERSON (0295 - 710213). An 11″ × 14″ drawing costs £75. After it's copied for the particulars and the ads you have a momento of your former residence.

- Read SOLD — WITH OR WITHOUT AN ESTATE AGENT? by NICHOLAS SAVAGE, pub ELLIOT RIGHT WAY BOOKS (0737 - 832202). £1.99.

- HOW TO MOVE HOUSE SUCCESSFULLY, by ANNE CHARLISH, pub SHELDON PRESS, £3.50; 'a friendly guide that will help reduce the pain', she hopes.

- THE PROPERTY EXCHANGE DIRECTORY (0273 - 608311) will, for a fee, (£175 for houses under £70,000 to £750 for those over £200,000) arrange for you to **swop** your home with someone else wanting to move into your area. By swopping not buying there is a saving on stamp duty, legal and conventional estate agents fees.

- The charity NATIONAL KIDNEY RESEARCH (01 - 928 5058) operates a similar, less expensive scheme, donating £40 per exchange to the charity.

- Did you know that you can gamble on house prices? I G INDEX (01 - 828 5699), the London financial bookmakers, offer a house futures/

hedge service. You hedge by betting on house prices moving **against** you. If they do, the bet has insured your loss (IGI pay out); if prices move **for** you, you lose the bet but gain on the price swing in your favour. However, not cheap.

• ACQUIRING YOUR COUNTRY PROPERTY

- The important thing to say under this heading is that in many rural areas rents are low compared to property capital values so seriously consider taking advantage of this financial imbalance. Two reasons:

- By relieving yourself of the capital commitment of buying you will revolutionise your financial requirement and consequently your **profitability.**

- In a volatile property market you cannot be sure that your property's value will increase. It may go down in value but meantime your **financial repayments** will probably not.

- You may well be able to find the property you want on rental because

- Many would-be sellers are forming the view that they may not be able to sell at their required price. Rather than take too low a sale figure letting out is therefore not unattractive.

- Your lawyer will guide you and confirm that legislation now properly protects both landlord and tenant.

- If the property you want is apparently only 'for sale' don't be deterred from putting up a rental suggestion, and maybe this could be coupled with

- An offer to take an **option to purchase** at some time in the future.

- This way you buy the property **after** you've proven that your business is a success, not before when nothing can be certain.

- Naturally, your intended landlord has to agree to the **business activity** that you intend to operate on his property and any **physical alterations** necessary.

- As between **buying** and **leasing** a property there are tax and other implications so check with your accountant as well.

- Other points to weigh:

- If dealing with an old building that you want to alter and repair you must have another professional, the **architect.**

- Repairs and furbishing will be costly; a good well-referenced architect will be expensive (however, remember his fees are negotiable) but will save you money because he will know the most reliable builders. This guidance could save you from potential

- Disaster. If you hit a **cowboy** builder unprotected you could be wiped out before you even begin.

- The right architect will save precious space and enable you to use everything you have more productively and more attractively.

- In the extreme he will know if it's even **worth** doing up an old building. With building costs the way they are it can sometimes make better sense to demolish and build anew or simply look elsewhere.

- This and other things you will want may involve **Planning Permission.** A good architect will "know" if you are going to get it or not.

- Chasing losers consumes more than money, it also eats time.

- He will also know about grants in detail.

- Your architect may recommend other professionals be involved on your project; e.g. **structural** and **quantity surveyors.**

- This may be the 'old boy' network in action but

- Maybe not. If you can't get independent advice you will have to use your own judgment. (But then a venturer's judgment, his 'nose', is his stock-in-trade.)

- If in doubt better check their references locally and employ them. If **properly briefed,** all your professionals are **insurance** and at the beginning that's worth paying for.

- When homing in on your ideal property be prepared to bargain like the devil on price or rent.

- The best way to get that right figure is to take advice, then make up your mind beforehand to let it **go** if the price is wrong because

- If you rent or buy at too high a price, with high building costs on top, you may be saddling your venture with an unsupportable burden.

- If you get the right place but with more acreage than you could possibly need don't necessarily sell the surplus (not easy anyway) but consider using it as a **Waste Dump.**

- Don't laugh; read the Waste Dump section of **RECYCLING** and see what we mean.

- Under **SPECIAL EFFECTS** (qv) you will find our comments on **Alternative energy sources.** If you can do so we recommend you use these to

319

contain energy costs. However, also consider the possibilities of using spare land to generate extra income by renting the rights to have **windmill energy generators** there. See **INFORMATION CHECK LIST.**

- Finally, if your local **dowser** doesn't charge too much, it's just worth checking to see if by chance your country land has a source of pure, **natural water.** Beneficial either for your own use or, if in sufficient quantity, as a commodity you could bottle and sell.

••• INFORMATION CHECK LIST

- Your solicitor will tell you where you stand as a tenant but get the landlord's point of view by reading PROFITABLE LETTING, by DAVIES & AIDIE, pub FOURMAT PUBLISHING, £9.95.

- Again, even though you will be employing professionals, it always pays to know something about a subject yourself; so, although you're not we trust going to become a farmer in the conventional sense, read PLANNING PERMISSION & THE FARMER, £4.50 from HM STATIONERY OFFICE (see your YELLOW PAGES).

- Similarly, read the Consumer's Association book, GETTING WORK DONE ON YOUR HOUSE, pub HODDER & STOUGHTON, £6.95 How to ensure value for money and, on the downside, how to get compensation.

- If your house is stately(?) enough, check with your architect, or speak to the HISTORIC BUILDINGS & MONUMENTS COMMISSION (also known as ENGLISH HERITAGE) on 01

- 734 6010 re the possibility that the house may be eligible for grant aid for its structural repair costs.

- Even if not that posh your country property is likely to be old and have some interesting history. Read HOW OLD IS YOUR HOUSE?, by P CUNNINGHAM, pub A & C BLACK, £7.95, and TRACING THE HISTORY OF YOUR HOUSE, by P BUSHELL, pub PAVILION BOOKS, £12.50.

- If you're really keen then you'll let those very top people DEBRETT ANCESTRY RESEARCH (0962 - 732676) discover the history of your house and the people who lived there. For a fee, of course. . . .

- See if you can track down THE SHELL BOOK OF THE HOME: DECORATION AND CONSTRUCTION OF VERNACULAR INTERIORS, 1500-1850, by J ARYES, pub FABER, ISBN 0 571 1162 56, and PERIOD STYLE, by J & M MILLER, pub MITCHELL BEAZLEY, £19.95.

- As appropriate contact, e.g., THE GEORGIAN GROUP (Ph: 01 - 377 1722), who run courses on restoration and give advice, e.g. "Old buildings weren't intended to be hermetically sealed; preventing moisture getting in and out causes real damage." So maybe no double-glazing but they will show you how to stop the windows letting in the draught.

- Or THE VICTORIAN SOCIETY (Ph: 01 - 994 1019). In which case read THE COMPLETE VICTORIAN HOUSE BOOK, by ROBIN GUILD, pub SIDGWICK & JACKSON, £19.95.

- Advice from such sources is aimed not just at

preserving your house but doing it in such a way that you will improve its **value.** Poor restoration has the opposite effect.

- Knocking old houses about should only ever be done under expert supervision, e.g. trying to put in a damp course can cause so many problems that it is often not worth the trouble.

- Better construct a cut-off drain nearby which will divert water before it reaches the property.

- Further points can be found under the **Architectural Salvage** section of **RECYCLING; NOSTALGIA** and **SPECIAL EFFECTS.**

- Check with the ALTERNATIVE TECHNOLOGY CENTRE (0654 - 2400) regarding 'growing' windmills for rent in your country acres.

- Finally, a caveat! In your researches you may come across a book called EMPTY QUARTERS: THE LISTED BUILDING OF YOUR DREAMS. Lest you find the title irresistible it may just be worth bearing in mind that this is a catalogue of listed buildings alright — but they're all in various states of **decay.** Financial arms and legs at severe risk here, we're afraid.

- **MARKETING PLAN**

- This involves putting together in fine **detail** 'the means of getting profits from the sale of a product/service', e.g.

- As **definite costs** must at this point be clearly visible, the ballpark (the general price you've been working on) must now give way to precision.

- So what **are** you going to charge the customer?

- Will this be based on **'market penetration'** thinking, therefore a **low price**?

- Or on a **'skimming the cream'** philosophy and **fat margins**?

- What **are** 'low' and 'high' margins to a new business? Analyse.

- In short, most marketing experts agree that for new entrepreneurs the **pricing decision** is the most difficult.

- However, we offer this one clue:

- The price you tag to your product/service is **your** signal to **your** market of the value that **you** place on **your** product/service. Who should know better?

- Precisely what means will be used to transmit what **message**? The **media mix**?

- Within what **budgets**?

- Beware costly campaigns, e.g. **direct mail** (use recycled paper for above-average results) and local advertising **might** be the most **cost-effective** way to go.

- Will you use a **public relations** company?

- If so, they must be well-referenced, **briefed in detail** and **tightly-budgeted.**

- Better still, spend perhaps less money by creating an exciting and worthwhile reason for getting potential customers to come and **meet you and your product/service.**

- If the occasion is made original enough the media will certainly come along; a good editorial is the next best thing to word-of-mouth by satisfied customers.

- Up to now everything has been concerned with dreaming, theorising, spending more and more money and preparing the product/service for the market.

- Now it is time to put it all to the test. And, of course, **it has to work.**

- There are **key elements.** Some of these are:

- **Having yourself and the right people in the right position,**
- **With the right training,**
- **With the right equipment,**
- **At the right time.**

- All too often promotional activity (PR, advertising, etc.) is launched **before** the product/service back-up is properly in place. This is commercial catastrophe in action.

- And your launch budget has been wasted.

- However, good thinking quickly reduces, conceivably even eliminates, a marketing budget.

- The marketing is done for you by your customers because they won't stop talking about it.

- Sounds crazy? Not really because the 'it' they will all be talking about is the best marketing plan of all — your commitment to

- **QUALITY.**

••• INFORMATION CHECK LIST

- Check **MAIL ORDER** for further detailed pointers.

- And (our final) **FINALLY**

- With all the planning in the world you will not be able to foresee every eventuality:

- No one connected with you and your venture will expect you to, so don't burden yourself unduly when the totally unexpected appears out of the woodwork.

- Examine it closely. Is it a genuine difficulty? If so, see it as a challenge to your ingenuity and solve it.

- However, it may not be a difficulty at all:

- Some **golden opportunities** come heavily disguised as **hard work.**

- Another useful tip concerns **sod's law** ('what can go wrong will go wrong').

- This tiresome law **does** operate, particularly in start-ups. Protect yourself against it by building in a **SL Factor:** give yourself 10, 15, even 20% leeway on every task. This method will not stop SL operating but, critically, you will be mentally prepared, so won't be devastated and so will rectify matters more speedily, more effectively.

- Sod's law is not all downside; intelligent people learn and profit from it!

- Also try hard to keep in mind that an awful lot of problems, indeed failure itself, can arise out of the easiest mistake anyone can ever make:

- **Trying to please everybody.**

- Someone once wrote:

FINALLY

> Life's battle doesn't always go
> To the stronger or faster man;
> But sooner or later the man who wins
> Is the fellow who **knows** he can.

● And, we might add, knows that he will win doing it **his way.**

BIBLIOGRAPHY

AGE OF UNREASON, Prof C Handy   5
UK CONSUMER SPENDING
   TRENDS & FORECASTS,
   Euromonitor   6
LEISURE COMPANIES & LEISURE
   MARKETS, Euromonitor   6
THE TIMES ATLAS OF THE
   SECOND WORLD WAR, Times
   Books   15
WORLD FURNITURE, H Hayward   18
SOTHEBY'S CONCISE ENCYCLO-
   PAEDIA OF FURNITURE,
   Conran Octopus   18
THE WHICH? GUIDE TO BUYING
   ANTIQUES, Consumers Assoc   18
MILLER'S ANTIQUE PRICE GUIDE,
   J & M Miller   18
BETTER THAN NEW, A
   PRACTICAL GUIDE TO
   RENOVATING FURNITURE,
   A Jackson   ·18
THE HERB BOOK, J Lust   26, *et al*
ULTRAHEALTH, L Kenton   26, *et al*
SEAWEED — A USER'S GUIDE,
   S Surey-Gent & G Morris   26
BACK ATTACK, Dr E Taylor &
   D D'Costa   26
THE BACK BOOK: HEALING THE
   HURT IN YOUR LOWER BACK,
   M Lettvin   26
BEATING BACK PAIN, Dr J Tanner   26
EXHIBITIONS & CONFERENCES
   DIRECTORY, York Pub   34
CALLIGRAPHERS HANDBOOK,
   ed H Child   36
MORE THAN FINE WRITING, ed
   H Child   36
PEN LETTERING, A Camp   36

AN ILLUSTRATED HISTORY OF
INTERIOR DECORATION, M Praz   52

PERIOD STYLE, J & M Miller   53, *et al*

THE COUNTRY HOME DECORAT-
ING BOOK, M Innes   53

NINETEENTH CENTURY DECO-
RATION, C Gere   53

RAGTIME TO WARTIME, THE
BEST OF 'GOOD HOUSE-
KEEPING 1922 - 1939',
Ebury Press   53

PAINTABILITY, J Innes   53, *et al*

DEBRETT'S ETIQUETTE &
MODERN MANNERS, Pan   58

DEBRETT'S CORRECT FORM,
Futura   58

(DEBRETT'S COMPANY
DIRECTORS)   58

GETTING IT RIGHT — A SURVIVAL
GUIDE TO MODERN MANNERS,
L Graham   58

ENQUIRE WITHIN UPON
EVERYTHING, M Bremner   58

BOOK OF TOTAL SNOBBERY,
L Jones   59

SPEED READING, Buzan   63

SPEED READING — THE HOW-TO
BOOK FOR EVERY BUSY
MANAGER, EXECUTIVE &
PROFESSIONAL, Fink   63

READING DYNAMICS, E Wood;
Nightingale-Conant   63

INCREASED READING SPEED;
Advanced Learning Systems   63

POWER MEMORY, A Butkowsky;
Advanced Learning Systems   63

BETTER CONCENTRATION;
Advanced Learning Systems   63

UNLIMITED MENTAL ABILITY;
Advanced Learning Systems   63

MAXIMISING MEMORY POWER:
   USING RECALL IN BUSINESS,
   A Brown   63
MASTER YOUR MEMORY, Buzan   64
MAKE THE MOST OF YOUR
   MEMORY, Ansell   64
THE MIND OF A MNEMONIST,
   A R Luria   64
YOU CAN REMEMBER, Dr Bruno
   Furst   64
THE DOWNWAVE, R Beckman   68
INTO THE UPWAVE, R Beckman   68
THE GAMBLER'S POCKET BOOK,
   D Spanier   70
HOW TO CHEAT AT CARDS AND
CATCH YOUR FRIENDS DOING IT,
   A D Livingstone   71
13 AGAINST THE BANK, N Leigh   71
THE BIGGEST GAME IN TOWN,
   A Alvarez   71
THE CHANNEL FOUR BOOK OF
   RACING, S Magee   72
BEGINNER'S GUIDE TO HYDRO-
   PONICS, J Sholto Douglas   83
ADVANCED GUIDE TO HYDRO-
   PONICS, J Sholto Douglas   83
THE ROYAL HORTICULTURAL
   SOCIETY GARDENER'S
   ENCYCLOPAEDIA OF PLANTS
   AND FLOWERS   84
THE GARDENING FROM WHICH?
   GUIDE TO SUCCESSFUL
   PROPAGATION; Consumers Assoc   84
HEALTH CARE IN THE HOME,
   Boots The Chemist   97
A BETTER MOUSETRAP, P Bissel   97
PATENTING: THE OPPORTUNITIES
   & PITFALLS, British Technology
   Group   98
THE EATING OUT SURVEY,
   Euromonitor   107

UK FOOD MARKETS, Euromonitor   107

CONVENIENCE & PREPARED
FOODS, Euromonitor   107

THE MICROWAVABLE FOODS
MARKET, Euromonitor   107

HEALTHY FOODS & HEALTHY
EATING, Euromonitor   107

FOOD TRADES DIRECTORY   107

SMOKING FOODS AT HOME,
M Black   107

EDIBLE GIFTS, C Clifton & M Nicholls   108

THE VEGETARIAN EPICURE,
A Thomas   108

FOOD COMBINING FOR HEALTH,
D Grant & J Joice   108

EAT TO WIN, Dr R Haas   108

DELIA SMITH'S COMPLETE
ILLUSTRATED COOKERY
COURSE, D Smith   108

THE READER'S DIGEST
COMPLETE GUIDE TO
COOKERY, A Willan   108

PROFESSIONAL CHEF'S GUIDE TO
KITCHEN MANAGEMENT, Fuller
& Knight   108

APPROACH TO FOOD COSTINGS,
R Kostas   108

FOOD FOCUS 1 & 2; British Food
Information Service   109

COMMON SENSE ABOUT
FOODCARE IN THE KITCHEN;
Food & Drink Federation   109

LANGUAGES IN BRITISH
BUSINESS: AN ANALYSIS OF
CURRENT NEEDS, S Hager   114

STUDY HOLIDAYS, The Central
Bureau   116

SMILE THERAPY, L Hodgkinson   120

ANATOMY OF AN ILLNESS,
N Cousins   120

MIND OVER ILLNESS, N Cousins   121

PRIMAL HEALTH, Dr M Odent 121

QUANTUM HEALING, Dr D Chopra 121

LAUGHTER IN THE AIR, B Took 121

PRESENT LAUGHTER, A Coren 121

NO-ONE ELSE HAS COMPLAINED,
C Freud 122

MAIL ORDER: HOME SHOPPING IN
THE 1980s, Euromonitor 131

BRITISH CODE OF ADVERTISING
PRACTICE; Advertising Standards
Authority 131

DO YOUR OWN ADVERTISING,
A Crompton 132

PRACTICIAL GUIDE FOR
ORGANISING YOUR OWN MAIL
ORDER BUSINESS, L Forshaw 132

SELL IT BY MAIL ORDER: MAKING
YOUR PRODUCT THE ONE THEY
BUY; Wiley 132

SUPERDRIVER, Sir John Whitmore 136

RUNNING YOUR OWN DRIVING
SCHOOL, N Stacey 136

THE DRIVING TEST: ESSENTIAL
INFORMATION, B Stratton 136

LEARNER DRIVER; Fourmost
Training 136

MICROWAVE COOKBOOK 1 & 2;
J B Fairfax 142

GLYNN CHRISTIAN'S MICROWAVE
COOKERY 143

A GUIDE TO MICROWAVE
CATERING, L Napleton 144

UK MUSIC INDUSTRY, Euromonitor 150

GETTING JOBS IN MUSIC, Cassell 150

MUSIC, Dorling Kindersley 151

SOUND SUPPORT ONE;
Nightingale-Conant 151

TETRABIBLOS, Ptolemy 155

I CHING (BOOK of CHANGES) 160

THE BIBLE 164, *et al*

FOOD IN ENGLAND, D Hartley 173

NATIONAL TRUST BOOK OF
FORGOTTEN HOUSEHOLD
CRAFTS, J Seymour   173
KEEPING HOUSE, S Stainton   174
DRAWING ON THE RIGHT SIDE OF
THE BRAIN, B Edwards   176
THE STUDENT BOOK; Macmillan   176
PHOENIX PERSONAL DEVELOP-
MENT COURSE, B Tracy   180
SELF-ESTEEM, POSITIVE SELF-
IMAGE; Advanced Learning Systems   181
RELAXATION, STRESS MANAGE-
MENT; Advanced Learning Systems   181
SELF-CONFIDENCE, ERASING
DOUBT; Advanced Learning Systems   181
MANAGING CHANGE; BBC
Enterprises   181
UK CAMCORDER MARKET
TRENDS, OPPORTUNITIES,
PROSPECTS to 1991, Euromonitor   186
STARTING YOUR OWN PHOTO-
GRAPHY BUSINESS, Schwarz   187
PROMOTING YOURSELF AS A
PHOTOGRAPHER, Rosen   187
GETTING JOBS IN PHOTO-
GRAPHY; Cassell   188
RECYCLED PAPER/PAPER
RECYCLING; Waste Watch   199
RECYCLING POLICY: ONCE IS NOT
ENOUGH; Friends of the Earth   200
PAPER: HOW IT IS MADE, Perrins   200
RECYCLED PAPER-MAKING,
P Brown   200
PAPER BASICS: FORESTRY,
MANUFACTURE, SELECTION,
PURCHASING, MATHEMATICS
and METRICS and RECYCLING,
Saltman   200
RECYCLE IT; Friends of The Earth   201
WASTE & RECYCLING, B James   201

334

DIRECTORY OF ARCHITECTURAL
  SALVAGE COMPANIES; Morgan
  Grampian   202
BARGAIN RENOVATOR'S GUIDE
  TO LONDON; Attica Press   202
HISTORIC HOME OWNERS
  COMPANION, M Saunders   202
PERIOD DETAIL: A SOURCEBOOK
  FOR HOUSE RESTORATION,
  J & M Miller   202
HOUSE RESTORER'S GUIDE,
  H Lander   202
FACTORY SHOP GUIDES   203
PHILLIPS GUIDE TO TOMORROW'S
  ANTIQUES, P Johnson   204
MILLER'S COLLECTABLES PRICE
  GUIDE: Miller Publications   204
20th CENTURY ANTIQUES: HOW
  TO BUY INEXPENSIVELY
  TODAY THE ANTIQUES OF
  TOMORROW, T Curtis   204
COLLECTING PRINTED
  EPHEMERA, M Rickards   204
CONFERENCE BLUE BOOK;
  Spectrum   217
SKI PERFECT, PARTS 1 & 2;
  Taylor Made Films   222
LEISURE DEVELOPMENT IN THE
  UK, Euromonitor   223
SPORTS & SPORTING GOODS,
  Euromonitor   223
FLOORS & MAINTENANCE, Salter   229
PAINT MAGIC, J Innes   230
PARDON'S VIDEOS ON SPECIAL
  DECORATION, L Pardon   230
COLOUR ATLAS OF PLASTERING
  TECHNIQUES, Kenneth, Mills, etc.   230
PLASTERING: A CRAFTSMAN'S
  ENCYCLOPAEDIA, Pegg & Stagg   230
HANDBOOK OF THATCHING,
  N Hall   231

FOLLIES & PLEASURE PAVILIONS,
  G Mott & S S Aall   231

AMDEGA BOOK OF CONSERVA-
  TORIES, Bradburn   231

SELF-BUILDER, Snelgar   231

NEGLECTED ALTERNATIVE —
  SELF-BUILD HOUSING; Poly
  of S Bank   231

BUILDING YOUR OWN HOME,
  M Armor   231

FOCUS ON ALTERNATIVE
  ENERGY, McGlory   231

NATURAL HOUSEBOOK, D Pearson   231

WORLD ENERGY, Euromonitor   232

ALL ABOUT TEA (2 vols),
  W H Ukers   238

CULTURE & MARKETING OF TEA   238

FILE ON TEA, Tea Council   238

HEALTHY DRINKS REPORT; Tea
  Council   238

A JAPANESE TOUCH FOR YOUR
  HOME, Koju Yogi   238

THE TEA CEREMONY, Japanese
  Centre, London   239

ZEN IN THE ART OF THE TEA
  CEREMONY; CHADO — THE
  JAPANESE WAY OF TEA, Japanese
  Centre, London   239

CONSTANCE SPRY COOKERY
  BOOK, J M Dent   239

ECCENTRIC TEAPOT, G Clark   240

BE YOUR OWN BOSS, D Lewis   245

YOUR TELEPHONE PERSON-
  ALITY: Ibis Information Services   245

GUIDE TO EFFECTIVE
  TELEPHONE TECHNIQUES,
  Pemberton   245

PHONE POWER, G Walther   245

THE COMPLEAT METEOR-
  OLOGIST, Mead   249

SOTHEBY'S WORLD WINE
· ENCYCLOPAEDIA, T Stevenson 255
STORY OF WINE, H Johnson 255
A TASTE OF ENGLISH WINE,
H Barty-King 255
DIRECTORY OF WINE SOCIETIES
and COURSES, P Barbour 255
1990 WHICH? WINE GUIDE,
Consumers Assoc 256
WORLD GUIDE TO WHISKY,
M Jackson 256
ALMANAC OF SCOTCH WHISKIES,
W Milroy 256
SCOTCH & WATER, N Wilson 256
WHISKY DISTILLERIES OF THE
UNITED KINGDOM, A Barnard 256
ALCOHOLIC DRINKS IN THE UK,
Euromonitor 257
WRITERS & ARTISTS YEAR
BOOK; A & C Black 261
WRITERS HANDBOOK, B Turner 261
HOW TO WRITE FOR PUBLICA-
TION, McAllum 262
BECOMING A WRITER, ed Chapple 262
YES! YOU CAN WRITE! E Neeld 262
LIVING CHOICES, Good House-
keeping/Open University 290
MANAGERS HANDBOOK, Arthur
Young International 296
UNDERSTANDING MARKETING,
A West 299
MAKING MARKETING WORK,
G Earls & P Forsyth 299
HOW TO UNDERSTAND & USE
COMPANY ACCOUNTS, R Warren 309
LENDING PACKAGES FOR SMALL
& MEDIUM-SIZED COMPANIES,
Robbie, Coulbeck & Moulds 309
THE BOTTOM LINE, A Warner 310
HANDBOOK OF MANAGEMENT
SKILLS, ed D Stewart 310

DEALING WITH YOUR ESTATE
AGENT: HOW TO PROTECT
YOURSELF, The Law Society   315
SOLD — WITH OR WITHOUT AN
ESTATE AGENT?, N Savage   315
HOW TO MOVE HOUSE SUCCESS-
FULLY, A Charlish   315
PROFITABLE LETTING, Davies
& Aidie   320
PLANNING PERMISSION & THE
FARMER, HM Stationery Office   320
GETTING WORK DONE ON YOUR
HOUSE, Consumers Assoc   320
HOW OLD IS YOUR HOUSE?,
P Cunningham   321
TRACING THE HISTORY OF YOUR
HOUSE, P Bushell   321
SHELL BOOK OF THE HOME:
DECORATION & CONSTRUCTION
OF VERNACULAR INTERIORS
1500-1850, J Ayres   321
COMPLETE VICTORIAN HOUSE
BOOK, R Guild   321
EMPTY QUARTERS: THE LISTED
BUILDING OF YOUR DREAMS,
Save Britain's Heritage   322

PERIODICALS

THE GLOBE & LAUREL   15
MARS & MINERVA   15
PEGASUS   15
COMBAT   15
ANTIQUE   18
ANTIQUE CLOCKS   18
ANTIQUE COLLECTING   18
ANTIQUE & COLLECTORS FAYRE   18
THE ANTIQUE DEALERS &
COLLECTORS GUIDE   18
THE ANTIQUE COLLECTOR   18
ANTIQUE TRADES GAZETTE   18
GP (US)   23

HERE'S HEALTH 26
SHAPE (US) 27
CRAFTS 34
THE CRAFTS REPORT (US) 34
The ASIAN WALL STREET
    JOURNAL 43
DESIGN 52
DESIGNERS JOURNAL 52
THE FINANCIAL TIMES 67
THE INVESTOR'S CHRONICLE 67
GROWER 85
FUTURE & THE INVENTOR 97
NEW PATENTS BULLETIN 97
CATERING 107
FOOD & DRINK 107
CATERER & HOTELKEEPER 107
THE LINGUIST 114
WHAT TO BUY FOR BUSINESS 146
JAZZ JOURNAL INTERNATIONAL 151
THE MUSIC TIMES 151
CLASSICAL MUSIC 151
MUSIC TEACHER 151
PSYCHIC NEWS 166
SPIRITUALIST GAZETTE 166
THE PHOTOGRAPHER 187
THE PHOTOGRAPHIC JOURNAL 187
IMAGE 187
PAPER FOCUS 199
WASTE PAPER NEWS INTER-
    NATIONAL 199
BUILDING REFURBISHMENT 202
TRADITIONAL HOMES 202
THE EPHEMERIST 204
SKI SURVEY 222
SKIING UK 222
WEATHER 249
JOURNAL OF METEOROLOGY 249
DECANTER 256
GRAPE PRESS 256
THE AUTHOR 261
WRITERS MONTHLY 261

ACKNOWLEDGEMENTS TO THE FOLLOWING WHO ASSISTED WITH OR ARE REFERRED TO IN THE TEXT

Gallup Polls Ltd	Intro
Henley Centre for Forecasting	Intro
Elizabeth, Lady Ashcombe, exclusive furniture maker	5
Mr & Mrs John Docker, dried flower producers	5
Lady Henrietta Gelber, fabric & wallpaper designer	5
Stephanie Donaldson & her Classes in a Country House	5
Christie's, auctioneers	5
Savill's, estate agents	5
Mr & Mrs MacLeod Matthews, herb growers	6
The Duchess of Devonshire, jams & chutneys producer	6
Viscount & Viscountess Cobham, business impresarios	6
Euromonitor, researchers	6, *et al*
The British Library	6, *et al*
OwnBase, home-workers' newsletter, club	6
Home-Start Consultancy, relocation easers	7
National Homeworking Unit	7
Schoolplan UK Ltd	7
Key Note, market researchers	8
Hilton Hotels	13, *et al*
Motivaction, activity specialists	13, *et al*
Trust House Forte	14, *et al*
Air Foyle Escapades, aerial special events	14
Gower's Clyne Farm Activity Centre, activity specialists	14
Outward Bound Trust, activity specialists	14
British Activity Holidays Assoc	14
Model Shop, wargames specialists	14

340

Model Masters, model makers 15
The Sports Council 15
Scalemead Arms Co Ltd 16
Sotheby's, auctioneers 18
British Antique Furniture Restorers
   Assoc 19
West Dean College of Arts 19
Victoria & Albert Museum 19
The Alternative Technology Centre,
   energy specialists 25, *et al*
Backswing Machines Ltd, therapy
   machines 25
Contactos Trading Corp, play machines 26
The Back Store Ltd, therapeutic
   equipment 26
National Back Pain Assoc 26
Royal Society of Arts 27
The Aquatic Exercise Assoc (US) 27
The Daniel Hotel & Spa (Israel) 27
Splashdance Ltd 27
The Rural Development Commission 33, *et al*
The Welsh Development Agency 33
The Scottish Development Agency 33
The Northern Ireland Industrial
   Development Agency 33
The Crafts Council 34
Contemporary Applied Arts, customer/
craftsman liaison 34
The Perfect Glass Shop, purveyors of
   recycled glass artefacts 34
College of Heralds (aka College of Arms) 36
The Calligraphy Centre 36
Society of Scribes & Illustrators 37
The British Computer Society 41, *et al*
Computing Services Assoc 42
Comprix Courseware, video interactive
   trainers 42
Maltron Keyboards 42
The Prisoner Appreciation Society
   ('6 of 1') 46
Portmeirion Hotel & Resort 46

ACKNOWLEDGEMENTS

The Prisoner Information Service	46
The Prisoner Shop	46
Elvisly Yours Emporium	46
Stagecraft, trainers in stage craft	47, *et al*
The Tate Gallery	51
The Design Council	52
Leeds Polytechnic	52
The Design Museum, London	53
Robertson Nash Textiles, commission weavers	53
Apple Computers Inc	53
C & J Antich Textiles, commission weavers	53
Nicola Wingate Saul, print room artist	53
The National Trust	54
Five Five Six Antiques, creators & purveyors of dummy boards	54
Nigel Dempster	56
The Historic Houses Assoc	57
The Polite Society	58
Leslie Kark, Lucie Clayton Grooming & Modelling School	58
Lady Style, etiquette guru	58
Ivor Spencer, The School for Butlers	58
The Guild of Professional Toastmasters	58
Nightingale-Conant (US), purveyors of self-improvement courses	63, *et al*
Gernella Communications Ltd, fast reading laboratory	63
London College of Business, speed-writing teachers	63
Advanced Learning Systems, self-improvement specialists	63
The Stock Exchange, London	66
Financial Times Business Information Ltd	67
Lamont & Partners, financial advisors	67
Gambler's Book Club (US)	71
Pro-Punter (DGA Software), purveyors of expert punting systems	72
Innovations, Mail Order sales	72

The British Gaming Academy, dealing
trainers   72

The British Gaming Board   72

Ladbroke plc, bookmakers   73

Macintosh School of Architecture,
Glasgow   78

National Aeronautics & Space Administration (NASA, US)   78

Dungl Centre Health Spa (Austria)   79

Rank Organisation plc   82

International Society of Soilless
Culture (Holland)   83

Institute of Horticultural Research   83

Food & Agriculture Organisation (FAO)   83

R Harris-Mayes, Cothi Engineering,
computer interface specialists   84

The Herb Society   84

New York Dept of Agriculture &
Markets (US)   84

Dr Peter Wilde, English Floral
Fragrances   85

D & D Bristow (Partners), purveyors of
exotic plants and trees   85

Dr Roger Leakey, Institute of Terrestrial
Ecology   85

Prof Malcolm Elliott, Leicester
Polytechnic   85

Daphney MacCarthy, British Food
Information Service   86

Agricultural Training Board   86

Institute of Horticulture   86

Antii Nurmesniemi, artist & designer   93

Boots The Chemists   93

Oscar Woollens Interiors International   97

Interlübke, furniture manufacturers   97

Harrods   97

The Design Centre   97

Society of Metaphysicians   97

Institute of Inventors & Patentees   97

Inventerprise Ltd, invention assessors   98

ACKNOWLEDGEMENTS

Association of Invention Managers
(AIM) 98
British Technology Group 98
Food Trade Press 107
City & Guilds of London Institute 109, *et al*
Hotel & Catering Training Board 109
Good Housekeeping Institute 109
Manchester Business School 113
Centre for Information on Language
Teaching & Research (CILT) 114
Institute of Linguists 114
Language Export Centre 115
British Institute of Management 115
Berlitz Schools of Languages Ltd 115
Council for the Accreditation of
Correspondence Colleges 115
The BBC 115, *et al*
The Esperanto Centre & Club 115
Assoc of Translation Companies 116, *et al*
Animatur (Spain), staff trainers 118
Dr Argyle, Oxford University 119
Dr John Chesney, Central Nottingham,
Health Authority 120
Jackson Lane Improvisation Workshop 123
Oval House Improvisation Workshop 123
British Rate & Data (BRAD) 131
British List Brokers Assoc 132
The Post Office 132
Department of Transport 135
The Driving Centre, instructor trainers 135
Driving Instructors Assoc 135
Institute of Advanced Motorists 135
The High Performance Club 135
The High Performance Course, driving
skill testers 135
Driving Management Ltd, driving skill
trainers 135
Bill Gwynne Rally School 136
All Wheel Drive Club 136
Rough Terrain Training School 136
Off Road Training Assoc 136

Royal Automobile Club 136

RDM Test Equipment Ltd, purveyors of
microwave testing equipment 142

Tricia Barker, Beaconsfield Microwave
School 142

Pamela Sparrow, microwave cookery
expert 142

Institute of Home Economics 143

Oxo Microwave Advisory Service 143

Lakeland Plastics, purveyors of
microwave cookware 143

Micro Cuisine Ltd, purveyors of
microwave cookware 143

Anchor Hocking, manufacturers of
microwave cookware 143

Royal Festival Hall 149

National Children's Wind Orchestra
Charity 149

Royal Academy of Music 150

Guildhall School of Music & Drama 150

Johnny Dankworth School 151

Incorporated Society of Musicians 151

Music Retailers Assoc 151

Mr & Mrs David Johnston, Musicale,
teachers of music 151

Theosophical Society 154

Society for Psychical Research 154

Wall St Journal 159

The Sorcerer's Apprentice, purveyors of
occult items 166

Mysteries Bookshop, purveyors of
occult items 166

Watkins Books, purveyors of occult items 166

W H Smith plc 166

Dot Griffiths aka Madame Morgana,
teacher of witchcraft 167

Dennis Severs & his Huguenot House,
Spitalfields 171

Spitalfields Trust & their Rodinsky
Room 172

Dicken's Old Curiosity Shop, London 172

ACKNOWLEDGEMENTS

National Trust for Scotland & their Georgian House, Edinburgh	172
The Tenement House, Glasgow	172
The Georgian House, Bristol	172
Flambard's Triple Theme Park, Cornwall	172
Reminiscence Centre, Blackheath	172
Guild of Guide Lecturers	173
Theatre Museum, London	173
Society of Genealogists	173
Metropole Hotel, Llandrindod Wells, Wales	173
Stapleford Park Country Hotel	174
Chilston Park Country Hotel	174
Tulloch Lodge Country Hotel	174
Brian Tracy and The Training College, personal development trainers	180
Canon (UK) Ltd	186
British Institute of Professional Photography	187
Assoc of Cinematograph, Television & Allied Technicians (ACTT)	187
Royal Photographic Society	187
Assoc of Fashion, Advertising & Editorial Photographers	187
Museum of the Moving Image, London	188
Mr & Mrs Jorge Lewinski, artists in photography	188
Rapid Results College, London	188
New York Institute of Photography	188
The Picture House, make-over specialists	189
Lord & Lady Guernsey	193
Shanks & McEwan plc	193
Jane Mansfield, recycled paper-maker	199
Community Support Anti-Waste Scheme (CSAWS)	200
Independent Waste Paper Processors Assoc	200
Cardiff, UK 2000 Recycling City	201
National Assoc of Waste Disposal Contractors	201
Aluminium Can Recycling Assoc	201

British Steel Tinplate   201
London Architectural Study Collection
    at English Heritage   203
Thirties Society   203
National Federation of Demolition
    Contractors   203
Alexa Rugge-Price of Mistakes, a posh
    recycler   203
Ann Lingard, Rope Walk Antiques   204
Ephemera Society   204
Assoc of Conference Executives   217
Expo-Sure, specialist insurance brokers   217
Neil Williams and his Snow & Ice Arena
    (Australia)   219
Biosphere 2 (US), space experiment   220
Piet Denksen & his Center Parc, covered
    holiday resort   220
Institute of Ecotechnics, London   222
Prof Keith Runcorn, Newcastle
    University   222
Richard Cass, Cass Associates, architect
    in winter sports   222
Ski Club of Gt Britain   222
British Assoc of Ski Instructors   222
National Skating Assoc of Gt Britain   222
English Curling Assoc   223
Phillip Bixby, Constructive Individuals
    Ltd, house self-build trainer   227
Construction Industry Training Board   228
Guild of Master Craftsmen   229
Building Conservation Trust   229
H & R Johnson Tiles   229
W B Simpson & Sons, also tile specialists   229
Tony Herbert, advisor on history of tiles
    & ceramics   229
Society for the Protection of Ancient
    Buildings   229
National Assoc of Master Masons   229
National Society of Master Thatchers   230
Thatching Advisory Service   230
Thatchers (Marketing) Ltd   230

ACKNOWLEDGEMENTS

Rockwell International Group	230
British Wind Energy Assoc	231
Tea Council	238
Mrs Takahashi, conductress of the Japanese Tea Ceremony	239
Michael Birch, international teacher of the Japanese Tea Ceremony	239
Ure Senke Foundation	240
Whittards, purveyors of fine teas	240
Meteorological Office	248
Reading University	248
Royal Meteorological Society	248
English Vineyard Assoc	256
Wine & Spirit Education Trust	256
John & Wallace Milroy of the Soho Wine Market, purveyors of fine wine & whisky	257
Scotch Whisky Assoc	257
Robert McKee, guru in the art of screen-writing	259
Rupert Downing, journalist, broad-caster, novelist & playwrite. RIP	260
Society of Authors	261
Institute of Journalists	261
Crime Writers Assoc	261
Romantic Novelists Assoc	261
David & Charles' Writers College	262
Institute of Translation & Interpreting	262
City University, London	262
Book House Training Centre, trainers in publishing	263
Amstrad plc	274
IBM Corp	274
Jack Mitchell, Psychological Pressure Points Ltd	290
Mobil Oil Co Ltd	295
Heineken Lagers	295
Marks & Spencer plc	297
Institute of Marketing	299
BBC Enterprises Ltd	310
Jane Anderson, artist	315

Property Exchange Directory, organisers
   of house-swops   315
National Kidney Research Charity   315
I G Index, dealers   315
Historic Buildings & Monuments
   Commission for England   320
English Heritage   320
Georgian Group   321
Victorian Society   321
Debrett Ancestry Research Ltd   321

INDEX

A

Abseiling, 11, 13

Accounts, 40, 127, 302, 307

Accountant(s), 43, 145, 303, 318

Acquiring your Country Property, 1, 218, 319

Acreage, acres, 3, 77, 82, 254, 319

Adams, A, 188

Adam & Eve, 122

Aerobics, 21

Age of Enlightenment, 251

Air Pursuits, 267

Allen, Woody, 121

Alternative
 – energy, 227
 – Technology Centre, 25, 228, 322
 – technology, 22, 231
 – therapy, healing, 24, 161

American War of Independence, 236

Amstrad, 274

Animal exotics, 267

Anon, 57

Answerphone, 244

Antique(s), 17, 268
 – Tomorrow's, 197, 204

Arad, Ron, 51

Archery, 12, 14

Architect, 318

Architectural Salvage, 195
 – yard, 196

Aristotle, 163

Armour, 30

Art Gallery, 176

Assault coursing, 14

Astrology, 155, 156
 – Conception theory of, 156
 – Chinese, 157

Auctions, 198

Ayran,
- bars, 104
- drink, 104

B

Babbage, Charles, 87
Baby breathing monitor, 90
Back
- chair, 24, 26
- problems & therapy, 22-26
Bailey, David, 188
Baird, J Logie, 96
Balance Sheet, 66
Baldness Cure, 90
Batman, 122
Battle, 11, 12, 13, 16
- games, 12, 15
- terrain, 12, 15, 30, 34
Beaumarchais, P-A C de, 120
Beauty, 146
Bedford, Duchess of, 235
Bedside table, 93, 97
Bell, Alexander, 241
BES (Business Expansion Scheme), 149
Biofuels, 228
Biosphere, 220, 222
Biscuits, 6
Blackjack, 72
Blavatsky, Helena, 154
Blechynden, Richard, 235
Blindfold, 214
Blowing – hot-and-cold-test, 289
Blue Badge, 172
Book   – design, 36
          – illustration, 36
Bookfinder(s), 18, 64, 71
Bored, 243
Borrowing needs, 287, 301
Brick (floor), 225

Bridge, 70
Brochure, 129
BSc (Bachelor of Science), 248
Butlers, 57, 58
  – School for, 58
Butler/Administrators, 57, 58
Buyer's Market, 311

C

Camcorder(s), 183
Camera, 183
Camp craft, 14
Car
  – accessories shop, 134
  – anti-hijack, 136
  – buying, 134
  – crammer courses, 134
  – criminal attack, 133
  – driving test, 133
  – E European, 134
  – 4WD, 134
  – old, 134
  – racing, 133, 134
  – radio recorder, 89
  – rally, 133
  – skid control, 133, 137
  – sub-agencies, 134
  – syphoning, 94
  – tank cap, 94
  – vizor, 94
  – women mobile security, 136
Card Index, 101
Cards, commemorative, 35
Carpets, 17, 29, 50
Cartier-Bresson, H, 188
Cartomancy, 157
Casino(s), 69, 70, 72
  – mobile, 73
Catherine, Queen, 235

Ceramics, 29, 32, 35
Certificates, 12, 215
Chado (The Way of Tea), 234
Charles I, 164
Charles II, 235
Chase Manhattan Bank, 159
Chasitsu (tea room), 235
Chauffeur, 57, 134
Cheques, bounced, 130
Chess, 70
Ch'i, 159
Children's food, 104
China, painting, 5
Chip-smoked foods, 102
Chiropody, 146
Chutneys, 6
Clairvoyant, 158
Clangers, 196
Clay Pigeon (shooting), 12, 14
Cleese, John, 122
Climate — controlled, 220
Climbing, 13, 14
Clocks, 6, 18
Coat of Arms, (service) 36
Collage maker, 30
Commodity trading, 66
Computers, 39-43, 50, 53, 77, 84, 87, 94, 101,
    273-275
Confuscius, 160
Conservatory, 5, 226, 231
Consultancy, 40, 49
Cookery books, 106, 108, 141, 239
Cooking, 99, 139
Copernicus, Nicolaus, 155
CTP (Correct Telephone Personality), 241
Correspondence course, 115
Cosindas, Marie, 188
Counselling, 146
Country house hotels, 268
Country pubs, 269
Country restaurants, 270

Coven, 167
Coward, Noel, 45
Cowboy builder, 318
Craftsman(men), 6, 29, 32, 33, 34, 95, 97
  – cooperative, 33
Credit line, 69
CSFs (Critical Success Factors),
Crossbow, 12
Crystal gazing, 157
Curling, 221, 222
Curtains, 49, 50

D

Dad's Army, 122
Damp Course, 322
Dandalos, Nick 'The Greek', 70
Darts, 70
Dean, James, 45
Decay, 322
Decision-maker, 290
Decision process, 290
Decor, 118, 209
  – decoratively, 209
Degas, 31
De-jargonising, 260
Dice, 72, 160
Diploma of Education, 150
Direct Mail, 129, 323
Disabled, 93, 209
Disraeli, Benjamin, 87
Divination, see Mysteries, 153
Dixon, Jeane, 154
Downside, 306, 307, 327
Dowse(r), 158, 320
  – (ing), 158
Drake, Sir Francis, 122
Draughtsman, 95
Dried flowers, 5
Drink, 211

Drunk, 212
Dummy Board, 51, 54

E

Earpe, Wyatt, 45
East India Company, 235
Edible Flowers, 81, 85
 – Gifts, 104
Education, 1, 7
Edward III, 55
Einstein, Albert, 179
Ennever, W J, 62
Ephemera, 198, 204
Erce, 153
Esperanto, 113, 115, 116
Evander, 164
EIS (Executive Information System), 39
ESP (Extra-sensory perception), 165

F

Fabric, 5
Falkland, 2nd Viscount, 164
Fancy Dress, 45
Fantasy, 314
Farming, 75, 271
Fellow, 187
 – ship, 187
Fencing, 11
Feng Shui, 158
Fields, W C, 119
Financial repayments, 301, 317
Flat Pack, 95
Floors, 53
     painted-, 225
Fountain Sculpture, 29
Franchise, 149, 151, 220, 227
Fraud, 154

Freephone, 130
Freepost, 130
Freud, Sigmund, 161, 163
Fu Hsi, Emperor, 160
Furniture, 5, 6, 17, 18, 19, 29, 32, 53, 92, 97
Fusion Power, 228
Futures, 66

G

Gaia, 153
Galbraith, J K, 68
Gall, Dr F J K, 163
Games, 70
Garnet, William, 188
Garway's Coffee House, 233
Gay, John, 277
Geller, Uri, 154
Genealogical trace service, 171, 173
Geomancy, 155
Gilding, 49
Glass, 17, 30
    stained-, 29, 32
    recycled, 30, 34
Grants, 37, 101, 131, 303, 319, 321
Graphic Design, 36
Graphology, 160
Green, 2, 193, 194
Griffiths, Dot, 167
Growing Things, 271
Guest Speakers, 217
Guillotin, Dr J B V, 88
Guillotin, Dr J I, 88
Guns, 6
  – hand, 11

H

Haas, Dr Robert, 105

Hair (care), 146
Halliday, Doc, 45
Handbags, 6
Handicapped, 43
Handley, Tommy, 122
Haruspicy, 154
Hay, Dr William, 105
  – System, 105
Health, 1
  – books, 25
  – care, 146
  – foods, 105
  – magazines, 26
  – shop, 25
  – -y eating, 105
Hedge (your bet), 316
Herbs, 6, 22, 26, 80, 81, 83, 84
  – -alists, 79
  – -al bath, 22
  – deep frozen, 80
  – delivery service, 80
Heritage, 17
Hiro, photographer, 188
Hitler, Adolph, 155
Hit List, 7, 39, 50, 75, 77, 265
Home, David, 154
Homework, 7
Hood, Robin, 47
Horoscopes, 156
Horse riding, 11, 14
    wooden-, 11
Hot rock power, 228
Hugs, 25
Hydromancy, 154
Hydroponics, 76, 77, 78, 79, 83, 86, 253, 254

I

IBM Computers, 274
Ice Skating, 221

Importing wine, 253
Infirmity field, 93
Inflatable brolly, 94
Instant plants, 82
Insurance, 275, 319
   – broker, 217, 276
   – companies, 275, 276
Iridology, 161
Isolation, 6

J

James, Clive, 122
James, Jesse, 45
Jams, 6
Japanese market, 210
Jardine Group, 159
Jargon, 66
     (de-ising), 260
Jazz, 149, 150, 151
Jewellery, 29, 32
Jogging, 21,
     stationary-, 118
Johnson, Dr Samuel, 83
Jokes, 119
Journalism (ists), 259
Jung, Carl, 161, 162
Junk, 195, 201, 268
   – bonds, 66

K

Karate, 11
Kayaking, 11, 14
Kennedy, J F, 61, 154
Keyboard skills, 40, 41, 42
Key elements, 324
Kilims, 50
Kitchen Factory, 271

Kitchenalia, 198, 204
Knitwear, 29

L

Ladies, 4, 13, 133, 136
  – (decisive role), 313
Lauda, Niki, 79
Laurel (Stan) & Hardy (Oliver), 122
Lawyers, 276, 277, 278
Lee, Bruce, 159
Leech, 91
LCG (Licentiate of the City & Guilds), 199
LRAM (Licentiate of the Royal Academy of
    Music), 150
Lighting, 53, 209
Life-plan, 287, 288
Lincoln, Abraham, 259
Litchfield, Lord, 188
Loan, bad, 305
    good-, 305
Lone Ranger, The, 45
Losses, 295
Loudmouth, 56
Lu Yu, writer, 234

M

Magna Carta, 122
Mahjong, 70
Mail Order, 13, 25, 36, 92, 106, 125, 238
Make-overs, 185, 189
Management buy-outs, 66
  – cop-out, 241
Manufacturers Agent, 32
Marble, 35
  – floors, 225
Marbling, 49
Market penetration, 323

Marks, Michael, 297
Marks & Spencer, 297
Martial arts, 16
MA (Master of Arts degree), 52
MBA (Master of Business Administration), 113
MSc (Master of Science degree), 248
Matisse, 31
Marx, Groucho, 119
McGoohan, Patrick, 46
Mead, G H, 177
Media, 127, 128, 323
Memorabilia, 30, 46
Memory, 62
Merchant Banking, 66
Metoscopy, 163
Micropropagation, 82
    tree plantlets, 85
Microwave Cookery, 271
Mili, Gjon, 188
Miniature (exotics), 82, 85
  – gardens, 80
Mix, Tom, 45
Miyake, Issey, 51
Mondeville, Dr Henri de, 118
Monroe, Marilyn, 45, 154
Morgan, J P, 65, 155
Moses, 122
Mountaineering, 11, 14
Murder evenings, 6
Music, 6, 21, 27, 77, 149-151
Mystique, 31

N

Napoleon, 12
Necromancy, 155
Nesting Tables, 93
New food, 82
Newton, Sir Isaac, 155
Niche, market, 40, 82

Niépce, J-N, 183
Nixon, Richard, 45
Numbered accounts, 66

O

Occult, the, 153
  – -ists, 153
  – -ism, 153
Oil essences, 81, 85
OK Corral, the, 45
Oneiromancy, 155, 161
On-the-spot professional, 145
Option (trading), 66
  – to purchase, 1, 317
Organic, 77, 236
Orienteering, 11, 14
Osteopathy, 24

P

Packaging, 102, 130
Paint brushes, throwaway, 91
Pallas, 164
Palmistry, 162
Paper-making, recycled, 191, 192, 199, 200
Paranormal, 166
Parapsychology, 165
Patents, 87, 95, 97, 98
Pellosotherapy, 24, 26, 27
Pelmanism, 62
Penn, Irving, 188
People business, the, 207, 212
Permasnow, 219
Perillos of Athens, 88, 96
Personal Development, 25, 177-181
PEP (Personal Equity Plan), 66
Pespedisology, 162
Pet carrier/home, 88

Phal'aris, tyrant of Sicily, 88, 96
Pharaoh, 122
PhD (Doctor of Philosophy), 248
Photography, 29, 183-189
Phrenology, 163
Physiognomy, 163
Physiotherapy, 24
Pianos, 6
Pilferage, 269, 271
Pistols, 12
Plant supply service, 79, 80
Plasma (power), 228
Plaster mouldings, 226, 230
Pleasure Principle, 117
Plumbing, 209
Poker, 71, 72
Pollution, control of, 194
Pony & trap, 212
Porcelain, 17
Portraits, 29
Power boom, 228
Presley, Elvis, 45, 46
Pricing decision, 323
Print Room, 50, 53, 54
Prisoner, The, 45, 46
Profit(s), 2, 3, 286, 297
 – ability, 317
Psychic, 154
Public speaking, 217
Punto Banco, 72
Pyromancy, 155

Q

Quality, commitment to, 325
Quorn, new food, 82
Quick dressing, 94

R

Rabelais, Francois, 117
Race tracks, 70, 72, 73
Racing, 72
Ragging & dragging, 49
Reagan, Ronald, 45, 155
Real World, 314
Recycling, 6, 77, 191, 268
 – mighty industry, 191
Reincarnation, 153
REM (rapid eye movement), 161
Renaissance, The, 149
Rent(al), 1, 3, 12, 42, 275, 311
    flexi-, 146, 147
    -ing out, 105, 127, 141, 142, 317
Repayment Holiday, 305
Research, 6, 8, 107, 126, 131, 150, 223, 299
Residential Care/Nursing Homes, 271
Reward Concept, 288
Richard II, 55
Rifle, 11, 12
Robots, redundant, 197, 198
Rockefeller, J D, 65
Rogers, Will, 277
Rolls-Royce, 145, 274
Roulette, 71, 72
Royalties, 95
Rugs, 17, 29, 50

S

Saddlery, 29
Salad, 81
    Hedgerow-, 81
    Miner's-, 81
Sales counter, 186
Salisbury, 4th Earl of, 87
Samurais, 235
Satanism, 153

SR (Saturday Richmond) Formula, 283, 285, 286
Screen painting, 49
Sculpture, 29
Scumbling, 226
Seaweed, 24, 26, 76
Seconds, 197, 203
Second-string business, 248
Self-build housing, 227, 231
Seller's market, 311
Selling your Present Home, 2, 311-316
Seminar, 3, 25, 45, 180, 205-218
    transition-, 290
Sen Rikyu, 238
Shakespeare, W, 122, 276, 289
Shamrock organisation, 5
Share buy-back, 307
Shaver light, 89
Shirts, 29
Shoes, 29
Shooting, 11
Shop, 33
Sick building syndrome, 78, 84
Side table, 92
Silk, painting, 5
Silver, 17, 29
  – smith, 34
Skiing, 219, 222
Skimming the cream, 323
Slate (floors), 225
Small arms, 12
Smith, W Eugene, 188
Snooker, 70
Snow & Ice, 219-223, 269
Snowdon, Lord, 188
Sod's law, 327
Solar power, 228
Soldiers, miniature, 12, 30, 34
Sortes, 164
Speedwriting, 62, 63
Spillage (let-it-all-hang-out-), 243
Spitting Image, 45

Spiritualist, 154
Sponging, 226
Sports cuisine, 105
Staff, 3, 7, 160, 269, 273
Stalemate, 312
Star Trek, 45
Start-up, 188, 193, 274, 275, 303, 307, 327
Stately home, 5, 169, 320
Stenciling, 49
Stingray, 45
Stone, 35
 – floors, 225
Stress, 1, 21
Suits, 29
Suppliers, 287, 293
Survival, 11, 13
Swimming, 21
 – pool, 21, 22, 27
Swop (your home), 315

T

Table coverings, 50
Tack(y), 30, 268
Takeovers, 66
Tarot, 165
Tea Ceremony, 233-240, 270
Telephone answering machines, 244
Telethesia, 165
Tesla, Nikola, 93, 97
Textiles, 29, 32, 50
Thallasotherapy, 24, 26, 27
Thatching, 226
Theatre, 47, 169, 170, 173, 214, 237
Theosophy, 154, 155
Throwaway paint brushes, 91
Tiles, 225, 226, 229
Timber (floors), 225
Toys, 30

Training (& re-), 2, 3, 33, 34, 37, 47, 52, 58, 63, 64, 72, 86, 133, 135, 136, 137, 172-3, 180, 187, 228-9, 230, 243, 256, 287, 324
    Dual-skill-, 113, 115
Transition course, 290
Translation service, 116, 260
Trekking, pony, 14
Trompe-l'oeil, 49, 50, 53
TV-video stand, 94
Two-box system, 104
Typewriter, 41

U

Under-cover, 76, 78, 220, 254
  – (covered), 21, 220
Unique Selling Factors, 312
Unit trusts, 66
Upholstery, 50

V

Value chain, 295
Vanderbilt, Cornelius, 65
Venturer's. . . nose, 319
Venture viability, 283
Victoria (Queen), 123
Vineyard, 253, 254, 255, 256

W

Walking sticks, 29
Walls & ceilings, 226, 230
Wall climbing, 14
Wallpaper, 5, 29
Wally, 306
War, 11, 12
  – games, 11, 14, 15, 30

Waste, 191
- ful, 192
- co's, 193
- dump, 193, 200, 319
- Digester, 195
- paper, 199, 200
Water, 12, 77, 208
- therapy, 21, 22, 23, 24, 27
Watersports, 272
Wave (power), 227
Weaver, commission, 50, 53
What To Do Now, 4, 281-323
Dr Who, 45
Wigs, 29
Windmill (power), 227
Windsurfing, 14, 272
Winstanley, Henry, 88
Wiping, 226
Wires, the curse, 93
Witch(es), 153, 166, 167
- craft, 167
Wodehouse, P G, 277
Wohl, Louis de, 155

Y

Yang, 157, 161
Yin, 157, 161
Your Personal Stocktake, 2, 287

Z

Zen, 239
Zoom, 221

To **SATURDAY RICHMOND PUBLISHERS,**
  Le Clos Fontaine, Little Sark, Channel Islands.

Please send details of/or a copy of your GUIDE
TO VILLAGE RICHES to my friends as detailed
below. Please send free greetings card to announce
each gift book from me.

Name ....

....

Address ....

.... Post Code...............

Name ....

....

Address ....

.... Post Code...............

Please debit my Credit Card No.

My name is ....

My address is ....

.... Post Code...............

NOTES

NOTES

NOTES

NOTES